CINDERELLA MAN

Cinderella Man

....

JAMES J. BRADDOCK, MAX BAER, AND THE GREATEST UPSET IN BOXING HISTORY

■

Jeremy Schaap

Houghton Mifflin Company
Boston ▪ *New York*

For information about permission to reproduce selections
from this book, write to Permissions, Houghton Mifflin Company, 215 Park Avenue South, New York, New York 10003.

Visit our Web site: www.houghtonmifflinbooks.com.

Library of Congress Cataloging-in-Publication Data
Schaap, Jeremy.
Cinderella Man : James J. Braddock, Max Baer, and the
greatest upset in boxing history / Jeremy Schaap.
p.   cm.
Includes bibliographical references and index.
ISBN 0-618-55117-4
1. Braddock, James J., 1906– 2. Baer, Max, 1909–1959.
3. Boxers (Sports) — United States — Biography.
4. Sports rivalries — United States. I. Title.
GV1131.S36 2005 796.83'092 — dc22
[B] 2004066085

Printed in the United States of America

Book design by Robert Overholtzer

QUM 10 9 8 7 6 5 4 3

For my father,
who wrote thirty-three
books — all of them
inspirations

In no list you will ever see will he be listed among the ten greatest, but that is as it should be. He had a good left hand but he was not a great boxer, and although he could bang with that right hand, he was not a great puncher. He may, however, in the sense that others could see themselves in him and read their own struggles into his, have belonged to more people than any champion who ever lived. His beginnings as a fighter were the beginnings of all fighters. What happened to him, though, happened to a whole country, and that is why I believe that no other fighter was ever as representative of his time.

— W. C. Heinz

Contents

Preface

Once I built a railroad, I made it run,
Made it race against time.
Once I built a railroad, now it's done.
Brother, can you spare a dime?

— E. Y. Harburg

In 1932, the song "Brother, Can You Spare a Dime?" achieved a unique distinction: it was a number-one hit for two crooners, Rudy Vallee *and* Bing Crosby. By capturing the despair of millions of Americans in the early years of the Depression, the song became a phenomenon. Harvey D. Gibson, the chairman of the Emergency Unemployment Relief Committee, said "Brother, Can You Spare a Dime?" "typified the plight of many men who toiled and helped build this country and who today could not understand why, through no fault of their own, they were forced to ask for aid."

The song's message was universally understood. On December 31 in London, the announcer on a special New Year's Eve radio broadcast said, "Now we take you to New York. They will be celebrating their own New Year in about five hours, in an effort to bring back prosperity." Then the engineer flipped on "Brother, Can You Spare a Dime?"

In the 1920s, Yip Harburg's elegiac lyrics would have meant nothing to most Americans, who were at the time drunk with prosperity. But by the mid-1930s, when families standing in soup lines had replaced flappers as the dominant cultural image, the song could have been the national anthem.

It floated through the air when James J. Braddock, fresh from the relief rolls, climbed through the ropes at the Madison Square Garden Bowl on June 13, 1935, to fight Max Baer. At odds of ten to one and higher, Braddock was the biggest underdog in heavyweight championship history. But when the ring announcer, Al Frazin, introduced him — "The challenger, from Jersey City, New Jersey, weighing in at one hundred ninety-one and three-quarters pounds, James J. Braddock!" — Braddock was engulfed in applause. Millions of Americans cheered for him that night, not because he was the betting underdog, not because the champion was unpopular, and not because Braddock was particularly exciting to watch, but because he personified their own struggles. Like so many of them, he had been humbled by forces beyond his control. Like so many of them, he had been devastated by a system that he assumed was stable. Like so many of them, he had been forced to ask for help. The decline in his personal fortunes mirrored the national collapse, perhaps more than that of any other American. Just before the crash, he had been one of the best young fighters in the world — everything was within his grasp. And then, when it hit, he tumbled from contender to tomato can to longshoreman to welfare recipient. "His time was the Great Depression and he was a man of his time," Red Smith wrote.

Only a boxer could have made the impact Braddock made, because in Braddock's time, boxing was the country's most popular sport and boxers were its most popular athletes. Little boys wanted to grow up to be boxers and plastered scrapbooks with images from the *Ring*, and their fathers spent what little disposable income they had to watch fights in cramped, smoky neighborhood arenas and enormous outdoor stadiums. Millions of people paid twenty-five cents to watch the fights they hadn't seen in person at the moviehouse. They went there too to watch enormously popular films in which the leading man played a boxer, such as *Golden Boy*, with William Holden, *The Champ*, with Wallace Beery, and *The Prizefighter and the Lady*, with Max Baer.

In 1935, the year Braddock fought Baer for the world heavyweight title, the New York Yankees played most of their games in an almost empty stadium; their average home attendance was 8,885 fans. But that fall, nearly 100,000 people crowded into Yankee Stadium to see Baer fight Joe Louis in a nontitle bout. In June, more than 60,000 fans saw Louis fight Primo Carnera in a nontitle fight at Yankee Stadium. And that May, more than 40,000 people attended the Barney Ross–Jimmy McLarnin *lightweight* championship fight at the Polo Grounds. Baseball may have been the national pastime, but boxing was the national passion.

Much of the sport's appeal was rooted in its ethnic and racial rivalries, which were exploited by promoters and relished by fans, many of whom were immigrants or first-generation Americans. The Irish versus the Jews. The Jews versus the Italians. The Italians versus the blacks. The blacks versus the Poles. The Germans versus all of them. Fighters changed their names to O'Brien or Goldstein to create ethnic matchups that would make their fights draw bigger crowds. And at a time when the heavyweight champion of the world mattered in a way in which no athlete now matters, Americans of all hues and ethnicities found inspiration in the story of a man who rose, in the words of his first biographer, from relief to royalty.

Damon Runyon, who knew a fairy tale when he saw one, dubbed Braddock "the Cinderella Man." At that time, to climb to the top of the heavyweight division was to ascend to the highest peak in sports, both in popularity and financially.

On September 22, 1927, for thirty minutes' work — plus nine minutes of catching his breath between rounds — Gene Tunney made $990,445 in his second fight against Jack Dempsey, more money than Babe Ruth had made in his fourteen major league seasons to that point. Eight years later, in 1935, in the midst of the Depression, the highest-paid player in the major leagues was Lou Gehrig, the Yankees' first baseman. The Iron Horse made $40,000, a significant sum to the average American but little more than pocket change for Max Baer, Max Schmeling, and the other pre-eminent boxers of the era. That fall, when Baer fought Louis, he earned $215,000, more than five times Gehrig's annual salary.

In the days of Max Baer and James J. Braddock, in a sports landscape lacking international basketball stars, soccer stars, and Formula One race-car drivers, the heavyweight champion wasn't just the best-paid or the most significant athlete in the world; he was — with the possible exception of a few world leaders, such as Stalin and King George V — the most famous person on the planet.

"Jack Johnson's impact on popular feeling was sharper than William H. Taft's," John Lardner wrote in *White Hopes and Other Tigers*. "Jack Dempsey overshadowed Calvin Coolidge. Taft and Coolidge accepted the situation meekly." In fact, after meeting President Coolidge, who enthusiastically shook his hand, Luis Angel Firpo, an Argentine heavyweight contender — not even a champion — turned to a bystander and said, "Who was that man?"

There were times, of course, when the heavyweight champion was trumped by presidents, kings, and field marshals — specifically, when the world was at war. But most of the time, the champ was king.

Someone, though, was needed to blow the champion's horn. In his later years, Dempsey, who was champion from 1919 to 1926, said, "I was a pretty good fighter. But it was the writers who made me great." Dempsey knew that the golden age of sport was an invention of the golden age of sports writing.

In the 1920s and 1930s, radio was in its infancy and television was a rumor. The vast majority of Americans got their information — about politics, sports, and entertainment — from newspapers. In New York City alone there were nearly two dozen thriving dailies — the *Times*, the *Herald-Tribune*, the *Post*, the *News*, the *Sun*, the *American*, the *Journal*, the *World-Telegram*, the *Wall Street Journal*, the *Daily Worker*, the *Mirror*, the *Staten Island Advance*, the *Brooklyn Eagle*, the *Star-Journal*, the *Bronx*

Home-News, the *Long Island Press*, and the *Forward*, among others.

In 1927, no one outside Soldier Field saw Gene Tunney as he rose from the canvas after the Long Count to defeat Dempsey. In 1932, no one outside Wrigley Field saw Babe Ruth call his shot against Charlie Root in the World Series. The pictures were painted by sports writers — giants such as Grantland Rice, W. O. McGeehan, Damon Runyon, Paul Gallico, Westbrook Pegler, and Frank Graham. Their syndicated columns were avidly read in the far reaches of the forty-eight states, and they used their talents to create legends. Rice, for example, was perhaps only slightly less instrumental than Knute Rockne in fashioning the mythology of Notre Dame football. The first few sentences of his account of the Army–Notre Dame game played at the Polo Grounds on October 18, 1924, remain the most famous and quoted lead in newspaper history:

> Outlined against a blue-gray October sky, the Four Horsemen rode again. In dramatic lore, they are known as Famine, Pestilence, Destruction, and Death. These are only aliases. Their real names are Stuhldreher, Miller, Crowley, and Layden.

Many years later, Jim Crowley, Destruction himself, stated the obvious when he said, "It was Granny who made us famous."

By the 1930s, Rice was making more money — about $250,000 a year — than any of the athletes he covered, with the exception of the heavyweight champion of the world and perhaps Gallant Fox, Omaha, and Count Fleet. He had a chauffeur.

To a man, the monarchs of press row considered Jim Braddock's impossible comeback the richest story they ever covered — it was one of the few they did not have to embellish to make resonate. "I don't want to sound trite," Runyon wrote, "but believe an old plot-maker, truth in Braddock's case is much stranger than fiction." But neither Runyon nor any of his contemporaries was paying much attention when the comeback started.

1

Corn and Hash

....

Queens, New York: June 14, 1934

On the night of June 14, 1934, James J. Braddock walked into the Madison Square Garden Bowl, an enormous outdoor arena in Queens, New York. His pockets were empty. A week earlier he had turned twenty-nine. He was a father of three, a washed-up fighter, and a part-time longshoreman. As feared as his right hand had once been — he was among the most powerful punchers in the light heavyweight division in the late 1920s — he was equally adept at taking a punch. In eighty pro fights, only one opponent had ever knocked him out, and that was a technical knockout. He had never been counted out. Beyond the ring, his toughest opponent had clearly been the Depression — which nearly knocked him out. But here he was, getting back into the fight game after nine months of inactivity.

By 1934, Braddock had outgrown the light heavyweight division's 175-pound weight limit and was fighting as a heavyweight, at about 180 pounds. He was six feet, two inches tall, with a head of thick, curly black hair. Ruggedly handsome, he looked every bit as Irish as his name, and he wore a shamrock on his trunks and was sometimes known as Irish Jim Braddock. He didn't talk much, but when he did the words were delivered from the side of his mouth in a thick, blue-collar Jersey accent.

His smile was always described as crooked. His parents, Joseph and Elizabeth O'Toole Braddock, had been born in England and immigrated to the United States in 1889, but they were both much more Irish than English or American, though there is no evidence that either ever set foot on Irish soil. They were raised in impoverished Irish enclaves in and around Manchester, where the Braddocks and the O'Tooles clung to their Irishness — mostly because the English never let them forget where they came from.

Forty-five years after Joseph Braddock escaped from the poverty and prejudices of northern England and made his way to America, his son James was struggling to clothe and feed his burgeoning family. He owed money to his landlord, the milkman, the gas and electric company, and his manager, to name just a few of his creditors. In the bitter winter of 1933–1934, he had trudged through the streets of North Bergen, New Jersey, in shoes that were falling apart. Most of the time he was hungry.

Braddock's decline as a boxer exactly paralleled the nation's descent into the Depression. After fighting for the light heavyweight championship in the summer of 1929, Braddock met defeat after defeat, first in big arenas, at the hands of top competitors, and then, gradually, at the hands of boxers only a couple of notches above club fighters — tomato cans and ham 'n' eggers, the dregs of the heavyweight division. He had lost sixteen out of twenty-six fights since the day the market crashed in 1929. Finally, on September 25, 1933, he broke his right hand, his only real weapon, on the jaw of a twenty-year-old heavyweight named Abe Feldman. The hand had been broken twice before, and Braddock thought it was unlikely that it would ever heal properly. If he somehow managed to scrape up enough cash to find a doctor who knew how to set the fracture, it would still take months to mend. By that time, he knew, he would be older and even slower than he already was, which was quite slow. Braddock announced his retirement — but virtually no one noticed.

Braddock was often called plodding. "Slow of foot" doesn't begin to describe the inadequacy of his speed and footwork. He could punch, he could take a punch, he could even box a little, but James J. Braddock couldn't move. Nor could he inflict much damage with his left hand.

Incapable of fighting, he sought work on the docks of Hoboken and Weehawken. The man who just five years earlier had come within one punch of winning the world light heavyweight championship was reduced to hauling railroad ties off ships coming from the south and loading them onto flatbed railroad cars. Initially he wasn't very good at it — not with a lame right hand. But Braddock was strong, and physical labor was something he never shied from. Not when he was training for a fight, and not when he was earning four dollars a day operating a baling hook.

Like tens of millions of Americans who had thrived in the 1920s, Braddock was wiped out by the economic collapse. Much of the money he had earned fighting at famous arenas like Boyle's Thirty Acres and Madison Square Garden disappeared when the Bank of the United States, in which he had deposited thousands of dollars, failed. He was far from alone. The men standing beside him on the docks in the shapeups, hoping to get picked by the hiring foremen for work, were lawyers and bankers and stockbrokers as well as laborers. The Depression took nearly everyone down a few pegs — or more. Unlike everyone else on the docks, however, Braddock was unknowingly building the strength he would need to get himself back in the ring.

Still, the work was irregular. There were days when he would walk the three miles from his apartment in Woodcliff down to the waterfront in Hoboken in vain. He would then turn north and walk another couple of miles to West New York, or farther, to Edgewater. Sometimes there would be work on the docks. Sometimes he would just turn around and head back home. It wasn't uncommon for him to walk ten or twelve miles in a single day. When there was work to be had, he would keep working until the job was finished. A double shift meant double pay. Fatigue was for sissies.

People who knew Braddock well thought that the nickname that best described him was Plain Jim, coined by John Kieran of the *New York Times*. Unlike John L. Sullivan and Jack Dempsey, the most popular heavyweight champions of the early days of gloved boxing, Braddock was as far as it was possible to be from a showman. He liked to go to pubs and have a few beers with the friends he had made growing up in West New York. But it concerned him not at all whether his dinner companions found him amusing. Or whether the sportswriters enjoyed his quips. Or whether the fans got a glimpse of his personality. On those rare occasions when he did speak, his words made an impact.

Braddock was teetering on the verge of anonymity as winter turned into spring in 1934. The talents he had displayed in the late 1920s were fading rapidly from the collective memory of the boxing community. When aficionados discussed the men who might challenge Primo Carnera for the heavyweight championship, the name Jim Braddock never entered the conversation. But Braddock remembered. So did his manager, Joe Gould. Perhaps a few of the men he had punished with his big right hand did too. Everyone else, though, thought of James J. Braddock — when they thought of him at all — as a broken-down, washed-up, one-time contender who just didn't quite have enough talent or power.

Even so, Gould continued to sell Braddock as a worthy opponent long after most promoters had decided he was through in the fight game. Gould spent hours pleading Braddock's case, insisting that all the fights he had lost were merely the result of a bad right hand. He reminded everyone who would listen that

Jim Braddock was still only twenty-eight years old and that he was, after all, the same young man who had broken the great Pete Latzo's jaw in four places, knocked out the heralded Tuffy Griffiths, and made mincemeat of Jimmy Slattery. He didn't mention that those events had taken place in the 1920s, half a decade earlier.

Meanwhile, Braddock's right hand was slowly healing. As he sweated on the docks, stripped to the waist, his strength was returning. The inner voice that had told him he was finished after the Feldman fight went silent. Now another voice told him that maybe his luck was about to change (for years he had considered himself jinxed). But if someone had made odds on the likelihood that Braddock would eventually capture the heavyweight championship, those odds would have been a million to one, or higher. Dozens of heavyweights were fighting regularly in New York, and virtually all of them were rated higher than Braddock, who was neither a solid veteran nor a talented up-and-comer. He was, like so many used-up fighters, damaged goods — literally. Unlike most, he had once had a shot at a title, but he had blown it and had never recovered from the disappointment. His time, it seemed, had passed.

Braddock, however, was not entirely worthless in the ring. His name still meant something to boxing enthusiasts. The boxing commission had twice refused to license him, fearing for his safety, but if it licensed him for this fight he could serve a purpose in the sport, as a human steppingstone for young fighters climbing the ranks — for a fighter like John "Corn" Griffin.

Unlike Jim Braddock, Corn Griffin spent the early years of the Depression gainfully employed, as an enlisted man in the United States Army. A big, bruising Georgian, he fought in the service and eventually caught the eye of a veteran manager named Charles Harvey. By 1934, Griffin was a civilian and Harvey was trying to position him in the heavyweight division. "Griffin," someone once wrote, "had the face of a loser, with a dented nose and scar tissue around his eyes." But he could punch.

In the spring of 1934, Griffin arrived in Pompton Lakes, New Jersey, to join the training camp of Primo Carnera as a sparring partner. Carnera, at six foot seven the tallest heavyweight champion ever, and at 270 pounds the heaviest ever — at least until George Foreman regained the title in 1994 — was an atrocious boxer and a relatively weak puncher. But in an era when many of the top heavyweights weighed no more than 190 pounds, Carnera's sheer size made him an attraction.

Born on October 26, 1906, in Sequals, Italy, near Venice, Carnera had won the championship in 1933 from Jack Sharkey under a cloud of justifiable suspicion. It was widely assumed that Carnera, who was controlled by the mobster Owney Madden, was the beneficiary of a fix. In later years, after the mob cruelly abandoned him, he became a pro wrestler, something he was much better at than fighting. Carnera was also the sad inspiration for the mob-controlled heavyweight in Budd Schulberg's classic boxing tale, *The Harder They Fall.*

When he is remembered at all, Carnera is remembered simply for his physique, which Paul Gallico described in *Farewell to Sport:*

> Carnera was the only giant I have ever seen who was well proportioned throughout his body for his height. His legs were massive and he was truly thewed like an oak. His waist was comparatively small and clean, but from it rose a torso like a Spanish hogshead from which sprouted two tremendous arms, the biceps of which stood out like grapefruit. His hands were like Virginia hams, and his fingers were 10 red sausages. His head was large, and he had a good nose and fine, kind eyes. His skin was brown and glistening and he invariably smelled of garlic.

History does not record what Gallico smelled like.

As far as Carnera's appetite was concerned, his publicity man wrote, "For breakfast, Primo has a quart of orange juice, two quarts of milk, nineteen pieces of toast, fourteen eggs, a loaf of bread, and half a pound of Virginia ham." Publicity men of the time were prone to hyperbole, but Carnera's flack might just have been telling the truth.

Carnera's handlers agreed to have him defend his title for the third time in seven months on June 14 at the Madison Square Garden Bowl. In preparation for the bout, Carnera trained at Pompton Lakes and sparred frequently with Corn Griffin. Because Griffin could actually fight a little, he often made Carnera look foolish — so foolish, in fact, that the writers who camped out at Pompton Lakes began singing Griffin's fistic praises, as those writers would have put it.

On June 3, Carnera sparred two rounds against Chester Matan, two rounds against Yuster Sirutis, and one round against Corn Griffin. "Carnera encountered his stiffest opposition in the round with Griffin," Joseph C. Nichols reported in the *New York Times*. "The latter, a former United States Army boxer, weighed little more than 185 pounds, but tore into the champion as if he were his own size."

"As a sparring partner, he is no mere catcher," Frank Graham wrote in the *New York Sun*. "He is a pitcher — and he pitches with both hands. He drives straight into Primo and his fists thud against the champion's jaw and into his stomach. Carnera fights back hard, but he cannot keep Corn away. The soldier piles him up in a corner, belts him savagely with both hands, and then drives him out."

Jimmy Johnston, the matchmaker at Madison Square Garden, which was promoting the Carnera-Baer fight, was paying close attention to the beatings Griffin was dishing out. He signed Griffin to fight on the undercard, in one of the preliminary bouts that both build up a crowd's bloodlust and provide value in the event that the main attraction is uninspiring.

"Two years from now," said Charles Harvey, Griffin's walrus-mustached manager, "Griffin will be the heavyweight champion. When I sent him up here to work with Carnera, I told him to be careful and not get hurt. Now all I am afraid of is that he will hurt Carnera."

Harvey wanted to get Griffin "started in New York with a flourish," Joe Williams of the *World-Telegram* said. "The best way to accomplish this was to get some washed-up name fighter and kick his brains out."

But as fight night approached, Johnston was having trouble securing an opponent for Griffin. The reports of his dominance in Pompton Lakes, whether or not they were exaggerated, scared off several would-be opponents and their managers. No one wanted to be the lamb offered up to Griffin for slaughter.

Except Jim Braddock.

On June 12, Joe Gould was waiting in his customary spot outside Jimmy Johnston's office. Nearly as broke as Braddock, Gould managed to keep up appearances, smoking, dining, and dressing well, although he could not afford to continue to indulge in his favorite pastime, golf. The secretaries at Madison Square Garden — which at the time was situated on Eighth Avenue between 49th Street and 50th Street, two miles north and west of its original location on Madison Square — liked Gould despite themselves. They took messages for him and signed for his packages. Like everyone else, though, they were growing weary of his favorite topic of conversation: James J. Braddock. Everyone knew that Braddock was washed up, but Gould persisted, badgering Johnston, relentlessly seeking fights that would put a little cash in Braddock's pockets — and his own.

Surrounded by a cluster of publicists, writers, managers, and trainers, Johnston loudly lamented the lack of a suitable opponent for Griffin. He wanted someone good enough to pique the fans' interest but not good enough to win — though that's not exactly how he put it.

Gould had slid into the crowd in Johnston's office. "Why not give Jimmy a chance?" he said, predictably.

"Don't mention Braddock again," Johnston said, as everyone

laughed at the joke that had already grown old. "I'm sick of hearing his name."

"Just give him a shot," Gould said. If he wasn't begging, he wasn't doing his job.

"Joe, Corn will kill him," Johnston said. "Ask any one of these guys. They've seen Corn in there with Carnera. I don't want Jimmy's blood on my hands."

"Listen," Gould said, his eyes zeroing in on Johnston, "no one's ever hurt Jimmy, you know that. He's cute that way. No-body hits him solid. And he's stronger now than he's ever been."

"Okay," Johnston said, relenting. "You've got me, you wore me down. But don't blame me if Griffin kills that old Irishman. And the purse is two hundred and fifty bucks. Don't even think about asking for more."

"It's a deal," Gould said.

Now all Gould had to do was find Braddock. He had a pretty good idea where he was.

Gould walked out of the Garden and headed south to 42nd Street and then west to the Hudson River. He boarded a New Jersey–bound ferry and a few minutes later landed in Hoboken. Braddock was only a few hundred yards away, laboring on the docks, sweating in the noonday sun.

"Well, champ," Gould said, after tapping on Braddock's shoulder. "I've got a fight for you."

Braddock, his face and chest red from the sun, his thick, curly hair drooping into his eyes, didn't say a word. He put down the baling hook in his left hand and peeled off his work gloves. He looked at Gould, waiting for the details.

"But the fight's Thursday night, on the undercard at the Bowl," Gould continued. "You've only got two days. Can you do it? Are you in shape?"

"Am I in shape?" Braddock said, wiping the grime from his brow. "Are you kidding? Look at me."

Braddock, who had turned twenty-nine on June 8, was in fact in the best shape of his life. He'd been walking several miles every day for months. He'd been unloading and hauling railroad ties. But even if his muscles weren't bigger than ever before, which they were, and even if his conditioning was lacking, which it wasn't, he would have jumped at the opportunity to get back into the ring.

"I had about two days' notice that I was going to fight Griffin," he later said. "Two hours — or an hour — would have been enough."

He needed the money — and he needed to fight. The gas and electric company had threatened to shut off his service again. He had been forced to move his wife and three children to a basement apartment in the building in which they were living because he couldn't pay the rent on the apartment upstairs. Most humiliating to Braddock, he had gone on the welfare rolls and each month was receiving twenty-four dollars from the Hudson County relief agency.

Johnston had approved a hundred-dollar advance on the purse, which Gould split with Braddock. For the first time in months, Braddock had a few — very few — dollars at his disposal. He handed over the money to his wife, Mae, and she in turn paid the milkman, the utility company, and the landlord.

On Wednesday, the day before the fight, Braddock took the ferry to 42nd Street, walked east to Ninth Avenue, turned left, walked fifteen blocks north to 57th Street, turned right, and entered Stillman's Gym, where Gould was waiting for him. The plan was to get in one solid workout with a sparring partner — to shake off the rust that had been accumulating for nine months.

New York's preeminent gym from the 1920s through the 1950s, and consequently the center of the boxing universe at the time, Stillman's was dubbed the University of Eighth Avenue by A. J. Liebling. It was opened in 1921 by two millionaires who hoped to civilize wayward youths by teaching them the rules of boxing that had been named for the marquis of Queensberry. But Stillman's was no Boys Town. Instead, it became simply a gym, albeit *the* gym. It is impossible to say how many spirits were lifted and how many were destroyed in its sweaty squared circles. Gene Tunney, the man who twice defeated Jack Dempsey in heavyweight championship fights, found the smell at Stillman's so appalling that he said he wouldn't train there unless the windows were opened. The featherweight champion Johnny Dundee responded by saying, "Fresh air? Why, that stuff is likely to kill us." Lou Stillman — born Louis Ingber (he changed his name after he bought the gym, to avoid confusion) — kept the windows shut. Tunney stayed away, but not for long. Every heavyweight champion from Jack Dempsey to Joe Louis trained at Stillman's.

Lou Stillman was successful because he never played favorites — except when he felt like it. "Big or small, champ or bum, I treated 'em all the same way — bad," he once said. "If you treat them like humans, they'll eat you alive." Irish, Italian, black, Jewish, Polish — it didn't matter to Stillman what you were, as long as you could fight.

Together, Gould and Braddock had spent thousands of hours at Stillman's — but the Jim Braddock whom Gould saw on June 13, 1934, was a stranger. Working in a ring for the first time since the Feldman fight, he fired off left hands with stunning precision and unexpected force. For years he had fought entirely from starboard. Now he seemed to be ambidextrous. His sparring partner wilted under the assault. He was also moving differently — up on his toes, heels off the ground, resisting the urge to settle into his customary flat-footed stance. No one was going to confuse Jim Braddock with Fred Astaire. Nimble he was not. But his movements could no longer be described as glacial. As a fighter, he had undergone a metamorphosis.

His longtime trainer, Doc Robb, looked at Gould from behind the heavy bag that Braddock was pummeling and shook his head in astonishment. The thought raced through Gould's mind that perhaps Braddock wasn't washed up. For years he had been droning on and on about Braddock's prospects, insisting that he deserved another chance. Every promoter in the business had at one time or another fallen asleep listening to Gould rattle on about the great James J. Braddock. There were times, though, when Gould would hear the words coming out of his mouth and not believe them himself. Joe Gould was no fool. He knew the fight game. He had grown up in it. He knew that no one had ever climbed to the top from the depths where Jim Braddock had toiled since 1929. But he had stayed with Braddock because they were friends and because he had no better prospects.

On the night of the fight, the gates opened at 5 P.M. at the Madison Square Garden Bowl, on the corner of 45th Street and Northern Boulevard in the working-class Long Island City section of Queens. A massive wooden structure erected in 1932, it could seat 72,000. Its life was brief but colorful. In its first year, Max Schmeling lost the world heavyweight championship by decision to the challenger, Jack Sharkey. Only the judges gave the fight to Sharkey. Coining a phrase known to sports fans from Brooklyn to Bangkok, Joe Jacobs, Schmeling's incensed manager, howled into a radio microphone, "We wuz robbed!"

Five times in seven years, the world heavyweight championship changed hands at the Madison Square Garden Bowl. Clearly, it was the arena where champions went to die.

For the Baer-Carnera showdown, 56,000 people filed into the Bowl — a significant turnout, considering just how few people had any disposable income in 1934. Ticket prices ranged from $25, at ringside, to $2.30 for the cheap seats. To attend a fight was an extravagance few could afford. Those who could spare a dime — movie stars, politicians, mobsters, athletes — showed up in droves. Postmaster General James A. Farley, one of President Franklin D. Roosevelt's closest advisers and the former chairman of the New York boxing commission, was there. So were former heavyweight champions Jack Dempsey,

Gene Tunney, and Jack Sharkey. Barney Ross, Benny Leonard, Tony Canzoneri, and Kid Chocolate — all legends in lighter classifications — were also in attendance.

The *New York Times* noted that of the two hundred policemen assigned to the task of ensuring public safety inside the arena, three were captains, three were lieutenants, and fifteen were sergeants. None was there working against his will.

In the hours leading up to a heavyweight championship fight, the crowd grows bigger, louder, and at the same time more solemn. The fans sense the danger, which distinguishes a fight crowd from crowds at every other sporting event except auto races. Today, only the most rabid fans pay close attention to the preliminaries. But in the 1930s, when boxing was still more important than every other sport except baseball and maybe college football, most fans watched the undercard fights with at least some interest. The newspapermen covered them closely, if only because the main events usually ended so late that the writers needed the undercards to fill their column inches.

After a few lackluster four- and five-round bouts, James J. Braddock and Corn Griffin prepared to step into the ring. Braddock was wearing old trunks and borrowed shoes. When he climbed through the ropes, the crowd was paying scant attention. Those who knew little about boxing were at the Bowl only to see the championship fight. Those who knew the sport assumed it would be a one-sided affair. If they had been following the goings-on at Carnera's camp, they knew that Griffin was considered an up-and-comer, and if they had been following boxing since the 1920s, they vaguely remembered Jim Braddock as a light heavyweight hopeful.

Gould, as usual, was chattering. "You feel good, Jim? You feel good?" he kept repeating. It was a tic, not a question.

"Yeah, Joe, I'm ready," Braddock said out of the side of his mouth. He had built up a sweat shadowboxing in his dressing room, and now, in the warm evening air, the sweat was pouring from him. His upper body was red and splotchy, his legs almost white. He looked out across the Bowl. Tens of thousands of patrons were already in their seats. His last fight, against Feldman, had also been outdoors, in Mount Vernon, New York, but only a few hundred people had been there. At the Bowl, none of those tens of thousands of people were there to see him fight, which was fine with Braddock. He had long ago adjusted his ambition to match his talent. Still, he needed a win, because a win meant another fight, which meant another purse, which meant another meal. Braddock had never felt uncomfortable in the ring — ever — and even nine months of inaction had not changed that.

"Remember, Jimmy," Doc Robb told Braddock just before the bell, "stay away from his right hand. He can punch."

At the bell, Griffin, well tanned, his hair close-cropped, went straight for Braddock. Within seconds he landed a right squarely on Braddock's jaw. Braddock staggered. He hadn't been hit that hard in years. As Griffin dominated him in the first round, Braddock simply tried to get his bearings.

"Come on, Jim," Gould said between rounds. "You look like you're sleeping."

Braddock stared straight ahead, refused the water he was offered, pounded his gloves together, and stood up.

In the second round, Griffin went for Braddock again. Braddock stood still, and Griffin followed a left jab with another right to Braddock's jaw. Braddock went down.

Watching from ringside, Lud Shabazian, the sports editor of the *Hudson Dispatch*, Braddock's hometown paper, winced. Shabazian was Braddock's Boswell, the only writer who had seen virtually all his East Coast fights since 1923. He wasn't at the Bowl specifically to cover Braddock — he was there to see the title fight — and he was more interested in Braddock as a friend than as a fighter. As Braddock writhed on the canvas, Shabazian felt his friend's pain. He and his colleagues on press row stayed in their seats, but the sharp report of Griffin's blow had alerted the crowd that something worthy of attention was now taking place in the ring, and thousands scrambled to their feet. No one would have blamed Braddock if he had closed his eyes, waited for the count of ten, and walked away from the ring forever. He was twenty-nine, a tomato can, better suited to life as a longshoreman. Maybe it was time to quit.

But a voice in Braddock's head urged him to get up — the same voice that had always urged him to get up when he was down. Too proud, too stubborn, and too broke to be counted out, he gathered himself, waited for the count of nine, picked himself up off the canvas, and waded straight into Griffin. He threw a jab that missed but followed with a short right to the chin. Griffin didn't see it and went down in a heap. Finally the Georgian got up, but he never recovered.

For the rest of the second round, with Gould screaming wildly and jumping up and down in his corner, Braddock continued to bludgeon Griffin. It had been years since he had fought so effectively. His punches — jabs, uppercuts, overhand rights — were crisper than they had been when *he* was the up-and-comer. His left hand, for years an almost vestigial extremity, was suddenly potent.

Maybe Braddock knew that he was better than ever. Maybe he could sense how far his comeback would take him. Probably not. What he did know, what he could sense, was that Corn Griffin was finished.

At the bell commencing the third round, Braddock went straight out to meet Griffin and jolted him with two more powerful right hands. Griffin was nearly out on his feet, his head still swimming from the punch that had knocked him down in the second round. But he kept fighting. Now Braddock was moving fluidly, throwing punches at a staggering target. Finally, with twenty-three seconds remaining in the round, the referee, Kid McPartland, stopped the fight. Braddock had his first knockout in eighteen months and only his second in more than four years.

Drained, Braddock stood in the middle of the canvas, waiting for Gould to throw a sponge full of icewater in his face. Gould took the sponge from the bucket, walked right past Braddock, and threw it in Griffin's face.

"What did you do that for?" Braddock said.

"Corn's in worse shape than you are," Gould said.

Before retreating to Braddock's dressing room, Gould found Johnston at ringside. "Hey, Jimmy," he said, his smile widening, "I hope Jimmy didn't hurt Corn. I know you've got high hopes for him."

"Tell Jimmy I'm proud of him," Johnston said bravely, trying to mask his disappointment.

Back in his dressing room, Braddock popped open a beer, embraced a few friends and relatives, and searched in vain for a shower. When Shabazian walked in, Braddock hugged him too.

"He had me on the deck," Braddock said as Shabazian scribbled. "He hit me with a right hand behind the ear. He's a left hooker, and I've always had a lot of success with left hookers. I have a fast right hand, and coming in with a left hook, you meet a guy with a right hand, and if you hit him in the right spot, which I done to him, I hit him right on the chin and that was it."

Then, turning to Gould, Braddock said, "I did that on hash, Joe. Wait till you see what I can do on steak."

2

The Battle of Nurge's Field

·······················

North Bergen, New Jersey: 1923

Just about every growing boy in the United States in the 1920s wanted to be either Babe Ruth or Jack Dempsey. Basketball? The game was no more recognizable to most Americans than lacrosse is today. Pro football? The National Football League was founded in an automobile dealership in Canton, Ohio, in 1920, and Red Grange had yet to make it a legitimate enterprise. Golf? Yes, Bobby Jones and Walter Hagen were stars, but the sport was strictly restricted not only to whites but to the privileged. All the important tournaments excluded professionals. The same was true of tennis, which was dominated by Bill Tilden, an Ivy Leaguer from Philadelphia's Main Line. If you were Italian, Polish, Irish, Jewish, or black, where were you going to play tennis and golf? You might play football, and even become a star — like Fritz Pollard, who was black, and Sid Luckman, who was Jewish — but first you had to attend college. If you weren't short and skinny, becoming a jockey was not an option.

There was baseball and there was boxing.

Unlike baseball, which is virtually synonymous with middle-class values, boxing was and has remained a sport of the underclass. When there are other plausible routes to financial security and elevated social status, no one of sound mind is going to choose to pursue boxing as a career. It is a hard way to make a living.

The great Jewish fighters of the 1920s and 1930s were the sons of impoverished immigrants from Eastern Europe. None of them was of German or Dutch or French extraction. The Western European Jews had come to the United States in earlier waves of immigration. They arrived with better education and more money. They did not congregate in ghettos like the Lower East Side, East Harlem, and Brownsville in Brooklyn. They built mansions. They were not shorter, weaker, or intrinsically more intelligent than their coreligionists from Poland and Russia. They were richer. So they didn't fight. They didn't have to.

But the Eastern European Jews, and the Irish and the Italians, turned to boxing. When they assimilated and prospered, they stopped boxing. But that wasn't until World War II.

In the teens and twenties, when Jimmy Braddock was growing up, boxing was a way out — one of the only ways out for a poor Irish kid from North Bergen. As a fighter, Braddock derived strength from his close-knit family, which had no money but was steeped in toughness.

His father, Joseph, had come to America from England as a twenty-two-year-old. According to family lore, he traveled on the *Adriatic*, the same steamship on which Jake Kilrain, the legendary bare-knuckle champion, was sailing. Kilrain, an American, was returning home to fight John L. Sullivan, the "Boston Strong Boy," the son of Irish immigrants, the heavyweight champion of the world, and probably the most famous man in America in the 1880s. On July 8, 1889, Sullivan and Kilrain fought the last meaningful bare-knuckle fight ever, in Richburg, Mississippi. The era of the ungloved fight ended honorably. Over the course of two hours and sixteen minutes, Sullivan and Kilrain fought seventy-five brutal rounds. When Kilrain failed to answer the bell for the seventy-sixth round, Sullivan was declared the winner.

From then on, the heavyweight championship was contested under the Queensberry rules, which were drawn up in London in 1865 not by the marquis of Queensberry but by John Graham Chambers, an English boxing enthusiast. The ninth marquis of Queensberry, John Sholto Douglas, was a Scot who in 1860 helped found the Amateur Athletic Club, of which Chambers was a member. In deference to Douglas, Chambers named the code after him. The rules — there were twelve in all — replaced an older code that had allowed wrestling and banned padded gloves. Significantly, in addition to ending bare-knuckle fighting, the Queensberry rules increased the duration of the rest period between rounds from thirty to sixty seconds and created the three-minute round. Before that, a round had ended only when one or both fighters were knocked down. (Most of the Queensberry rules are familiar to fans of modern boxing; a few, though, are obscure. For instance, rule eleven states, "No shoes or boots with sprigs allowed.")

Soon after his arrival in New York, Joseph Braddock found work as a laborer in Hell's Kitchen, the teeming ghetto on Manhattan's West Side that had become the center of Irish life in New York City. (In the 1880s, 40 percent of New Yorkers were of Irish extraction.) Stretching from 34th Street to 57th Street and from Ninth Avenue to Twelfth Avenue, Hell's Kitchen was a dirty, dangerous, squalid place dominated by vicious street gangs — a place where a man who couldn't use his fists couldn't call himself a man. Even the priests knew how to throw a punch. "Dad was a fighting Irishman who used to relish taking part in battles himself," James J. Braddock once said, and Joe Braddock sometimes boasted that he could carry a baby grand piano up three flights of stairs without pausing to catch his breath.

Between fights, Joe found time to meet and court Elizabeth O'Toole, who immigrated from England when she was twenty-three. Braddock and O'Toole had been born only ten miles apart, she in Manchester, the gritty industrial hub of northern England, and he in the village of Mottram. They married in 1893.

Elizabeth spent much of the first twelve years of her marriage pregnant, giving birth to Nellie, Julia, Ralph, Joseph Junior, Jack, and, on June 8, 1905, James Walter, who would one day become James J. Braddock. James was born in a tenement at 511 West 48th Street, two blocks west of the heart of Hell's Kitchen, and was by far the biggest of the Braddock clan, supposedly weighing seventeen and a half pounds at birth. Within weeks of his arrival, the Braddocks, eager to escape the filth and crowds of the city, packed up and boarded a ferry that took them across the Hudson River to West New York, New Jersey, a town just a few hundred yards west of their New York flat. It was here that Elizabeth eventually delivered her seventh and last child, Alfred, and it was here that James W. Braddock grew up.

Joe, tall and stout, found work in the moving and trucking business and somehow earned enough money to feed his seven children and send them to parochial school. His son Jimmy entered St. Joseph's Parochial School in West New York as a six-year-old. Jimmy never wavered in his aversion to schoolwork — to math in particular. From the beginning he was much fonder of recess, which on most days was an improvised battle royal on the playground. The nuns intervened only when it seemed that real damage was being inflicted, which was rare, since young hands are generally too fragile to withstand more than one or two solid strikes. Still, the boys fought, because there was little else to do, because it was expected of them, and because it was, for most of them, fun. Sometimes they played baseball, emulating Christy Mathewson of the Giants and Zack Wheat of the Dodgers. Sometimes they swam in the Hudson, in swimming holes protected from the river's strong current. But mostly they fought.

It was on the St. Joseph's playground that James J. Braddock developed both his skills and his passion for boxing. The poise he later displayed in the ring was learned there too, in countless scraps. "There were thirty-five boys in my class," he explained, "and every one of them could fight a bit."

Braddock, of course, could fight better than most. He was born with a hard punch, a solid chin, and, most important, a fighter's desire to inflict pain. Though the other boys might hesitate to punch with all their might, Braddock reflexively used all his strength. Though other boys might flinch when presented with the opportunity to strike someone in the face, Braddock aimed his fists directly at his opponent's nose, where a punch would hurt most and result in spurting blood. In the schoolyard, strength and athleticism weren't what separated the fighters from the other boys; gameness was the distinguishing characteristic. Braddock's most persistent opponent was a boy named Jimmy Morris. The two Jimmies fought more than thirty times, apparently splitting the series.

When Braddock was ten years old, his family moved again, this time from West New York — a town that was getting tougher by the day — to North Bergen, which was less congested and urban, just a few miles away. A year later, in 1916, Jimmy and his best friend, Marty McGann, decided that they had had enough of school and were going to see the world by tramping the trains. First stop, Chicago.

On the appointed day, the boys told their parents they would be late returning from school — which was technically true — and not to worry. At recess they walked to a nearby rail yard and boarded a boxcar of the New York, Ontario, and Western Railroad. Late that night, hungry and cold, they disembarked, not in Chicago but in Washingtonville, New York, only about seventy miles from North Bergen.

"It was so cold, we had to keep running to keep warm,"

Braddock later told his friend Lud Shabazian. "While we were bouncing around, the freight started to go again. We yelled to one another and headed again for the train. But by the time we got to the caboose, we had been noticed and all our efforts to hitch on were in vain. We were beaten off by a trainman with a lantern."

Braddock and McGann trudged along in the darkness. Eventually they were taken in by a farmer, who fed them and put them to bed. In the morning the authorities were alerted, Joe Braddock was summoned from New Jersey to retrieve his wayward son, and the two-hour train ride home passed in total silence. Back in North Bergen, Jimmy received a beating that kept him off the trains for several years.

Meanwhile, at St. Joseph's, where he was still attending school, Jimmy continued to hone his pugilistic skills on a daily basis. "If I happened to be anywhere near where there was a fight," he once recalled, "I soon found myself in the middle of it. Many times I didn't know what it was all about, but I always managed to wind up getting the blame for it."

Trading punches with his classmates every day, Braddock grew accustomed to fighting — perhaps as much as any man who ever made his living with his fists. No matter the opponent, no matter the situation, he exuded confidence and a preternatural calm. Long after his retirement, Jimmy Cannon, the great columnist of the *New York Post*, wrote in typically eloquent fashion, "Serene was Braddock and unafraid. There was about him an inspiring calmness that transcended his ability."

Once, though, Braddock was afraid — he was afraid that he had killed a classmate.

One day in the schoolyard, he and Elmer Furlong got into an argument — apparently over a game of marbles — which quickly escalated into a full-blown fight. When Braddock landed a solid right to the jaw, Furlong went down hard.

"Elmer is dead!" another boy screamed.

The boys summoned a doctor, who revived Furlong — but

only after he had been lying unconscious for thirty minutes. While the boy was lying motionless in the schoolyard, Braddock's stomach was churning and he was thinking about how he might be punished. Staring at his hands, he was forced to consider, for the first time, the power within them.

The incident made a deep impression on Braddock — he told the story to several writers after he turned professional. In the wake of the Furlong knockout, Braddock and the nuns at St. Joseph's came to a meeting of the minds. They decided that Jimmy Braddock, at the age of fourteen, had had enough education.

In 1919 it was not unusual for a fourteen-year-old to quit school and hold down a steady job. The muckraking journalism of the era, embodied by Lewis Hine, with his camera, and Upton Sinclair, with his pen, had not yet succeeded in outlawing child labor. High school was for scholars. Jimmy Braddock was no scholar.

He found work quickly, as a messenger delivering Western Union telegrams. On the Fourth of July, 1919, he was carrying a stack of telegrams in downtown Union City, New Jersey, when he noticed an enormous throng that had gathered outside the offices of the *Hudson Dispatch*. Hundreds of men in summer suits and starched collars were listening intently to two *Dispatch* staffers who were trading a megaphone back and forth. Braddock realized at once what he was hearing — a blow-by-blow account of the world heavyweight championship fight that was taking place at that moment in Toledo, Ohio.

For four years an overgrown cowboy from Kansas named Jess Willard had held the title — since the steamy day in Havana when he had knocked out Jack Johnson in the twenty-sixth round. (Johnson later claimed he threw the fight. Willard retorted, "I hardly think he would have waited twenty-six rounds before taking a dive.") But now Willard, at six foot six and 250 pounds, was wilting under the staggering assault launched by twenty-four-year-old Jack Dempsey, of Manassa,

Colorado. In the first round, fighting with the unrestrained brutality that would make him a legend, Dempsey knocked Willard down seven times. It was said that Willard "managed himself, trained himself, and tossed in his own towel," so he had no one to turn to for advice when the round ended, because he was too thrifty to share his purse. Also, he thought that Dempsey didn't have a chance.

At thirty-seven, though, Willard was too old, too rusty, and too tired to withstand the ferocity of Dempsey's attack. With his lip split and his jaw broken, he refused to answer the bell for the fourth round. For the rest of his long life — he lived until 1968 — he claimed that Dempsey's hands were so destructive only because they had been dipped in cement.

Dempsey's seven-year reign at the top of the heavyweight division had begun. The Manassa Mauler, as he came to be known, was the defining figure of the Jazz Age, rivaled only by Babe Ruth, whom he outearned by a margin of more than ten to one. His fights against Georges Carpentier, Luis Firpo, and Gene Tunney were the most significant sporting events of the decade — bigger than any horserace, bowl game, or World Series.

The fight, which lasted less than twenty minutes, was the first significant heavyweight encounter in the United States since the Johnson-Jeffries bout in Reno nine years earlier. No one could have known it at the time, but Dempsey-Willard inaugurated boxing's golden age. A few months later, with the passage of the Walker Act, New York City's twenty-year ban on prizefighting was lifted. The city quickly reestablished itself as the center of the fistic solar system. There would be no more big fights in Toledo.

That night Dempsey dreamed he had been knocked out. At four in the morning, in a state of denial or delirium or both, he left his hotel in search of a newspaper, to find out who had actually won the fight.

"Give me a paper, kid," he said to the first paperboy he encountered. "Who won the fight?"

"Aren't you Jack Dempsey?"

"Yeah."

"You damn fool. You did! Don't you know?"

His curiosity satisfied, Dempsey turned around, went back upstairs to his room, and fell asleep.

Dempsey's thrilling victory so distracted young Jimmy Braddock that he entirely forgot his appointed rounds. He visualized himself as a professional boxer, fighting a giant like Willard and winning.

Braddock soon gave up his job as a messenger and went to work as a printer's devil, setting type in a press shop in Manhattan. Over the course of the next few years, from 1920 to 1923, he also worked as a teamster and as an errand boy in a silk mill. But none of these positions held his interest, and he grew restless. Emulating Dempsey, his hero, whose adventures as a teenage hobo had become part of his myth, Braddock hit the rails again, this time accompanied by several friends. Their westward progress was halted in Chicago.

After getting a taste of life in Al Capone's town for a few weeks, Braddock returned home to North Bergen. When he arrived, he set out to meet some friends at a place called Nurge's Field, and he had the temerity to throw on a brand-new sweater his older brother Joseph Junior had just purchased. It is quite conceivable that if Jim Braddock had selected another sweater, or a jacket, or anything other than his brother's sweater, he never would have become a prizefighter.

Legend has it that Joe, four years older than Jimmy, was furious when he got home and realized that his brother had borrowed his sweater. He tracked Jimmy down at Nurge's Field and, in a rage, flew at him. Without saying a word, he came up on Jimmy from behind, spun him around, and punched him in the face. The ensuing set-to was a classic.

Back and forth, up and down Nurge's Field, Joe and Jimmy punched and parried — to the delight of the assembled gang, which logically anticipated a quick knockout for the twenty-two-year-old Joe, who had just turned pro after an amateur career highlighted by capturing the New Jersey welterweight championship. Joe should have walloped any novice — even one, like his brother, who outweighed him by fifteen pounds.

Joe was peeved not only because Jimmy had borrowed his sweater without permission, but because Jimmy had worried their mother so much by tramping to Chicago. As a family, the Braddocks believed wholeheartedly in the educational value of a good, sound beating.

But Joe was matched blow for blow by his brother. He was stunned by the sting of Jimmy's fists, the swiftness with which they landed, and most of all the quality of Jimmy's chin. His brother could absorb punishment like no one Joe had ever fought. Jimmy was also completely unfazed by the situation. There was no wildness or fear in his eyes; he breathed steadily. He coldly sized up the situation and let his fists fly.

Joe and Jimmy traded punches for nearly an hour, by which time the sweater that had started the fight was torn and stained with their blood. Finally the police arrived and broke up the battling Braddocks.

For years the brothers argued about who won the fight, which became legendary in north Jersey. Whether or not Jimmy got the best of Joe, he had held up much better than expected. He realized that if he could fight his brother to a draw, he had a future as a boxer, an idea reinforced by the praise of those who witnessed the fight and spread the story throughout the county.

In and around North Bergen, Jimmy Braddock was suddenly a celebrity. When his neighbors realized that the ne'er-do-well tramp with no future could actually fight a little, they treated him with more respect — and Braddock noticed. His self-esteem surged.

Embarrassed by his inability to clobber his brother, Joe

stopped speaking to Jimmy after their brawl. But on November 27, 1923, as Joe was preparing to enter the ring to fight Battling Walker at Moose Hall in Grantwood, New Jersey, two of his closest friends told him that Jimmy was in the building and was itching for a fight.

The promoter that night, Harry Buesser, needed an opponent to square off against Tommy Hummel in a four-round bout. Jimmy Braddock was eager but hadn't dressed for the occasion. If his career was going to begin right then and there, he would need to borrow his brother's six-ounce gloves and homemade trunks. Grudgingly, Joe obliged — on the condition that Jimmy fight under an assumed name, Jimmy Ryan, which would enable him to fight under his real name as an amateur in the future.

"Don't get any blood on 'em, got me?" Joe said. It was the closest thing to encouragement he offered.

That night Tommy Hummel whipped Fighting Jimmy Ryan. But for an eighteen-year-old making his debut in organized fighting, Ryan/Braddock was impressive. He took Hummel's best shots and was unfazed. He was raw but unafraid. He kept wading in, never backing down. When he landed his right hand, flat-footed, without even generating half the power he was capable of delivering, Hummel took it hard. For his efforts, Jimmy Braddock made three dollars. And there was almost no blood on Joe's trunks.

Seated at ringside, Lud Shabazian, who had been elevated to sports editor at the *Hudson Dispatch* a year earlier, at the age of twenty, made a mental note: Find out more about Jimmy Ryan. Why, Shabazian wondered, were Joe Braddock and his manager, Barney Doyle, so interested in young Ryan?

After the fight, Joe — who was again on speaking terms with his brother — told Jimmy that he might have a future as a boxer. Jimmy Braddock had spent four years delivering telegrams, setting type, and running errands for a sweatshop.

Fighting was hard, but not that hard. He was eighteen, and for the first time in his life people were paying attention to him, admiring him, complimenting him. If he had been half as gifted as he was, he would still have chosen boxing over the drudgery of his other options.

What kind of life did he have to look forward to without boxing? At best he would find steady work in a factory or as a union truck driver — not the kind of career that would satisfy a man with his drive and his wanderlust. No one would have called Jimmy Braddock an egotist, but by the same token, he wouldn't mind being rich and famous. He was not afraid to dream.

The same night he sprang into the ring, Jimmy Ryan ceased to exist. Joe Braddock and Barney Doyle made it clear: if Jimmy was serious about boxing, he would have to pay his dues as an amateur, just as Joe had. It was impossible, they thought, to learn to fight on the job. An amateur apprenticeship was required. So Jimmy Ryan was laid to rest — career record 0–1 — and Jimmy Braddock, amateur light heavyweight, was born.

For the next few months, Joe and Jimmy Braddock spent most of their time in the gym. Joe would put on oversized gloves and Jimmy would wade into him. Slowly, Jimmy started punching more crisply, more like a pro. Joe made him practice his footwork and defense. Jimmy was an eager pupil and a quick study, picking up the finer points instinctively, despite his slowness. It helped that nothing outside the ring interested him — not even women. Yet. Boxing became his life, and he developed a profound respect for the sport. He was drawn to its ancient code, which he had learned as a schoolboy — the code that told him to stay on his feet no matter how hard he got hit. He was comfortable with the rigor of the boxer's life: the monkish devotion to training, the hours in the gym and on the road. He also liked to use his fists, because he was good at it.

He would become a fighter's fighter, not an enormously gifted boxer but a professional as familiar with defeat and disappointment as with triumph and glory. The notion that there is something honorable about trying to punch another man until he is senseless strikes some as ludicrous. But there is something undeniably admirable about men who display so much discipline and so much courage, who take so much pride in what they do and are willing to fail in full view of the rest of mankind. The most beloved fighters aren't the undefeated automatons, rare though they are. The fighters the fans love are the fearless, the vulnerable, and the game. Jimmy Braddock was all three.

From 1924 to 1926, Braddock was the terror of the Garden State's amateur ranks. With each quick knockout, Barney Doyle got louder and louder. He was convinced that in Jim Braddock he had finally landed a fighter of championship caliber.

On March 21, 1925, fighting at the National Turners Club in Newark, Braddock knocked out Johnny Emerson and won the New Jersey amateur light heavyweight championship. The fight lasted 107 seconds.

Two nights later, to burnish his reputation, he fought for the state's heavyweight championship — even though he was fourteen pounds under the *light* heavyweight limit. Weighing in at 161.5 pounds, he knocked out 209-pound Tom Burns in the first round of their semifinal bout. After only a few hours' rest, he fought 211-pound Roy Bodman in the finals. Bodman succumbed to a Braddock right hand one minute and fifty-seven seconds into the fight. Nineteen-year-old Jimmy Braddock was New Jersey's amateur light heavyweight and heavyweight champion.

At the same time, Joe Braddock was facing the biggest fight of his own career, against his archrival, Andy Lake, who like Joe had once held the New Jersey amateur welterweight title. Locally, Braddock versus Lake was one of the most anticipated events of 1925. Everyone in Hudson County knew they would fight to the finish. For weeks it was the talk of Union City, North Bergen, and every hamlet in between. Bragging rights were at stake. This was what boxing was like in the 1920s. It wasn't just about a few world-beaters on television. You could go see your neighbor fight, or your grocer's son, or your daughter's beau. Local grudge matches were deadly serious. There were fights everywhere, from Elks Clubs to baseball stadiums, all the time. Braddock-Lake mattered not at all in the world rankings. It mattered because the fighters knew each other and their friends and their priests knew each other. In those days, all boxing was local.

In the first round, Joe Braddock hit Andy Lake hard with a right hand. In the second and third rounds, his lead and his confidence grew. In the fourth round, he got sloppy and Lake knocked him out. Going into the fight, Barney Doyle had had his sights set high; now he was seething. He thought Joe had ignored his advice. While Joe was still unconscious on the canvas, Doyle stormed out of the arena, and when his brother revived, Jimmy told him that Doyle had bolted. Even though Joe continued to work with Doyle, he never forgot the slight.

Even as he worked various odd jobs to feed himself, Jimmy Braddock continued to spend most of his time in the gym, leading up to a repeat of his rare amateur championship double. On the night of February 28, 1926, he successfully defended his light heavyweight championship. Then, a few hours later, he defended the heavyweight championship against 212-pound Frank Zavita, who outweighed him by a staggering 50 pounds. At 162 pounds, Braddock had gained just eight ounces since he had won the title the year before.

The first punch Zavita threw was a perfect left hook to the body, which nearly crumpled Braddock, who somehow managed to stay on his feet. Years later, after he had fought Max Baer and Joe Louis, two of the most feared punchers ever, Braddock would say that no one ever hit him harder than Frank Zavita.

"What's the matter?" Zavita said. "Are you going to quit?"

It was the wrong question to ask Jimmy Braddock.

As Zavita continued to pummel him, Braddock did what he had been instructed to do: he jabbed. Every time Zavita threw his right, Braddock stuck out his left hand in defense. Quicker to the punch, he kept stinging the bigger man in the face, clinching, trying desperately to overcome the pain he was feeling in his midsection.

At the bell, Braddock staggered to his corner. His brother and Doyle managed to revive him. In the second round, he kept popping his jab into Zavita's now bloodied face. The bigger man was frustrated. None of his punches were landing. Then he did what tired, frustrated fighters always do: he made a mistake. Braddock was waiting. When Zavita threw a sloppy haymaker, a lazy, looping right hand, Braddock countered with a crisp right to the head. Down went Zavita. Then he went down again. Again. And again. And again. By the time Braddock knocked him out in the third round, Zavita had become quite familiar with the taste and texture of the canvas. It was the eleventh time he had gone down.

To anyone who was watching, it was clear that Jimmy Braddock was more than an ordinary fighter. He could punch, he could take a punch, and he had heart — the three prerequisites for greatness in the ring.

It was also clear that the apprenticeship of Jimmy Braddock was over. There was nothing left for him to prove as an amateur. It was time to turn pro.

From the southern tip of Cape May to West New York, Jimmy Braddock was the premier amateur fighter in the state of New Jersey. By this time Barney Doyle knew that Joe Braddock would not be a contender; all his hopes were now pegged to Joe's little brother, who was not only talented but fearless. Of course, it would be nice, Doyle must have thought, if the skinny Irishman would fill out a little. A fighter shouldn't make a habit of giving up fifty pounds to his opponents. Eventually he was going to run up against someone who could use that extra weight against him. It hadn't happened yet, but the day would come, Doyle thought. Still, he saw in Jimmy Braddock a future beyond the local fight clubs that at the time dotted every neighborhood.

Much to Doyle's surprise and consternation, however, he was exiled from Braddock's camp — by Joe, who had decided that he would personally guide his brother's career and who had never forgiven Doyle for abandoning him after Andy Lake had knocked him out.

When Jimmy went pro, Joe told him that he was giving up fighting to manage him. It made sense that Jimmy would want his brother as his manager. Joe wasn't looking to get rich from his talents; he was protecting him from the parasites he knew so many managers to be.

Turning pro was a momentous event in Jimmy Braddock's life. He was twenty years old. His future was boundless. His first fight, though, was typical of his early career. In other words, he was both brilliant and ordinary. Fighting an otherwise forgotten black heavyweight named Al Settle on April 14, 1926, at an otherwise forgotten arena known as Amsterdam Hall, Braddock could not score a knockout. He couldn't win either. He and Settle settled for a no-decision draw. For his four rounds of hard work, Braddock received fifteen dollars. No one could say he was overpaid.

Wasting no time, Joe quickly found a less formidable opponent who might boost his brother's ego: a baker from Union City named George Deschner. "I feinted him with a left in the second round," Braddock told Shabazian, "and *boom!* — the right hand finished him." For the knockout, Braddock was rewarded with thirty-five dollars.

With some cash in his pocket, Jimmy now took his brother's advice and started training regularly at Joe Jeannette's gym in West Hoboken. Born in North Bergen in 1879, Jeannette had been a leading heavyweight contender in the first two decades of the twentieth century — although to call him a contender is perhaps misleading. A contender, after all, is someone who can plausibly fight for the championship. Jeannette, who was black, was constantly passed over for title shots in favor of white men, as was his black contemporary Sam "the Boston Tar Baby" Langford. Even Jack Johnson refused to defend his title against Jeannette or Langford, opting instead for less dangerous opponents.

By 1926, Jeannette was eking out a living operating his gym, a hole-in-the-wall sweatbox filled day and night with aspiring pugilists. He was also a referee. Like most gyms, Jeannette's was filthy and decrepit. It is one of the charms of the fight game that even champions train in gyms that hygiene has forgotten. A clean gym is for dilettantes.

Jeannette's gym happened to be situated not far from the home of a young fight manager and reformed bantamweight named Joe Gould. Though Gould had fought a little as a teenager, he was better suited to a life outside the ring — in fact, just outside the ring. By the age of thirty, Gould, short, feisty, Jewish, and exceedingly verbal, had established himself in the very dirty and very competitive field of fight management. The most valuable boxer in his stable was Harry Galfund, a gifted Jewish welterweight from Brooklyn who, unfortunately for Gould, was also notoriously quarrelsome and demanding.

Speculating on fighters is always a tricky business. Measuring just how many punches a boxer has left to throw and how many he has to take is a matter less of science than of intuition. If nothing else, Joe Gould had intuition. He could look at a fighter the way a good rancher could size up cattle, measuring his heart, his skill, and his future.

Gould looked at Galfund and thought his future was behind him. Eager to rid himself of a fighter he considered unworthy of his talents, Gould found a group of investors from Hoboken — bootleggers — interested in purchasing his stake in Galfund for $2,500. There was only one catch: before they would pay, they wanted to see their prospective purchase in action. They too suspected that Galfund might be more trouble than he was worth. Accordingly, Gould arranged for Galfund to work out at Joe Jeannette's gym.

The gym was busy but not overflowing when Gould and Galfund showed up on a Wednesday afternoon in June 1926. The typical assortment of broken-down bums and eager novices were pounding away on punching bags and one another. Galfund changed into his trunks, and then Gould taped up his hands and laced on the gloves. Now all they needed was a sparring partner — someone who would make Galfund look good.

Up against the wall, a tall, skinny, impossibly pale young man was shadowboxing. He looked like he was fifteen.

Gould approached him, and the young man put down his fists. "You want to make five bucks?" Gould said.

"Sure," Jimmy Braddock said, wiping the sweat from his eyes.

"All right," Gould said. "I just want you to box three rounds with this fellow over here."

"Sure," Braddock said, as though Gould had asked him what time it was.

Gould walked back to Galfund. "Now listen," he said. "Knock this bum out as quick as you can. Understand?"

Galfund nodded. "Okay," he said.

For all his instincts and all his savvy, Gould picked the wrong guy to spar with Harry Galfund. Like nearly everyone else, he made the mistake of underestimating Jimmy Braddock on first sight.

With the potential investors standing within inches of the ring, Harry Galfund, famous welterweight, bore down on Jimmy Braddock. Like Gould, Galfund needed an impressive performance; he would receive 50 percent of whatever the investors paid for his contract. But as soon as he moved within range, Braddock clipped him with a left to the head, causing the lighter man to stagger. *Anyone can get lucky,* Galfund must have thought, and he waded in again. Again Braddock hurt him with a left. Then a right. Then a left. Struggling when he should have been dominating the action, Galfund slowed Braddock down in the clinches, fired off a few shots of his own, and at the bell retired to his corner.

"What are you doing, trying to ruin the sale?" Gould said to him. "These guys are laughing at me."

"I'll knock the bum out right now," Galfund said, breathing heavily.

But in the second round, Braddock embarrassed Galfund — and Gould — again. Every time Galfund threw a punch, Braddock countered with a harder punch. Easily warding off Galfund's blows, he stayed on the offensive, punishing Galfund with shots to the head and body.

The third round was much the same, and Gould ended it abruptly, explaining to the investors that Galfund was under the weather. He agreed to accept $1,200 for the rights to Galfund, less than half the original price. He and Galfund split the amount evenly.

Six hundred and fifty dollars poorer than he thought he would be, Gould approached the young man who had refused to play possum for Harry Galfund.

"Here is ten dollars for you instead of five," he said as he tried to calculate Braddock's height and weight. "What's your name?"

"Braddock," Braddock said. Gould noticed that he hadn't broken a sweat.

"You know who I am?" Gould asked, in a way that suggested Braddock should know.

"You're Joe Gould," Braddock said. Braddock knew plenty of Irishmen named Gould, but he could tell that this Joe Gould wasn't Irish.

"You've got a manager?" Gould asked.

"My brother Joe," Braddock said.

"Oh, the welterweight," Gould said. He had seen Joe fight

many times. He was hoping that Jimmy was more talented than his brother. "When can I see him?"

"He works during the week," Braddock said. "He's a plumber. But he'll be here Saturday."

"Tell him I'll be here at noon to see him," Gould said. "I want to talk about your future."

The Meat Inspector

Jersey City, New Jersey: 1926

Only a few Jewish athletes have been heroes to the vast majority of American Jews. In the 1960s, there was Sandy Koufax. In the 1930s and 1940s, there was Hank Greenberg. In the teens and 1920s, there was Benny Leonard.

"Our superhero was Benny Leonard," wrote Budd Schulberg, who was born in 1914. "'The Great Benny Leonard.' That's how he was always referred to in our household. There was the Great Houdini. The Great Caruso. *And* the Great Benny Leonard . . . I had only one ambition, to become a world champion like the Great Benny Leonard."

Schulberg was far from exceptional. Leonard's fans were legion. Born Benjamin Leiner in 1896 in Brooklyn, raised on the Lower East Side and in East Harlem, Leonard was to the lightweight division what Jack Dempsey was to the heavyweight division — a singular, spectacular talent. He was, however, much more active than Dempsey. In 1919, as the lightweight champion, he fought twenty-six times. Over his career he participated in more than two hundred official fights, not including scores of exhibitions. He held the title for almost eight years, from 1917 to 1925. His success made him a hero to hundreds of thousands of American Jews who were still struggling to shed their foreignness. Though he was only five foot six and weighed just over 130 pounds, Leonard gave them strength and hope.

Long before Leonard became an icon, when he was just learning to scrap on the streets, one of his best friends was Joe Goldstein, a tough little kid who lived next door. Goldstein was even shorter and lighter than Leonard, but he loved to fight, both with his mouth and with his fists. Like almost every other Jewish boy in East Harlem, he looked up to Leonard, who would clearly someday fight for a living. Naturally, he wanted to do the same.

Several years before Joe was born, his father, Benjamin Biegel, stepped off a boat at Ellis Island. His world had changed from a shtetl in Poland to New York City in just thirty days. Somehow, for reasons best known to the Immigration Service, Benjamin Biegel became Abraham Goldstein at Ellis Island. He never bothered to correct the error.

Carrying only his new name and a few shirts and socks, Abraham Goldstein found his way to Poughkeepsie, a city sixty miles up the Hudson River from Ellis Island. It was there that Joseph, the fifth of Abraham's nine children, was born, on August 14, 1896, late in the second term of President Grover Cleveland. When Joe was two, the family moved to 49 East 112th Street in Harlem.

Joe Goldstein, Benjamin Leiner, and a boy named Robert Lippman grew up together in this East Harlem neighborhood, scrapping in the streets, cutting class, and causing trouble. Unlike their siblings, they had little or no interest in scholarly pursuits. They would not attend services on Saturday morning. They did not want to be lawyers, doctors, or accountants. They did not want to play baseball. They wanted to fight.

Eventually, each would assume a nom de guerre: Goldstein became Joe Gould, Leiner became Benny Leonard, and Lippman became Doc Robb. Gould would manage a world champion, Leonard would become a world champion, and Robb would train three world champions. Clearly, something was in the water.

The Jewish community in East Harlem was much smaller than those in the ghettos of the Lower East Side and Brooklyn. There was no uptown equivalent of Delancey Street, bustling with immigrants from Russia and Poland. But like their counterparts downtown and across the East River, the Jews of Harlem lifted themselves up from poverty and into the halls of academia and commerce in one generation.

Joe Gould, though, was an exception. He was as disdainful of book learning as Braddock was. He ran with the wrong crowd. His brother Irving went to the Ivy League, entering the University of Pennsylvania to study ophthalmology. His brothers Aaron and Sam passed the bar exam. Joe, in contrast, quit school and enlisted in the navy before the United States entered World War I.

While he was in the service, Gould fought as a featherweight and made matches between his shipmates. It became painfully clear to him that he was a better matchmaker than fighter. "They put us on an oil tanker," he later told Lud Shabazian, "and that's where I learned to schmooze those matchmakers and promoters into giving my fighters good fights."

But back on shore, living with his family now in Jersey City, Gould couldn't decide what he wanted to do with his life. Naturally, he opted to take a civil service test for meat inspectors — a growth business in 1916, when standards were just being implemented and enforced at American abattoirs. Woefully unfamiliar with the butcher's arts, he failed the exam by a wide margin.

However, fortunately for Gould, the United States declared war on Germany on April 6, 1917. Suddenly most certified meat inspectors were "over there," safeguarding the doughboys' right to untainted beef. Since the qualified inspectors had been drafted, Gould was in luck — and at work. "Just imagine, I got sixty-five dollars a week as a meat inspector," he later said, "and what I didn't know about meat would have filled a whole stock-yard."

Then came November 11, 1918. The Treaty of Versailles not only ended the war; it may have saved the lives of those who might have eaten bad meat rubber-stamped by Joe Gould.

Out of work, Gould went to see his old friend Sammy Diamond, with whom he had grown up in Harlem and served in the navy. Sammy's brother Lew was making a name for himself as a boxing manager. His best fighter, a Jersey City lightweight named Johnny Buff, had just claimed two championships. Lew agreed to teach Gould the business.

Instantly Gould knew that he had found his calling. No clock to punch. No boss to flatter. No degree required. All he would need was his brains and his mouth — which were certainly Harvard caliber.

By the mid-1920s, Gould had built a strong stable of fighters and was among the more successful managers in boxing. He wasn't rich and powerful, like Doc Kearns, Dempsey's manager, but he seemed to be on his way.

Unlike most managers today, Gould had been a fighter himself. He respected the sport and he respected boxers. But as a young manager, by his own admission, he was sometimes less concerned with his fighters' health than with their — and his own — wealth.

Gould liked to tell a story about the time when Tex Rickard, the preeminent promoter of the era, wanted Joe Herman, one of Gould's boxers, to fight Luis Firpo in Havana. Gould agreed to the bout without consulting Herman. He soon found out that Herman was in the hospital, though, which Gould did not see as a deterrent to his fighting Firpo a few days later.

"What's the matter with you?" Gould asked.

"I had a pain in the belly," Herman said, "and the doctor says I'm going to get appendicitis."

"Are you?" Gould asked.

"I don't think so," Herman said. "I feel great."

"Then what are you lying here for," Gould said, "when you are boxing Firpo in Havana on Wednesday?"

"I am?" Herman yelled.

Then, the story goes, Herman jumped out of bed and pulled on his pants.

Frank Graham of the *New York Sun* was perhaps the greatest boxing writer ever. Joe Gould would become his favorite manager. In *The New Yorker*, John Lardner ranked Gould among the great managers. "In spite of a compulsion to find the 'angle' in everything he did," Lardner wrote, "he had legitimate gifts that entitled him to a place . . . at the top of his profession."

Gould agreed. "I take my hat off to no manager," he said once, within earshot of Dumb Dan Morgan, another legendary manager. "Your hat means nothing," Morgan responded. "You don't even take it off when you eat." (Morgan, incidentally, was neither stupid nor incapable of speech. Rather, he was called Dumb the way you might call a short man Stretch. Like Gould, Doyle, and most other managers, he could talk until his audience passed out.)

Lardner, whose father, Ring, virtually invented modern sports writing, loved fight managers. "The manager may be a racketeer or a parasite," John Lardner wrote, "but, in his best form, he is a man of wit and skill, as exhilarated by a sense of his own personality as any fighter could be, and proud, as no other kind of agent or 'easy rider' is, of the thought that he makes his way by what Jimmy Johnston called 'the sweat of my imagination.'"

Dapper, debonair, and street-smart, Joe Gould sweated for Jim Braddock, badgering promoters, courting writers, lining up opponents. Decked out in the finest suits, smoking the most expensive cigars, and dining at the classiest restaurants, Gould was as slick as Braddock was simple. He loved to promote himself and therefore was the ideal man to guide Braddock, who was constitutionally incapable of self-promotion. The partnership they formed was unique: the tall, quiet, powerful Irishman and the short, fast-talking Jew were the sport's favorite odd couple.

"They looked like Mutt and Jeff and behaved like Damon and Pythias," W. C. Heinz wrote. At five foot five, Gould was about nine inches shorter than Braddock. Lean in his youth, he was cultivating a potbelly by the mid-1920s, obscured by his well-tailored suits but immediately apparent when he was in less formal attire, like the T-shirts he wore when working Braddock's corner. He talked a lot, loudly, and liked to stick his chin into the air to emphasize certain well-considered points.

When Gould talked, Braddock sometimes listened and sometimes didn't, but he never interrupted him. There was no way to get a word in.

"Listen," Gould told Braddock shortly after they signed with each other, "I've got a fight for you. At Boyle's. You ever fought outdoors?"

"Not with gloves on," Braddock said.

Within a few weeks of their initial encounter, Gould signed Braddock to fight Leo Dobson at an enormous outdoor arena called Boyle's Thirty Acres. Just five years earlier, Boyle's had been the site of the fight that had generated the first million-dollar gate — Jack Dempsey versus Georges Carpentier of France. But by the time Braddock and Dobson were supposed to fight there, the arena was a white elephant. The taxes were costing Tex Rickard, who had built it for the Dempsey-Carpentier showdown, more than he could recoup.

Braddock and Dobson were to fight on the undercard of a bout between Tiger Flowers and Young Bob Fitzsimmons, on June 18, 1926. Early that afternoon, Braddock, ecstatic to be making seventy-five dollars for a night's work, showed up for the weigh-in. Curiously, his opponent did not. Fighting as a light heavyweight, Braddock could have weighed up to 175 pounds, but he weighed only 163. At most, he thought, he would be giving up 12 pounds to Dobson, about whom he knew virtually nothing.

Hours passed, and still Dobson was a no-show. Gould began to get suspicious. He wondered what Charley Doessereck, the matchmaker, was hiding.

As it turned out, Doessereck was hiding Dobson's girth — and his record. Sniffing around for information about Braddock's missing opponent, Gould found out that Dobson had won fourteen straight fights by knockout. Suddenly he felt sick.

"What's wrong?" Braddock said.

"Idontlikeit," Gould said. When he was anxious, he spoke very quickly. "I don't know what Charley's got up his sleeve."

When Dobson, who was black, finally showed up at the arena, he tipped the scales at 189 pounds, 14 more than the light heavyweight limit and 26 more than Braddock.

Now Gould was in a rage. Not only was Braddock climbing into the ring to fight a heavyweight, he was fighting a heavyweight with a stunning recent record. He told Braddock to get back into his street clothes. No one was going to make a fool of Joe Gould.

Watching Gould storm around, Braddock wondered what he had gotten himself into. Gould, it was clear, had an uncontrollable temper and a highly developed sense of persecution. He was loudly berating Doessereck, and alternately himself. "If he thinks he's dealing with a rube, well, I'll show him," Gould said, stabbing his finger in the air, his face turning red. But Braddock decided he wasn't going to let Gould ruin his night. When he was an amateur, he told Gould, he had fought men who outweighed him by more than fifty pounds. And won. A twenty-six-pound difference meant nothing to him.

This was his first fight in a big arena, with thousands of spectators, among them dozens of friends and relatives. And he was looking forward to it. Jersey City was his back yard. *Trust me*, Braddock said. *I'll knock the bum out.*

It bothered Gould that he had been conned. Doessereck had known that once Braddock was in the building, it would be all but impossible for him to back out of the fight. Why would he walk away from seventy-five bucks?

Against his better instincts, Gould relented. "Fine," he said. "Get in there and knock him out."

Usually in manager-fighter relationships, the fighter is the hothead and the manager spends large chunks of every day undoing the damage caused by his rash gladiator. But when the fighter burns slowly, like Braddock, or not at all, the manager is the one who has to be aggressive, protecting their interests and making sure they get respect. Gould was congenitally aggressive, a fighting bantam with his chin out and his tongue wagging. Most often Braddock had to calm *him* down.

At about nine o'clock — there was still ample daylight — Braddock climbed through the ropes. He was twenty-one years old and about to fight in front of a large outdoor crowd on a splendid summer evening in the famous pine bowl where the great Dempsey had fought. This was everything he had ever wanted.

Jack Merity, the ring announcer, grabbed the microphone and said, "And from North Bergen, New Jersey, entering the ring at one hundred sixty-three pounds, James J. Braddock!"

Braddock couldn't hear the cheers of his friends and family through the din. Still, he wondered what they thought of his new name, which was Gould's idea. A few days earlier, Gould had bumped into the former heavyweight champion James J. Jeffries on the street in Manhattan, and it had occurred to him that it would be a good idea to link Braddock with boxing's great James J.'s. So Gould ditched the *W* for a *J*.

In fact, three of the first eight men to hold the world heavyweight championship after the advent of the Queensberry rules in the 1880s were named James J. In 1892, James J. Corbett, invariably described as a mild-mannered San Francisco bank clerk, stunned the boxing world by defeating the great John L.

Sullivan. Two years earlier, in a charity exhibition, Corbett and Sullivan had fought in evening wear.

At the turn of the century, boxing's biggest star was James J. Jeffries, who wrested the title from Bob Fitzsimmons. At six foot two and 220 pounds, Jeffries was a huge man, especially for his time. He is best remembered for coming out of retirement at the age of thirty-five — at the urging of writers such as Jack London, who dubbed him the Great White Hope — to fight Jack Johnson for the title in Reno, Nevada, on July 4, 1910. Johnson, the first black man to reign as heavyweight champion, tore Jeffries to shreds, and Jeffries's defeat sparked antiblack riots and lynchings.

James Joseph Tunney was born in Greenwich Village in 1897. In 1926, Tunney, known as Gene, won the title from Jack Dempsey in Philadelphia, and a year later he defended it in Chicago. The rematch was probably the most anticipated sporting event in American history. More than 100,000 people attended, and the gate, $2.6 million, was a record for almost fifty years. In the seventh round, Dempsey knocked Tunney down but failed to retreat to a neutral corner, which delayed the beginning of the count. Tunney was down for about thirteen seconds before he stood up. The Long Count, as it was instantly known, tainted Tunney's victory in many minds and made Dempsey a bigger hero than he had ever been as champion.

In 1928, a year after his victory in Chicago, Tunney retired from the ring, leaving the championship vacant and throwing the heavyweight division into turmoil for nine years.

Three months before the first Tunney-Dempsey fight, Braddock waited for the bell to ring. He had thought that he would be nervous, but when he climbed through the ropes, he realized he wasn't. When the fight started, he moved forward to meet Dobson cautiously, feeling him out, looking for his weaknesses. In the second round, he exploited what he had found. First he went to the body with his left, breaking two of Dobson's ribs, then to the head with a thunderous right. Dobson — all

189 pounds of him — fell at the feet of James J. Braddock. Numerous Braddocks who were in the crowd leaped to their feet and shouted. For the first time in his life, Jimmy Braddock heard an enormous crowd cheering for him. Gould jumped into the ring and hugged him.

"See, Joe," Braddock said, grinning, "big guys don't scare me."

Paddy Mullins, who had managed the great black heavyweight Harry Wills, was awestruck by Braddock's performance. It was reported that after Dobson was counted out, he said to Braddock in his thick brogue, "Sure, bye, and you're the next champeen!"

Three weeks later, Braddock fought again at Boyle's Thirty Acres, against Walter Westman. Joe Jeannette was the referee. Braddock hurt Westman badly, and Jeannette stopped the fight in the third round. James J. Braddock was 2–0. Braddock for Galfund, Joe Gould said to himself, was a hell of a trade.

4

The Livermore Butcher Boy

....

San Francisco: 1930

The man Jim Braddock would eventually face in the most significant fight of his life had the physique of a Greek god and the mentality of a circus clown.

At six two and a half and 210 pounds, with a waist as slim as a bride's and shoulders as wide as a doorframe, Max Baer was built to box. His cranium was the only problem. "That's right," he once said, "I got a million-dollar body and a ten-cent brain."

But Baer was by no means stupid. On the contrary, he was charming and quick-witted, especially for a man whose formal education had ended after one year of high school. He simply did not possess the mental qualities that the old-timers said great champions had to possess: ferocity, cold-bloodedness, and gameness. In several crucial fights during what should have been his prime, he was neither ferocious nor cold-blooded, much less game. More than anything else, he liked to make people laugh, which he did frequently.

None of this is meant to suggest that Baer only looked like a boxer. His arms weren't just muscled, they were powerful. His shoulders weren't just broad, they generated tremendous force. His chin wasn't just chiseled, it was famously solid. He was no Primo Carnera or Jess Willard, who added up to significantly less than the sum of their respective physical attributes.

Max Baer was much more than a pretty physique. Everyone agreed that he should have been a great champion. But everything that Jim Braddock would come to personify — stability, stoicism, determination, doggedness, and resiliency — was foreign to Baer.

So much came so easily to him; so many gifts were showered on him; women and money and fame sought him out. Who could blame him for laughing hard all the time? It's hard to find a picture of Baer in which he is not smiling broadly, with his eyes narrowed to slits — even when he was in the ring. He lived his life in a state of perpetual amusement.

In an era when sports figures almost always had a nickname — the Sultan of Swat (Babe Ruth), the Manassa Mauler (Jack Dempsey), the Wild Horse of the Osage (Pepper Martin) — Baer may have had the most, and the most colorful. Madcap Maxie, the Livermore Larruper, the Merry Madcap, the Livermore Butcher Boy, the Fistic Harlequin, the Larruping Lothario of Pugilism, the Pugilistic Poseur, the Clouting Clown, the Playboy of Pugilism, and the Magnificent Screwball are but a sampling of the flights of poetic fancy that he inspired.

Before the writers and promoters turned on him, they made a killing from Baer. During the Depression, when attendance at baseball stadiums dipped precipitously and after boxing had been marred by the mob, his antics kept fans interested in the fights. He helped erase the putrid taste of the suspect bouts that gave the heavyweight championship to Jack Sharkey in 1932 and to Primo Carnera in 1933. Grantland Rice, the preeminent sports writer of the era, called Baer "the New Deal for bored fight fans."

Nearly twenty years after Baer died, in 1959, *Sports Illustrated*'s Ron Fimrite, who as a child had fallen under his spell, captured the essence of the Livermore Larruper:

"Above all else, he was a lover, not a fighter. That such a man should have become heavyweight champion of the world and a principal in some of the ring's bloodiest conflicts, including one — purportedly two — that brought about the death of an opponent, is one of the most remarkable paradoxes in the history of sport."

The former light heavyweight champion Tommy Loughran defeated Baer before Baer went on a four-year winning streak that culminated in his championship victory over Carnera. A brilliant and elegant boxer, Loughran, the Philadelphia Phantom, lived to the age of seventy-nine. He claimed that "Max was the most misunderstood fighter of them all. He was the nicest guy. He had the heart of a lion."

Maximilian Adelbert Baer was born in Omaha on February 11, 1909. In 1915, little Max and his family moved to Denver, then to Durango, Colorado, where his father, Jacob, worked for Swift, the meatpacking giant.

Jacob Baer was an accomplished butcher and slayer of cattle who had once won a national meat-trimming contest at the Chicago stockyards. "Our father's a champion too," Buddy Baer, Max's younger brother and a top heavyweight contender, once said. "At dressing a steer. That's opening the steer, removing the insides, splitting him, and turning back the hide. In a contest once Dad dressed a steer and carved the American flag on the hide in three minutes and thirty-six seconds."

In 1922, when Max was thirteen, the Baers relocated again, this time to northern California. Jacob soon purchased the Twin Oaks Ranch in Livermore, forty-five miles east of San Francisco. Raising hogs and cattle, the family thrived.

By all accounts, Jacob, of German and Jewish extraction, and his wife, Dora, who was Scotch-Irish, provided a loving home for their five children, including a Portuguese ranch hand whom they adopted. For their biological children they also provided genes that, when properly mixed, produced some extraordinary specimens. Jacob and Dora were both six feet tall and weighed about 200 pounds. Their children were bigger.

Working on the family ranch, Max developed his famous muscles, swinging an ax and hauling the heavy carcasses of cattle and pigs. If the ranch had been in Zanzibar rather than Livermore, his life could not have been further removed from life in North Bergen, where Jimmy Braddock was living.

Unlike Braddock, Baer grew up without knowing how to throw a punch. He claimed that when he was attacked by schoolmates, his sister Frances — who eventually grew to six feet and more than 200 pounds — defended his honor. When she was unavailable, he simply fled. But one night, outside a dance hall near Lodi, when Baer was seventeen, he and some friends found a parked truck full of bottles of homemade wine — the kind of swill that only Prohibition could have made potable. Back inside the hall, Max's friends passed the bottles around, although Max never took a sip.

The swill was contraband, but it was the property of a stout lumberjack who stormed at Baer and his friends when he spotted the bottles being passed from across the dance floor. Terrified, Baer made a run for it, but before he could reach the door the lumberjack grabbed him from behind. In an instant the man pulled back his right fist and struck Baer flush on the jaw with a powerful blow. To the considerable surprise of his attacker and himself, Baer didn't budge. The punch hadn't hurt him at all. Reflexively, he pulled back *his* right fist and let fly. The lumberjack collapsed at his feet, unconscious. Baer had registered the first knockout of his career.

The dance came to a standstill. No one could believe what had just happened.

"Are you wearing brass knuckles?" one of Baer's friends asked.

"No, I just punched him," Baer said, examining his right hand.

"Well, that was a helluva punch."

"A lucky punch, I guess," Baer said.

But luck had nothing to do with it. Baer had discovered the weapon that would shape the rest of his life.

*   *   *

Until that moment, Baer had been interested in fighting purely as a fan — of Jack Dempsey's. He was only ten when Dempsey defeated Jess Willard — too young to appreciate the Mauler's fighting qualities. But by 1923, when Dempsey fought Luis Firpo, the Wild Bull of the Pampas, Baer was fourteen and, like virtually every other teenage boy in America, paying close attention.

In 1949, when the Associated Press polled 374 sports writers and commentators to determine the most thrilling sports event of the first half of the century, Babe Ruth's called shot in the 1932 World Series didn't win (it placed second). Neither did the match race between War Admiral and Seabiscuit (not in the top fifteen). Neither did Jesse Owens's four victories at the Olympics in Berlin (eleventh). Or Joe Louis's one-round knockout of Max Schmeling in 1938 (tenth). Or the Long Count in Dempsey-Tunney II (third). Instead, Dempsey-Firpo won an easy decision.

More than 85,000 people jammed the Polo Grounds in northern Manhattan to see Dempsey defend his title on September 14, 1923. The receipts were $1,188,603. For weeks fans had debated the relative merits of the champion and the challenger. The city was gripped by heavyweight fever. "Even the subway and elevated guards fell in with the spirit of the occasion," the *New York Times* reported. "A guard on one of the elevated trains was heard to remark: 'Step lively, lady; we mustn't keep Jack waiting.'" Twenty-five thousand fans stuck outside the Polo Grounds rioted when a sign went up to tell them that the fight was sold out. If they had known what they were about to miss, they would have been even angrier. Even Jess Willard waited forty-five minutes to get through the turnstiles.

"It was not a boxing match — not a civilized fistic encounter," Frank Menke wrote. "Two wild men were tossed into the same ring, each with an intent to murder the other — or be murdered in his failure. And 85,000 persons, imbibing the spirit of madness, arose to their feet, and 85,000 voices howled and shrieked in a delirium that made a din which rivaled a thousand Niagaras."

The first round was the most thrilling round ever seen in a heavyweight championship fight. Dempsey knocked Firpo down seven times, Firpo knocked Dempsey down twice, and when a Firpo punch hurled Dempsey out of the ring, some writers seated at ringside saved the champion by shoving him back onto the canvas. "I fell right on top of the press," Dempsey said. "When I fell I could have hurt myself pretty badly. I had to go to the hospital after. It tore my whole backside open. The bell rang about the time I got back in there. I got a break. If the bell hadn't rung, it might have been a different story."

In the second round, Dempsey knocked Firpo down again, but Firpo got up. Then, with a short right uppercut, Dempsey laid out the gallant Argentine.

The entire fight, including a total of eleven knockdowns, lasted three minutes and fifty-seven seconds. "The crowd saw four minutes of action," John Lardner wrote, exaggerating only slightly, "at a rate of three hundred thousand dollars a minute. There is no record that any member of it complained."

As Nat Fleischer, the Homer of boxing writers and the founder of *Ring Magazine*, put it, "It was the most dramatic fight in the history of modern pugilism. It was a gripping, nerve-shaking contest between lion-hearted, heavy-hitting ringmen."

It was also Dempsey's defining moment, the fight that cemented his place in boxing history — although it did not make him beloved; only his losses to Tunney would achieve that effect. Still, Dempsey without Firpo is like Ali without Foreman or Truman without Dewey.

Back in Livermore, with the lumberjack lying unconscious at his feet, Max Baer realized that up until that moment he hadn't known his own strength, that he could perhaps pursue Dempsey's line of work. As Fleischer later excitedly put it, "The fighting instinct was awake, never to slumber again!"

Soon enough a local man named Percy Madsen took an interest in Baer's boxing aspirations. Madsen recruited Ray Pelkey, a veteran fighter from Oakland, to tutor Baer, who was already six feet tall and 190 pounds.

This was the beginning of a pattern in Baer's early career. He never had to seek out mentors. People just had to look at him to see championship belts and dollar signs. In gyms crowded with hopefuls, Baer stood out. Fighters, trainers, managers — they all wanted to help mold him. Some were motivated by greed; others had purer impulses.

Baer showed enough aptitude in his early training to warrant a change of venue. He wasn't going to progress as a fighter living in Livermore. He needed expert training and solid competition. Fortunately, the Bay Area was a breeding ground for boxers, with a proud tradition dating to Gentleman Jim Corbett and beyond.

Before Baer turned eighteen, not long after the fight at the dance hall, he moved to Oakland and found work in a factory that produced diesel engines. One of the factory foremen happened to be a boxing enthusiast and gave him permission to set up a makeshift gym in the basement, which was soon outfitted with a twenty-five-dollar punching bag filled with sand. When his shift ended on the assembly line, Baer would immediately head for the basement and proceed to demolish anyone foolhardy enough to lace up a pair of gloves and trade blows with him. If opposition dried up — broken noses and sore ribs tended to discourage rematches — Baer would shadowbox, hit the bag, and jump rope.

Max Baer's boxing skills were a gift he loved to share — and to show off. During his shift he would punch the air with his fists, working on his form, strengthening his already substantial muscles. It was inevitable that he would attract the attention of J. Hamilton Lorimer, an avid boxing fan whose family owned the factory in which Baer labored. Wherever he was — in the company of machinists or in the company of film stars

— Baer stood out. Men and women gravitated to him, not simply because he was good-looking but also because he exuded warmth.

Like virtually everyone who met him, J. Hamilton Lorimer developed an instant fondness for the young man from Livermore. He knew Baer wanted to box. He also knew that good machinists were a sounder investment than aspiring heavyweights. But when Baer urged him to find him a fight through his boxing connections, Lorimer reluctantly consented.

"Max worked for me," Lorimer told a newspaper reporter in 1930. "He was always talking fight. I listened, and when he began to train in an amateur sort of way, he asked me to hold the watch for him. He was big and powerful, but I thought him too good-looking to go in for fighting. I wanted to cure him of his nonsense. So I matched him with Chief Caribou, an Indian heavyweight in Stockton, the toughest fellow around."

Just before the fight, at the Oak Park Arena in Stockton, Baer, who had just turned twenty, was desperately thirsty. It was a hot, muggy night. Unaware of the deleterious effects of carbonation, Baer quenched his thirst by downing five bottles of Coca-Cola. As he prepared to enter the ring, the soda was turning his stomach inside out. When the fight started, Chief Caribou struck him in the stomach. Baer nearly threw up. He realized that he had no time to spare — if he didn't knock out Chief Caribou soon, his nausea would make it impossible for him to continue. So he chased Caribou around the ring, winding up his haymakers and utterly disregarding his own defense. The crowd went crazy. Who was this mad bomber? For his part, Chief Caribou, who thought he had seen everything in the ring, was bewildered. Never had he encountered a fighter who flailed across the canvas so recklessly.

Baer was raw and wild but effective. Four times in the first round, he knocked Caribou down. In the second round, as Caribou was calculating just how long his opponent could keep up his constant attack, he was struck on the temple by Baer's right hand. At that moment Chief Caribou's mind went blank, his heart momentarily stopped beating, and his big body toppled over. He had never been hit with such force.

Maximilian Adelbert Baer had claimed his first victim — and thirty-five one-dollar bills. Coca-Cola was eliminated from his prefight routine.

Now Lorimer was stuck. He had lost his gamble. Baer would not toil on the assembly line anymore, and Lorimer had promised to manage him. But Lorimer was not yet convinced that Baer had the makings of a champion. To determine just what he had, he matched him not against the usual fare of punch-drunk has-beens but against legitimate, well-respected tough guys. Like Sailor Leeds.

According to Nat Fleischer, Leeds was "a hard-bitten hombre with a sinister rep for icing opponents in the opening round of a squabble." Baer had every reason to worry. When he fought Leeds, his entire ring career consisted of the two-round knockout of Chief Caribou and a one-round knockout of Tillie Taverna in his second fight.

But Baer, Lorimer was learning, was fearless. The man-child who had never thrown a punch in anger was now mesmerized by the power of his right hand. Discovering it was like waking up one day to find that you are a world-class pianist. It was like striking gold. And Baer knew it. He was eager to show off his phenomenal punch, eager to jump in the ring against anyone. Boxing meant nothing to him, but punching was his narcotic. He had been warned to be wary of Leeds and his arsenal. Instead he emerged from his corner in a rage, swinging wildly, overwhelming his opponent with right hands. When the first big punch landed, less than ninety seconds into the first round, Leeds went down and did not get up.

Word of the wild man from Livermore was spreading, from Stockton to Oakland to San Francisco and San Jose. In just three fights, Baer had established a reputation and a following.

In 1929 he fought a total of sixteen fights, winning the first twelve (including a rematch against the always game Chief Caribou) by knockout, winning the next three by decision, and losing the last, against Jack McCarthy, on a foul. For his ninth fight, against Alec Rowe, Baer earned $4,000. For his fourteenth, against Benny Hill — decidedly *not* the English comic — he earned $7,500.

As quickly as Baer caught on with the fisticuffs crowd, he was even more popular with what was then referred to as the fairer sex. Among the many who pursued him, the first to capture his heart was Olive Beck, a waitress. She was also the first woman, but not the last, to sue him for breach of promise. She thought they were getting married until one night at the movies when she saw him with another woman — in the newsreel. After Baer left Olive, he sent her a postcard:

> Hello, I'll bet you're surprised to hear from me. I am sure feeling fine. And know you are always trying to forget. Excuse the writing — never was much as you know. Always, Max.

Eventually Baer paid off Olive Beck and went on to make and break promises to other women.

Even the Depression could not stop Baer from having his fun. As an up-and-coming boxer, he was basically immune from the hard times. He was in demand, and people needed their diversions, even if fewer and fewer could afford them. A crowd pleaser, Baer knocked out virtually every opponent unfortunate enough to step in his path. As his fame spread from the Bay Area to points south, his instinctive showmanship flowered. He arrived in a sixteen-cylinder limousine, attended by both a chauffeur and a footman, for the contract-signing ceremony that preceded his first fight in Los Angeles, in April 1930. He was dressed like an English nobleman at leisure, in tweeds, riding pants, and boots.

There were two fights in January 1930 — a loss to Tiny Abbott, the Eureka Giant, who stood six foot eight and weighed 240 pounds, followed quickly by a rematch and a knockout win.

Then there were two fights in April — one win by knockout, one by decision. In May, two more fights, both won by knockout. Jack Linkhorn, Baer's victim on May 28, had knocked out eighteen consecutive opponents. Baer knocked him out in the first round. In June, Baer registered two more knockout victories. Then, in July, fighting a solid veteran named Les Kennedy in Los Angeles, he lost a decision. But he and his fans were far from discouraged.

As it became clear that Baer was no ordinary fighter, Lorimer sought the assistance of Ancil Hoffman, a veteran West Coast manager and avocado farmer from Sacramento. Hoffman soon supplanted Lorimer, who had his business to run. One of the first fights Hoffman lined up for Baer was to take place on August 25, 1930, in San Francisco's Recreation Park, against an experienced twenty-six-year-old heavyweight named Frankie Campbell. No less an authority than Jack Dempsey had rated Baer and Campbell the two best heavyweights in the state, even though Campbell was really a blown-up light heavyweight who was much more effective against men who weighed less than 175 pounds. The fight was the most hotly anticipated contest in California in years, and each fighter would receive 27.5 percent of the gross — about $10,000.

Campbell's real name was Francisco Camilli; he had changed it to prevent his mother from discovering he was a boxer. He had been a good semipro infielder, though not as good as his younger brother, Dolph, who at the time was playing first base for the Sacramento Solons in the Pacific Coast League and who went on to win the National League Most Valuable Player Award in 1941, when he was the Brooklyn Dodgers' first baseman. In twelve major league seasons, beginning in 1933, Camilli was named to two all-star teams and hit 239 home runs.

At the time of the Baer-Campbell fight, San Francisco, though a traditional bastion of boxing, was gripped by an antiboxing sentiment fanned by the *Examiner*, the West Coast flagship of William Randolph Hearst's newspaper empire. Just the week before Baer and Campbell were to fight, an eighteen-year-old named Johnny Anderson died after Red Ruehl knocked him out at National Hall. It was Anderson's second pro fight, and the *Examiner* railed against the state boxing commission in particular and the sport in general.

Nationally, the movement to ban boxing had really peaked in the early years of the century, after Jack Johnson's victory over Jim Jeffries sparked race riots. In the 1920s, Dempsey — through the sheer force of his charisma and with the assistance of Doc Kearns, his manager, Tex Rickard, his promoter, and the writers who made a god of him — lifted the sport out of the shadows. When Dempsey fought Georges Carpentier at Boyle's Thirty Acres in 1921, thousands of women were in attendance; it was the first time women attended a fight en masse. Perhaps the horrors of World War I that their husbands and brothers had endured had somehow inured them to violence. What they saw in Jersey City — another brutal Dempsey assault — was a typical though concentrated example of the fights of the era, which were characterized by a bloody savagery that bears little resemblance to most of today's fights. In the 1920s, fighters were urged not just by the crowds but by referees to engage each other constantly. Boxers who did not keep punching risked being disqualified. They were taught to be constantly aggressive. Each knew that every time he stepped into the ring, he might be fatally injured — and that there would probably be no doctor or ambulance nearby to save him.

Campbell and his wife, Elsie, had become parents the December before Campbell's fight with Baer, and perhaps the sleeplessness of new fatherhood contributed to the sluggishness he displayed when he trained. Elsie was also pregnant again. Campbell had won fourteen consecutive fights but was still a two-to-one underdog. "Frankie had better not leave himself as open to attack in the ring with Baer, for it may prove disastrous to him," Harry Smith wrote in the *San Francisco Chronicle* after attending one of his workouts.

In fact, Campbell weighed only 179 pounds at the weigh-in, 6 pounds lighter than his manager had said he would weigh for the fight and 15 pounds lighter than Baer, who was a solid 194 pounds. At the weigh-in, Baer and Campbell were told to "keep fighting as long as the other man is on his feet."

Baer did not take the instructions lightly.

For a nontitle bout between two local fighters staged at a time of enormous economic distress, a big crowd turned out at Recreation Park: 15,000 people. In the second round, Campbell clipped Baer and Baer slipped to the canvas. Thinking that he had knocked Baer down, Campbell drifted to a neutral corner and waved to the crowd. He was leaning over the ropes with his back to the ring when Baer flew at him in a fury. At the sound of his approach, Campbell turned his head, and Baer instantly walloped him with a thundering right hand. Blood flew from Campbell's mouth and he collapsed onto the canvas.

Dazed and wobbling, he somehow managed to regain his feet. But he was clearly hurt. "Something feels like it broke in my head," he said after the round to his trainer, Tom Maloney.

Nevertheless, in the third and fourth rounds, he fought effectively, though Baer's punches "seemed to carry about twice as much power as those of his opponent." In the fifth, Baer's superior strength overwhelmed Campbell. At one point Baer had him up against the ropes and unleashed a vicious torrent of blows. Pinned against the ropes, Campbell absorbed punch after punch, hooks, uppercuts, and overhand rights. Baer battered him, each blow carrying the full force of his tremendous strength. Campbell's head was bobbing like a speed bag, presenting itself as an easy target. But because the ropes were supporting him, he couldn't fall. Even as his body went limp, the referee, Toby Irwin, stood watching, allowing Baer to continue hammering him. When Campbell's head smashed into one of the metal turnbuckles that connect the ropes to the ring posts, Irwin finally stepped in and ended the carnage, and Campbell sagged to the canvas.

Seconds later, Irwin raised Baer's hand in victory. Baer then noticed that Campbell was unconscious. His own seconds rushed to help Campbell, while Campbell's seconds stood idly by. "As the fans milled around the ring," Rudy Hickey reported in the *Sacramento Bee*, "crowding over the fallen boxer for a peep at him in mere curiosity, neither the police nor the state boxing commissioners, who were seated less than thirty feet from the senseless youth, took steps to clear the ring or rush the patient to a hospital. For exactly a half hour Campbell lay on the ring floor." When it seemed safe to do so, Baer helped carry Campbell to his stool. But the ambulance that had been called was stuck in traffic. Finally it arrived and took him to the hospital.

When Baer later got a phone call informing him that Campbell was near death, "he just stood there, tears as big as golf balls rolling down his cheeks," his adopted brother, Augie Silva Baer, said. He returned to San Francisco and went to St. Joseph's Hospital, where he paced the hallways praying that Campbell would survive. He met Elsie Campbell in the hallway. She was cradling her baby.

"I'm sorry," Baer said.

"It's all right," Elsie said. "It might have been you. It wasn't your fault."

The morning after the fight, thirteen hours after Baer knocked him out, Frankie Campbell died. "Campbell's brain was knocked completely loose from his skull," said Dr. T. E. Tillman, the attending physician. "If it had been a case of one cerebral hemorrhage or two, or even three, we might have saved his life. But his brain was literally one huge mass of bruises. There was nothing to be done."

When Campbell died, a warrant was issued for Baer's arrest for manslaughter, even though neither Elsie Campbell nor Eliza Camilli, Campbell's mother, would sign the complaint. (The complainant was Sergeant Patrick Shannon of the San

Francisco police, who witnessed the fight.) Baer surrendered to the police at the Whitcomb Hotel and was led to the Hall of Justice in Portsmouth Square. After he spent several hours behind bars, Hoffman posted $10,000 bond and he was released. The bail money included $9,171.63 in small bills and coins — Baer's share of the gate receipts from the fight.

Walking out of the Hall of Justice, Baer told reporters, "I went into the ring to do my best. I can't express how sorry I am that the fight ended as it did."

Most of the critics directed their anger at Irwin, not Baer. "He should have stopped the contest before he did," Carol Working, Campbell's manager, said a few hours after Campbell died. "After my boy was out on his feet, he took enough punches to have done for ten other men. The referee was on the other side of the ring instead of being on top of the fighters to see what was doing. I asked commissioner [Charles] Traung not to appoint Irwin referee. I objected to Irwin because he had refereed several of Baer's previous bouts. The commissioner paid no attention to me, although I asked him again at the weighing-in to name either Willie Ritchie or Jim Griffin."

The *San Francisco Examiner* launched another crusade, condemning the sport, Irwin, and Baer, who was criticized for throwing the punch in the second round and for continuing to pummel Campbell in the fifth. Hearst's headlines blared, "Butcher! Murderer!" and "Jury Will Sift Ring Butchery" and "Men Who Abet Murder in Ring Must Be Disciplined."

Of course Baer had only followed the explicit instructions he had received, and the rules of boxing. "According to the ethics of the ring, Baer was entirely in the clear," Rudy Hickey, who covered the fight, wrote in the *Sacramento Bee*, referring to the punch in the second round. "Campbell had merely left himself unprotected."

But Governor C. C. Young appointed a five-man panel to investigate the matter, and the state athletic commission conducted its own inquiry. At the commission's hearing, Irwin testified that Baer had done nothing improper. He also said that he stopped the fight when it should have been stopped. But the commission suspended Irwin, Baer, Hoffman, Working, and the five other men who had been in the fighters' corners.

The commission's decision to suspend Baer was particularly silly and probably politically motivated. The fact was, and remains, that even in the cleanest, best-refereed bout, it is possible that one of the fighters will die. Most ring deaths cannot be attributed to the incompetence of referees or to illegal punches. Most fighters who die in the ring die because their opponent did what he was trained to do.

Baer had done nothing more than fight with all the aggressiveness that was expected of him. Yes, he had punched Campbell when his back was turned, but it is every fighter's obligation to protect himself at all times, and Campbell had not. And that blow probably had nothing to do with his death, which was a direct result of the punches Baer landed in the fifth round.

"Max is heartsick," Lorimer told the papers. "He can't sleep and he can't eat. He tells me he doesn't want to fight again." Adding to Baer's sadness, Elsie Campbell, who had been unexpectedly kind to him after Frankie's death, lost the baby she was carrying.

Finally, after four months of hearings, inquiries, and headlines, all the charges against Baer were dropped and his boxing license was reinstated.

At the time of Frankie Campbell's death, Baer was twenty-one years old and had only eighteen months' experience as a pro. Suddenly he was under attack — his character assassinated, his reputation sullied by newspapers eager to link a name with the so-called evils of boxing. Certainly boxing was more savage in Baer's time than it is today. Today most referees will stop a fight as soon as it appears that one fighter is incapable of defending himself. In the 1930s, a referee might wait until a man was entirely senseless to stop a fight — if he stopped it at all. Today most states stipulate that when a fighter is knocked down three times, the fight is over. In the 1930s, the three-knockdown rule did not exist. Fights today are no longer than twelve rounds. In the 1930s, most championship fights were scheduled for fifteen rounds, and some went even longer; Baer himself fought two twenty-round fights in Reno. Perhaps most crucially, in the 1930s there were very few regulations compelling promoters to have doctors and ambulances standing by in the event of serious injury. And fighters fought far too frequently, often more than once a week.

There were some very sound reasons for the Hearst syndicate and others to launch a crusade against boxing. The sport needed reform. But vilifying Max Baer as public enemy number one was unfair. And arresting him was ludicrous.

For Baer, the scandal came as a shock. Despite the power he knew he packed in his punches, he had never considered the possibility that his hands were literally lethal weapons. Boxing had given him his identity, as well as several big paychecks. He loved nothing more than lacing up his gloves and showing off his remarkable strength. But when Frankie Campbell died, Baer lost his passion for boxing. Rather than bringing him joy, as it had when he was just learning to box, fighting became a means to an end; fighting was the price he paid for his wealth and fame. No other heavyweight champion has ever publicly expressed as much ambivalence about boxing as Baer did.

Sometimes when a fighter kills a man, he can accept it and move on. After Ray Robinson killed Jimmy Doyle in Cleveland in 1947, for instance, Robinson had to appear at an inquest investigating the circumstances of Doyle's death. At one point he was asked accusingly, "Did you know you had him in trouble?" "They pay me to get them in trouble," Robinson said coolly.

But for the rest of his life Max Baer had nightmares about the events of August 25, 1930. Later in his career, he mysteriously refused to press his advantage against wounded opponents on several occasions. He would hammer someone with his right hand, then step back and wait for his opponent to recover his senses. It was almost as if he were making sure the man could withstand another attack before he threw another punch. He lost two fights to Lou Nova, who said that Baer would have knocked him out if he hadn't pulled his punches after Nova was hurt.

"Nothing that ever happened to me — nothing that can happen to me — affected me like the death of Frankie Campbell," Baer later said. "It was almost a week after the fight before I could get more than an hour or so of successive sleep. Every slightest detail would come racing back to mind, and I couldn't blot from my eyes the last scene — Frankie unconscious in the ring, his handlers working on him. And then the news that he was dying . . . dead."

Baer's son, Max Junior, who was born in 1939, said that when he was growing up, his father often cried about what happened to Frankie Campbell.

5

Spooked by the Phantom

....

New York: 1929

Like most gyms, Joe Jeannette's gym in West Hoboken was a loud and boisterous place. In the summer of 1926, when Joe Gould started working there with Jim Braddock, it got much louder.

"Here's the plan," Gould said to Braddock shortly after they formed their partnership. "We're gonna fight everyone we can. We're gonna fight every week if we can. We're gonna build up your record and then we're gonna fight for the title."

Braddock just kept punching the heavy bag.

"We gotta put some weight on you," Gould said. "You're too skinny to fight as a light heavyweight — and you're too slow to fight as a middleweight."

Gould's speeches were the same as Barney Doyle's and Joe Braddock's, but they were louder and delivered with more conviction.

With Gould tirelessly making matches, Braddock fought fifteen times in 1926. He registered twelve knockouts, one in the third round, three in the second round, and eight in the first round. He won one fight by decision, and two fights were draws. He did not lose. After the draw with Al Settle in April, his maiden campaign could be considered an unmitigated success. He had proved that he was capable of winning as a pro, and his knockout power was a drawing card in northern New Jersey, where, as everywhere else, fight fans preferred strength to artistry.

But as 1927 dawned, Joe Gould had a tough decision to make. Did Braddock need further seasoning in the small clubs and arenas where his reputation was growing, or was it time to venture across the Hudson into Manhattan and Madison Square Garden, the Mecca and Medina of boxing? A manager has to know when to groom and protect his fighter and when to let that fighter risk everything. By nature and inclination, Gould was a risk-taker. He thirsted for the big time — the big venues and the big fights. Unlike most managers, he was not intimidated by Tex Rickard and the other giants of the boxing business. He thought, rightly or wrongly, that he could hold his own with them in any negotiation. His confidence was rooted in his friendship with Benny Leonard, in whose company he had seen the sport at its top. Of course, when Gould made a fight, it wasn't his jaw that was in the line of fire or his brain that might be concussed. But his livelihood and his pride were at stake.

Gould decided that Jim Braddock was ready for his closeup and signed him to fight an opponent whose résumé suggested he would make easy work of Plain Jim. Jess McMahon, the matchmaker at Madison Square Garden, Rickard's right-hand man, wanted a fight that would showcase George LaRocco, a light heavyweight who was living in the Bronx and who had already won twenty-eight pro fights. LaRocco looked the part: he was a magnificent fighting specimen. His handlers had high hopes. But Braddock dashed them. In his Madison Square Garden debut, he knocked LaRocco out in the first round.

Insisting that their man was the victim of a lucky punch, LaRocco's managers demanded a rematch. Gould consented. Braddock and LaRocco shouldn't have bothered. In the rematch, they fought to a dull draw. Nevertheless, LaRocco's honor was still at stake, and he successfully pressed his case for a third shot at Jim Braddock.

The rubber match took place on July 21 at Yankee Stadium — the Yankees were on the road, in the midst of their historic 110-victory season — on the undercard of a main event featuring Jack Dempsey and Jack Sharkey, who five years later would claim the heavyweight championship. A crowd of 80,000 gathered at the stadium to see Dempsey in action for the first time since he had lost his title to Gene Tunney the previous year.

To help the crowd identify the fighters, the athletic commission was enforcing a new rule stipulating that opposing combatants wear contrasting brightly colored trunks. In each of the six scheduled bouts, one fighter would wear purple trunks and the other red trunks. Jim Braddock and Jack Sharkey were placed in the purple camp. LaRocco and Dempsey both wore red. Consequently, the fans — even those in the upper deck — had no trouble distinguishing Braddock from LaRocco as they fought six hard rounds.

Outweighed by fourteen pounds, Braddock thrilled the crowd with his right hand, landing it several times on LaRocco's jaw. In the second round, Braddock's right sent LaRocco to the canvas. "The punch was a Firpo-like club blow which descended to LaRocco's jaw," the *New York Times* reported the next day. "The latter was cool under fire, taking the nine count in order to recover. The third was pretty even, but in the fourth Braddock again smashed the right to the Bronxite's jaw for a knockdown. Again, LaRocco took the count of nine, while resting on one knee, before getting up for the battle."

Two rounds later, Braddock won a unanimous decision. The Braddock-LaRocco saga was at its end. They would not fight each other again.

About an hour after Braddock left the ring, Dempsey and Sharkey squared off. Sharkey, a former sailor, was Boston's most celebrated heavyweight since John L. Sullivan, and he outpointed Dempsey into the seventh round. Dempsey responded by fighting in close, throwing body shot after body shot, maybe landing a few punches below the belt, maybe not. After what he considered a very low blow, Sharkey turned to the referee to complain, "He's hitting me low." At that exact moment, Dempsey fired a left hook at Sharkey's exposed chin. It landed full and flush. The fight was over.

Later, when Sharkey suggested that it was unfair to strike him while he was addressing the referee, Dempsey said, "What did he want me to do? Write him a letter?"

Before the year was out, Braddock fought the first of his three career bouts against Joe Monte of Brockton, Massachusetts. Mean and strong, Monte also possessed a hard skull, against which Braddock broke his right hand en route to a ten-round draw. It was the first of many injuries to the hand, which never quite healed. For the next eight years, as Braddock's right hand went, so went his career.

Braddock was more than stoic in the face of pain. He knew he had fractured his hand, but he refused to acknowledge the discomfort he felt when he landed it. After the Monte bout, he continued to train without telling Gould how much his hand ached. Finally Gould demanded to know what the problem was, why Braddock always winced when he punched. "You stupid Irishman," Gould said when he got an answer. "You can't fight with a broken hand. We've got to see a hand doctor."

He dragged Braddock into Manhattan to see Dr. Wilfred G. Fralick, who was to damaged hands what Freud was to damaged psyches. Fralick's patients included Jack Dempsey and Gene Tunney. The doctor had Braddock's hand X-rayed and then delivered the bad news first: the hand was severely fractured and would not heal properly unless it was rebroken and reset. He would gladly do this for $1,400. There was no good news.

Braddock certainly didn't have $1,400. And neither did Gould, for whom saving money was anathema.

"Say, doc," Braddock said to Dr. Fralick as Gould stood beside the examining table, "I couldn't raise a thousand dollars or a hundred dollars now if my life depended on it, and if I could, it would go to my mother. But what's the matter with breaking the hand in a fight? Ain't that as good a way as any? If it's got to be broken, why not bust it against some guy's jaw and get paid for it? That's the only way out for me, as I can see."

"Well," Fralick said, "I suppose that might work. We can reset it when you break it again."

Stunned that Fralick had given Braddock his blessing to break his own hand, Gould searched for an opponent whose skull was harder than his punch. He settled for Paul Swiderski of Syracuse. On January 6, 1928, at Madison Square Garden, on the undercard of the light heavyweight championship between Tommy Loughran and challenger Leo Lomski (Loughran was fighting his third fifteen-round fight in three months), Braddock fought Swiderski.

Unsure how long he could keep punching with his lame hand, Braddock, at the opening bell, stalked out to engage Swiderski, waited for an opening to counterpunch, threw his right at Swiderski's head, and landed it. The punch both staggered Swiderski and shattered Braddock's hand. For the next seven rounds, he fought only with his left, and he still managed to claim the decision.

This time Braddock had the fracture set immediately.

The following spring, after four months' rest, Braddock began winning some and losing some. Meanwhile, a fighter named Tuffy Griffiths rose from the plains like a twister, devastating every opponent in his path. In the New York papers, he was described as nothing less than a force of nature. So eager were writers and fans to embrace a bona fide puncher that they abandoned all reason and proclaimed Griffiths the second coming of Jack Dempsey, who had announced his retirement in March. Something about what the East Coast boxing press thought of as the frontier was endlessly appealing to them. Fighters who learned to box anywhere west of the Alleghenies were often given the attributes of mythological beasts. Of course, this was partly because none of the writers had actually seen them fight. For their accounts, the writers relied on unreliable local stories and the even less dependable boxing grapevine.

In any event, not since Dempsey himself had come east had an unknown quantity been so lavishly praised as Griffiths was. Out west — which in those days meant anything west of Pittsburgh — he beat opponent after opponent, fifty-four of them in a row. Every promoter in every big city wanted to get Tuffy Griffiths to fight for him, in his arena. Every manager wanted to avoid matching his fighter with the cyclone from Sioux City.

Tex Rickard in particular was hoping to cash in by fashioning Griffiths into the next Dempsey. Like Dempsey, Griffiths was a westerner. Like Dempsey, he was a one-punch knockout machine. Like Dempsey, he looked the part of the toughest man on the planet. Rickard marshaled all his considerable talents to sell his protégé to the press and to boxing fans.

But Pete Latzo was unimpressed with Griffiths's clippings. Latzo, the former world welterweight champion, was gaining weight in midcareer and had moved up to fight as a light heavyweight. In June he had fought Tommy Loughran, the Philadelphia Phantom, for the light heavyweight championship and lost a fifteen-round decision. If he could defeat Griffiths, he would get a rematch. He thought he would have no trouble handling a relative novice, no matter how hard he could punch. Rickard was pleased when Latzo agreed to fight Griffiths on November 30 at Madison Square Garden.

Before getting into the ring to face Griffiths, however, Latzo thought he could use a couple of tune-ups. Nothing too challenging — just a few rounds of live action to supplement his sparring and roadwork. First he fought Charlie Belanger in Detroit on October 5 and won a ten-round decision. Next he wanted James J. Braddock, who had done nothing so far as a pro to suggest that he could handle a world-class talent such as Latzo and who had recently fought poorly.

In May 1928, Braddock had scored consecutive wins against Jack Darnell and, nine days later, Jimmy Francis, a pretty good fighter. But then he had stumbled badly. The pattern would repeat itself throughout his career: big win followed by mystifying loss, followed by another loss, followed by a win, over and over. It was once said, accurately, that if his career had been charted on a graph, it would have resembled a sine curve. In the summer of 1928, Braddock was dipping toward the bottom of the curve, and Gould was wondering if he had rushed his development. Braddock was losing to or drawing against fighters he should have dominated. On June 7 he fought another ten-round draw with Joe Monte (this time without fracturing his hand); on June 27 he and Billy Vidabeck — a future policeman — fought to a no-decision; on July 25 he underperformed again, drawing with an Italian fighter named Nando Tassi; and on August 8 he lost in lackluster fashion to Joe Sekyra at Ebbets Field. Outweighed by Sekyra 177 to 168, Braddock impressed no one, least of all James P. Dawson of the *New York Times*. "Almost exclusively a counter-fighter," Dawson wrote, "he looked good starting the bout, when he outboxed Sekyra in the first round and crossed a sharp right hard to the jaw, sending Sekyra back on his heels, but thereafter Braddock was heavy-footed, slow in thinking and acting, and altogether awkward. He missed like a novice at times, when he went on the attack, and appeared ludicrous at times."

Heavy-footed. Slow. Ludicrous. No one could say that James Parnell Dawson pulled his punches.

Braddock's reputation was so hurt by his performance that Gould considered suing Sekyra for a portion of the purse — technically, on the grounds that he had failed to make the 175-pound weight limit; in reality, to erase the stain on Braddock's record.

Braddock frequently fought at the level of his opponents. For instance, three days before looking terrible fighting Nando Tassi, he sparred with Tom Heeney, the New Zealander who was preparing to fight Gene Tunney for the heavyweight championship. Training outdoors in Fairhaven, New Jersey, on July 22, Heeney was in peak form. He was so impressive that Jack Dempsey told reporters, "Only a superman can beat him."

But Braddock made Heeney look feeble. He rattled Heeney with a left hook and had him on the defensive for the two full rounds they sparred. "The youngster gave indications that this was not to be entirely Heeney's day," one reporter wrote.

To Pete Latzo, who was looking around for someone to loosen up with before the Griffiths fight, Braddock seemed less than formidable. Braddock, meanwhile, couldn't understand what had happened. His progress had been halted, and he didn't know why. It wasn't as if any of his opponents had hurt him. No one had knocked him out or even down. He was a powerful, quick puncher, but his slowness of foot and his reluctance to use his left hand made him incomplete.

Gould did what he could, urging Braddock to work on his speed and his left. "Come on, Jim, show 'em the jab," Gould would say as they passed their days at Jeannette's. "Get your left up."

In the gym Braddock would oblige, but when the bell rang to signal the start of a fight, he fell right back into his bad habits. Like so many fighters with a good right hand, he would simply stand around waiting for an opening to use it. When the Latzo fight was proposed, Gould and Braddock had serious doubts about Jim's future in the ring. One more bad performance and his career might become unsalvageable.

It was at times like this that Jim Braddock was invariably at his best. The prospect of ultimate failure scared him. He knew he did not want an ordinary life or a real job. He had no degree or patronage position to fall back on. As far as he was concerned, everything was at stake.

Fighting in front of a hometown crowd in Newark on October 17, 1928, Braddock started the bout slowly. A much smoother, quicker man, Latzo piled up points in the first three rounds. Gould, standing in Jim's corner, wondered if he was witnessing the end of a career. He wondered if they had proceeded too quickly and fought too many fights. Then, in the fourth round, Braddock found an opening. When Latzo let his guard down for an instant, Braddock hammered a right hand to his jaw. Braddock could see the bone crumple inside the cheek. With one punch, he had fractured Latzo's jaw in four places. Typical of the fighters of the era, Latzo, in agony, kept fighting. In the ninth round, Braddock caught him with three consecutive right uppercuts. Somehow Latzo stayed on his feet and went the full ten rounds.

James J. Braddock had salvaged his career and earned three hundred dollars. Once again he had pulled himself out of a slump.

In the dressing room after the fight, Gould was already making plans. He told Shabazian and Howard "Poke" Freeman of the *Newark Evening News* that Braddock deserved a shot at Tuffy Griffiths. "After all, we beat the guy [Griffiths] was supposed to fight," Gould said. Like many managers, Gould made frequent use of the first-person plural when describing the achievements of his fighters. When they lost, *we* became *he* and *us* became *him*. But Gould, more than most, truly felt as if he were one with his fighters. Unlike many of his peers, he had been a fighter himself. Even though, as a manager, he didn't have to throw punches anymore, he remained a fighter.

After losing to Braddock, Latzo naturally was deemed unworthy of a shot at Griffiths. Even if the Garden had wanted him to fight, however, he would not have been able to. Eleven feet of fine wire was the only thing holding his jaw together. For months he could not eat solid foods, and he fought only once in the next fifteen months.

*   *   *

As the public clamored for a fight, Rickard cast about for a worthy — but not too worthy — opponent. First, of course, he wanted Latzo. Then he and his matchmaker, Tom McArdle, tried to line up the former light heavyweight champion Jack Delaney. A few days later, they set their sights on Jimmy Slattery, an eccentric light heavyweight from Buffalo who, forty years before Mike Tyson was born, liked to walk into car dealerships in his dungarees and astound skeptical salesmen by whipping out an enormous wad of cash to buy fancy cars on the spot. Predictably, Joe Gould badgered Rickard and McArdle about Braddock. Then he badgered the writers, who made sure his rants were printed.

"Jimmy deserves this fight," Gould told anyone with a notebook while sticking out his chin. "He broke Latzo's jaw, and he'll make Tuffy wish he'd never left Iowa." Braddock, standing nearby, would usually nod his agreement. He liked to let Joe do the talking. He liked to watch his friend hustle, because no one derived more pleasure from hustling than Joe Gould.

Finally Rickard relented. He expected Braddock to get flattened. So did virtually everyone else. The odds were against Braddock when the fight, scheduled for November 30, was announced, and only got steeper, climbing to seven to one.

Griffiths was much more than a figment of Rickard's imagination. He was truly spectacular. In September he knocked out the former light heavyweight champion Mike McTigue in one round. In November, in the three weeks leading up to his fight against Braddock, he knocked out three opponents. Just eight days before the fight, he knocked out Jackie Williams in one round in Davenport, Iowa.

When he rolled into New York on November 27, he was greeted like a conquering hero. He went straight to Stillman's Gym, where he was accorded all the honors normally reserved for reigning champions. Lou Stillman made him feel welcome, and so did the writers, who were nearly as eager as Rickard to find the next Dempsey. In five rounds, Griffiths beat up two sparring partners, Gene McCue and Jimmy Moore.

By 1928, Braddock had abandoned Joe Jeannette's gym for Stillman's, which at the time was at 919 Eighth Avenue, between 54th and 55th Streets, its home for all but a few years in the early 1930s. Its proximity to Madison Square Garden made it *the* place to train, as clearly evidenced by Tuffy Griffiths's presence there in the days leading up to his hotly anticipated New York debut.

Stillman's was vast, 125 feet long and 50 feet wide. It had two rings on the main floor, which was one flight up from the street. For three days Griffiths monopolized one of them, a ring circled by writers who dutifully recorded his every movement. Sparring partners were thrown at him like raw meat. They waded onto the canvas hesitantly, felt the sting of his wrath, and then were carried out.

On one occasion, in the space of just a few minutes Griffiths knocked two sparring partners unconscious without even breaking a sweat. Even the old hands — the trainers and cut men who had not been impressed by anyone since John L. Sullivan — were crowding around for a look at him.

When the sparring partners were carried unconscious from the ring, Jim Braddock was standing just a few feet away, punching a heavy bag, with Joe Gould and Doc Robb, his trainer, at his side. Robb had spent most of the morning massaging and taping up Braddock's right ankle, which he had twisted badly while sparring. No one except Braddock, Gould, and Robb knew how serious the injury was. Braddock, typically, ignored it, because if it was discovered, the fight might be postponed or canceled.

Only Robb tended to Braddock's injuries at this time. At age twenty-three, Braddock was still a bachelor. By the standards of his time, he was an old bachelor, but by the standards of boxing, he was right on track. For the most part, young fighters had no room in their lives for wives, who, it was thought, would only distract them from their calling. Most of the great heavyweight champions had been single at their peak. They were expected to consort with the opposite sex but not to marry. There was something monkish about the fighter's life — not just in the days and weeks leading up to a big fight but at all times. Certainly there were notable exceptions — playboys like the great middleweight champions Stanley Ketchel and Harry Greb, for instance. And there were times when even the most virtuous young men strayed — maybe even Gene Tunney, the clean marine.

By all accounts, young James J. Braddock was a man whose only vice was an occasional beer with his friends Howard Fox and Marty McGann (the same Marty McGann with whom he had run off when he was eleven). He was shy around women, especially those he found attractive, like Howard's sister Mae.

When Howard invited his friends over to his house, Mae was usually there. She was a telephone operator in Manhattan, but in the 1920s young women who lived alone were viewed with suspicion, so she lived in New Jersey with her brother. She kept house and cooked for Howard, and when his friends showed up, she cooked for them too. No matter how much she fed Jim Braddock, though, he never gained any weight.

Slowly the relationship between Jim Braddock and Mae Fox expanded beyond the culinary realm. But it was slow going. With Tuffy Griffiths on his mind, Braddock had no time for romance.

Griffiths got top billing in the main event on Friday, November 30, 1928. The ad in the *Times* looked like this:

> Madison Square Garden
> Friday, Nov. 30th
> MAIN BOUT — 10 ROUNDS

TUFFY GRIFFITHS
JAMES J. BRADDOCK

SEMI-FINAL — 10 ROUNDS
Kid Chocolate vs. Joe Scalfaro
Vince Dundee vs. Izzy Grove, 10 Rounds
Terry Roth vs. Al Beauregard, 6 Rounds
Al. McGillory vs. Al. Gafner, 4 Rounds
Prices: $1, $2, $3, $4.40 and $5.40
INCLUDING ALL TAXES

It was a fairly typical night of boxing at the Garden — except for the fact that the rafters were packed with more than 19,000 fans, all aching for a look at the new sensation from the West, who, they had read in the papers, would thump Braddock.

The fans waited anxiously for the preliminaries, which included a draw for Kid Chocolate, a sensation from Cuba, to end. Braddock and Gould waited in a dressing room, Braddock silently thinking about the significance of the moment, Gould talking nonstop, releasing his nervous energy through his mouth. Braddock was confident. Even the most accomplished boxers are anxious in the minutes leading up to an important fight, but Braddock was usually an exception. No one he had ever fought had scared him. No situation had cowed him. He was meant, he thought, to fight big fights against the likes of Tuffy Griffiths.

With a shamrock on his trunks, Braddock finally climbed through the ropes at about 11 P.M. He listened to the instructions of the referee, Kid McPartland, who reminded both fighters to keep their punches up and to retreat to a neutral corner in the event of a knockdown, then went back to his corner. When the bell rang, he moved out to meet his fabled opponent and promptly took a shot to the stomach. It didn't hurt. Any slight degree of uncertainty that had built up inside him instantly dissipated. Tuffy Griffiths was no Dempsey.

Griffiths kept working on Braddock's body, throwing lefts and rights at his ribs, but Braddock easily deflected most of them. Griffiths was snorting and charging like a bull; Braddock was calm and steady. He parried punch after punch, waiting for Griffiths to wear himself out. By the end of the round, Braddock had taken charge.

The fans, of course, couldn't feel Griffiths's punches, so they couldn't know what Braddock knew — that it was only a matter of time before Griffiths made a mistake and went down. They thought they were about to witness a brawl. What they got was a beating.

In the second round, Griffiths again charged out of his corner, firing wildly at Braddock. Braddock waited for a sloppy left — for an opening. He got it. With Griffiths's guard down and his face exposed, Braddock reached back slightly, cocked his arm, and delivered a devastating straight right, solidly on target. Griffiths collapsed to the canvas. Dazed, he got up at the count of three instead of waiting so he could gather his senses. Braddock waited patiently for another opening, found one, and threw another right that sent Griffiths to the canvas again. Again Griffiths rose at the count of three, staggering. Now the Garden was engulfed by a deafening roar — the sound of 19,000 fans jumping off the Tuffy Griffiths bandwagon.

Shabazian, sitting in press row, marveled at Griffiths's gameness. "No one who saw that fight will ever deny that Tuffy Griffiths had heart," he wrote. "In the midst of a din that shook the Garden to its very foundations, Griffiths rolled around the ring like a drunken sailor, his arms by his side, absolutely helpless, while Braddock leaped close and fired a steady, ceaseless, withering bombardment at his chin."

With Griffiths listing in front of him, Braddock was aiming at a moving target — a slow-moving target. He threw another right, and down went Griffiths again. Disoriented, the westerner staggered to his feet, once more failing to take the count. Braddock reached back with all his strength and threw another straight right that exploded on Griffiths's chin, knocking him down for the fourth time. Finally McPartland stepped in and ended the fight.

Braddock, who had barely warmed up, smiled and pumped his fist. Gould was jumping up and down. At ringside, Tex Rickard and Tom McArdle had their heads in their hands. Braddock had killed their golden goose. All they could do was embrace their new goose, whom they immediately matched with Leo Lomski, a light heavyweight known colorfully as the Aberdeen Assassin. The winner would fight Tommy Loughran, the world light heavyweight champion. Jim Braddock was suddenly two wins away from the title.

Braddock's unexpected win caused a sensation in the boxing world. He hadn't just won the fight — he had won thousands of new fans, including William Muldoon, "the Solid Man," the eighty-three-year-old New York State boxing commissioner and former bodybuilder who a half-century earlier had been one of John L. Sullivan's closest advisers.

Just a few days after the fight, Muldoon summoned Braddock and Gould to his office. "Young man," he said, pointing his finger at Gould, "I am going to hold you accountable for the development of this fighter. I saw him knock Griffiths out the other night, and I enjoyed the fight. With a little weight on him, I predict he will someday win the world's heavyweight championship. But he must not be rushed along too rapidly."

Braddock and Gould never forgot their meeting with Muldoon, or his prediction. Gene Tunney was also impressed with his fellow Irish-American. In one of his frequent newspaper commentaries, he too predicted that Braddock would one day win the heavyweight championship.

While Muldoon and Tunney were talking about Braddock's future as a heavyweight, Braddock himself was still struggling to fill out as a light heavyweight. Gould marveled at the enormous quantities of food he consumed, only to see all the calories burn off at Stillman's. He was still a light heavyweight, fighting well under the 175-pound limit, and Leo Lomski was all that was standing between him and a shot at the title.

Braddock's total purse for fighting Griffiths was $8,860, a sum more than sufficient to pay off his parents' mortgage and repaint the house, which were the first things he did. He remained devoted to his tightly knit clan, who followed his career keenly. Shortly after he upset Tuffy Griffiths, a story appeared in the *Ring* under the headline "Braddock's Mother Behind His Startling Rise."

The headline was at least slightly misleading. The story was less about Elizabeth O'Toole Braddock than it was a recapitulation of Braddock's career up to that point. Francis Albertanti, who wrote the piece, moonlighted as a boxing publicist, which as a rule is not a vocation that places a great deal of emphasis on the truth. It was Albertanti's thesis that the vast majority of boxers' mothers recoiled at the sight of their sons' blood being spilled. He cited the example of Benny Leonard's famously squeamish mother, Minnie Leiner, who, it was said, succeeded in talking her son into premature retirement, even though he was arguably the greatest lightweight ever. She may have been the original stereotypical Jewish mother.

Elizabeth Braddock, in contrast, thrilled to the sight of her son in the ring. Of course, she had had plenty of opportunities to see Joe Junior fight, and later Jim's younger brother, Alfred, would fight too. In a fighting family, there is no place for the weak of heart.

When Jimmy told his mother that he wanted to be a boxer, she did not try to steer him to the law or the priesthood. Instead, she reportedly said to him, "I am happy at the thought that you have decided to box for a living. I may know very little about your profession, but I do know that in order to be successful you must lead a very clean life, train hard, listen to your manager, but most important, save your earnings."

Before Braddock's fight against Tuffy Griffiths, she said, "Looks like they are picking a casket for you. Don't let that stuff worry you. Go in there and try to knock him out with the first punch." Which was exactly what James J. Braddock always tried to do.

Like Tuffy Griffiths, Leo Lomski was a westerner, in this case a real westerner, as he was from Aberdeen, Washington. Lomski had grown strong chopping down trees in the thickly forested Northwest. For a century fighters have made a habit of posing for publicity shots with axes in their hands; Lomski was one of the few who actually knew how to use one and trained for fights by swinging it at defenseless trees. "Nobody chops wood," the legendary trainer Ray Arcel said in 1982. "The only one who came close to that was Leo Lomski, a nurseryman in the 1920s who chopped trees for exercise."

Two years older than Braddock, Lomski had learned to fight in the navy and by 1927 was fighting in big arenas in California and New York. He went 9–1–1 that year, beating two Hall of Famers, Tiger Flowers and Maxie Rosenbloom. He delighted fans with his aggressive style.

On January 6, 1928, at the top of the card on which James J. Braddock broke his hand on Paul Swiderski's head, Lomski had fought Loughran for the light heavyweight title at Madison Square Garden. In the first round, he twice knocked down the Philadelphia Phantom, but he was outboxed for the rest of the fight, losing a fifteen-round decision. Over the next few months he and Braddock traded opponents back and forth.

To a much greater degree than Braddock, Lomski was a pure puncher. In fact, as the fight approached, in contrast to Lomski, Braddock was characterized as a master boxer, which he was not. In the *Ring*'s first long profile of Braddock, Albertanti wrote, "In more ways than one Braddock reminds some of the old-timers of a similarity of his fighting stance to that of Jim

Corbett's [sic]. He is a pretty picture to watch in action. He is a great counterer, and hits with deadly precision. If he wants to box, there is no light heavy in the racket, with the possible exception of the champion, Tommy Loughran, who can box better."

At this time, after his wins against Latzo and Griffiths, Braddock was a star. When he walked into the pubs in North Bergen, he was the center of attention. When he worked out at Stillman's, fighters, trainers, and managers gathered nearby to watch him. Everyone wanted to shake the hand that had felled the mighty Tuffy Griffiths.

A few days before the fight against Lomski, Gould was typically brash. With Braddock shadowboxing behind him, he said to the reporters who had assembled at Stillman's, "Those fights against Latzo and Griffiths were the battles in which James J. found himself. He was better than an ordinary fighter before those two contests, and the fact that he knocked out both Latzo and Griffiths gave him just the confidence he needs."

None of the writers bothered to correct him when he said that Braddock had knocked out Latzo. He was on a roll, and they let him keep talking.

"Lomski can be hit with a right hand," Gould continued. "That's one of his weaknesses. And James J. can hit with a right hand. That's one of his strongest points, as Griffiths and Latzo will attest. He'll knock out Lomski Friday night and go right on until he establishes himself as the world's light heavyweight champion."

With that, Gould wheeled around to face Braddock, who was listening to his speech but whose mouth was shut. Gould wondered how anyone could say so little.

The fight, on January 18, 1929, was scheduled for ten rounds. Braddock weighed 172 pounds, Lomski 172.5. More than 18,000 people — almost all of them men — packed the Garden to see for themselves just how tough Jersey Jim was. Still, most of them believed he would lose to Lomski, who was a two-to-one favorite. To the fans in the Garden's far reaches, Braddock would have been barely discernible if not for his distinctive paleness. He was whiter than his white trunks.

In the first round, Braddock boxed masterfully and hurt Lomski with left hooks and straight rights. In fact, Braddock entirely dominated the first three rounds. But then he started to tire. In the previous three months he had spent less than five minutes in the ring, all against Tuffy Griffiths. He wasn't used to the inactivity that is customary when a fighter starts climbing the ranks. The Lomski fight was his forty-fifth as a pro but his first in seven weeks. He was used to fighting two or three times a month.

Lomski hurt Braddock with body shots, slowing Braddock's momentum and chipping away at his will to fight. He took control of the fight in the fourth round, hammering Braddock with jabs and more body shots. Suddenly Braddock slowed to a crawl. His legs started to wobble, and his punches weren't landing. When they did, Lomski was in trouble, but Braddock couldn't follow up. He was too weary; his aggressiveness had drained him. He lost the fourth, fifth, and sixth rounds.

"The trouble with Braddock's work for this part of the fight was that it lacked consistency," James P. Dawson wrote in the *New York Times*. "He seemed to be saving himself, only occasionally striking out with rights. Three times in the sixth session he grazed Lomski's jaw with his right, but his punches never stopped Lomski's rush."

Braddock won the eighth and ninth rounds, but Lomski took the tenth. One of the judges, Charles F. Mathison, saw the fight as a draw. But the other judge, Tom Flynn, and the referee, Arthur Donovan, gave the decision to Lomski.

Braddock was disappointed. Gould was beside himself. It was the biggest fight of Braddock's career, and he had botched it. He hadn't disgraced himself — he hadn't lost by much. But he had blown his shot at the light heavyweight championship.

Braddock spent the night in New York with Gould, drinking contraband liquor.

"Don't worry, Jim," Gould said, trying to sound upbeat, "you're still in the picture."

"But now Lomski gets another shot," Braddock countered.

"You'll get your shot," Gould said. A good manager has to be a good psychologist. After a loss, he has to convince his fighter that it never happened and at the same time explain to him how to prevent it from ever happening again.

Returning to his previous habits, Braddock got active again. Two weeks after the loss to Lomski, he knocked out George Gemas in one round. Then, five weeks after that, he fought Jimmy Slattery, the fighter who liked to buy cars with wads of cash.

One of the more colorful fighters of the era, Slattery, the Buffalo Adonis, was either amusingly eccentric or seriously disturbed, depending on your point of view. He was also a gifted fighter, a favorite of Gentleman Jim Corbett's. "He was a brilliant boxer," Shabazian wrote, "a flitting will-o'-the-wisp, who, when he was good, was (like the little girl with the curl) very, very good."

On March 7, four days before the fight, while Braddock was working out at Stillman's, Slattery was still at home in Buffalo. "Reports from there state that he is in fine shape and predict dire things for Braddock when he meets him," one New York newspaper reported.

On the night of March 11, Manhattanites had several entertainment options. Al Jolson was starring in *The Singing Fool* at the Sam Harris Theater. One hundred and fifty "charming hostesses" were available as dance partners at Roseland. And in the main event at Madison Square Garden, two Irish light heavyweights named Jimmy were squaring off. More than 12,000 people attended the fight, which Braddock, an eight-to-five underdog, won rather easily by technical knockout in the ninth round, when Lou Magnolia, the referee, stopped the fight. Slattery never came close to hurting Braddock, while Braddock hurt Slattery with a barrage of body shots and headshots.

Typically, the coverage of the fight focused less on Braddock than on Slattery, whose gracefulness made much better copy than Braddock's toughness. In the *New York Times*, running alongside a photograph of Braddock — a handsome twenty-three-year-old with a thick shock of dark wavy hair framed by prominent ears — James P. Dawson's story of the fight began, "James J. Braddock advanced a step in his march toward light heavyweight championship honors last night at Madison Square Garden and wrote finish to the career of Jimmy Slattery, Buffalo boxer . . . Slattery gave only flashes of the form which once caused him to be hailed as a successor to James J. Corbett in style." With the win, only Leo Lomski was rated ahead of Braddock as a contender for Tommy Loughran's title.

Dawson also noted the result of a ten-round fight on the undercard between Maxie Rosenbloom and Osk Till. Rosenbloom won the decision. Seven days later, in Philadelphia, Rosenbloom was back in the ring, this time to fight Lomski for the third time. After losing twice to the Aberdeen Assassin, Slapsy Maxie, a decided underdog, stayed out of Lomski's reach all night and hung on to gain the decision. Now Lomski had fallen behind Braddock in the title picture, despite having beaten him in January.

Just ten days later, in an effort to regain his designation as the top contender, Lomski fought again, in Chicago, against none other than Tuffy Griffiths. Again Tuffy was invaluable to Jim Braddock, winning a controversial decision. From that point on, Lomski was out of the running.

It was at just about this time that Braddock suffered the first of what would be several devastating financial setbacks. He had saved his purses — nearly $20,000 — and deposited them in the Bank of the United States. Six months before the stock market collapsed, plunging the country into the Depression, banks everywhere were already failing. When the Bank of the United States went under, Braddock's savings were lost. Of course, there was no such thing as depositors' insurance.

Braddock took the loss with aplomb. He could afford to — he was the top contender for the light heavyweight championship, and he was only twenty-three. A champion could make $20,000 a month if he wanted to.

On May 14, three weeks before his twenty-fourth birthday, Jimmy Braddock signed a contract to fight Tommy Loughran for Loughran's world light heavyweight championship. Gould decided that Braddock would train in Saratoga Springs, far from the noise and distractions of Stillman's and Manhattan. The camp was a success. The writers who went upstate to watch him train were impressed by his fitness and his aptitude. Still, only three years had elapsed since his first pro fight. Despite the wins over Pete Latzo, Tuffy Griffiths, and Jimmy Slattery, Braddock was considered a relative novice. Joe Gould might have disagreed with that assessment, but he would have been wrong.

Caught up in the excitement of his win over Slattery, Braddock forgot how Leo Lomski had found a way to defeat him. Heading into the Loughran fight, he was filled with youthful arrogance — and ignorance. This time his opponent wasn't fighting out of his customary weight class, as Latzo had done, or been overhyped, like Griffiths. Nor was he crazy, like Slattery. In Tommy Loughran, Braddock was, for the first time in his life, matched against a truly great fighter — more than a world champion, a future Hall of Famer.

Only three years older than Braddock, Loughran was already a legend. Six times he had fought the fierce and dangerous — and soon to be dead — Harry Greb. The results: two wins for Greb, one win for Loughran, and three no-decisions. (Just stepping into the ring six times to fight the unstable Greb was a testament to Loughran's uncommon valor. Gene Tunney called

Greb the dirtiest fighter he ever fought.) Loughran had defeated Slattery, Latzo, Lcomski, and the great middleweight champion Mickey Walker. He had even fought Tunney to a draw. And on October 7, 1927, Loughran had wrested the light heavyweight championship of the world from Mike McTigue.

Known as the Philadelphia Phantom, Loughran was so agile he could barely be touched. As Braddock later said, "He was a guy you could never hit with a good solid punch." If Loughran had wrestled a polar bear, he would have walked away without a scratch. The only thing he couldn't do was punch. In 227 career fights, he knocked out only 18 opponents. It didn't help that his hands were chronically sore. For several reasons, many observers were betting that there would be a new champion. Most important, Loughran, who was five-eleven, was struggling to get down to the 175-pound weight limit. Even in the days leading up to the fight, he was training in thick sweatshirts to melt away the excess pounds. A desperate race was on — if he weighed one ounce over 175, the fight would not be a title defense and Braddock would have the right to back out. Gould told the newspapers that if Loughran didn't make the weight, he would insist on a larger share of the gate. As it was, Loughran was getting 37.5 percent to Braddock's 12.5 percent.

The constant sweating and dieting took their toll. In his workouts just before the fight, Loughran was uncharacteristically sluggish and weak. John Kieran, for one, was already preparing to bury him. "Tommy won't be 27 years old until November if the records are correct," Kieran wrote the day before the fight, "but he has been fighting a long while and close observers say that he hasn't been getting any better of late. In ten years, he has had approximately 120 bouts, which averages a fight a month over a decade. Perhaps an athlete has only so many years when he can travel along at a brisk pace, and Tommy began traveling at an early age. He may be due to slow up."

Still, some voices of reason were crying out, warning not to take a Loughran defeat for granted. In the *New York World-Tele-*

gram, Joe Williams wrote, "A gent who doesn't care to be hit isn't the easiest target known to man, woman, or beast."

Jim Braddock, meanwhile, appeared to be in peak physical condition — until a few days before the fight. His problem was the opposite of Loughran's. No matter how much he ate, he could not keep weight on. In the days leading up to the bout he lost three pounds. He was down to 170, and Gould and Robb were worried.

At this point in his career, Braddock wasn't sophisticated enough to respect a fighter of Loughran's rare abilities. "That guy will be duck soup," he told his girlfriend, Mae. "He's only got that jabbing left, and he couldn't knock over a flea with his right. Just watch and see." Braddock thought, *If he can't hurt me, I can't lose.* It was the mentality of a puncher.

Joe Gould and Doc Robb should have disabused him of his notions of superiority, but they did not. "Braddock is the picture of confidence," the *Times* reported two days before the fight. "He is more certain of annexing the light heavyweight crown by a knockout before ten rounds have elapsed than at any time during his training siege."

On July 18, 1929, at Yankee Stadium, Braddock climbed through the ropes to fight Loughran. Still more cocky than nervous, he bounced up and down, waiting for the opening bell. When it came, he rushed Loughran and fired a short right at the champion's head. The punch not only landed solidly, it opened a deep gash over Loughran's right eye. "The fight had hardly started," Shabazian wrote, "and here Loughran's eye was spouting blood like water out of a hydrant! A technical knockout seemed imminent."

"Go for his eye, Jimmy!" Joe Gould screamed from his perch in Braddock's corner.

Eager to press his advantage, Braddock kept throwing rights at Loughran's eye, hoping to finish him off before he could recover his senses and stem the tide of blood gushing down his face. Loughran, however, did not panic. He did all that he could to stay out of Braddock's range — feinting, ducking, circling away from Braddock's right. For his part, Braddock just kept throwing rights, but with each miss his arm got heavier and his frustration grew.

When the first round finally ended, Loughran was bloodied but still on his feet. As his seconds patched up his eye, he cleared his head. Braddock had lost the initiative. "Throw more lefts," Gould said. "Don't just throw the right."

The challenger, however, didn't listen to his manager. Right-hand happy, he won only one more round. He spent most of the rest of the fight chasing Loughran around the ring, stumbling, tripping, punching from awkward angles, trying desperately to reopen the gash above his opponent's eye. It was as if his boots had been tied together, while Loughran danced into range, unleashed a quick flurry of lefts and rights, then darted back out of the range of the big right hand that had nearly blinded him.

"Why aren't you throwing the left?" Gould said to Braddock between rounds five and six.

"The left?" Braddock said. "I can't touch him with my right."

But in the seventh round, Braddock finally caught up with Loughran again. This time the punch landed right in the middle of the champion's forehead. Again blood spurted forth. But this time Loughran followed up with an assault of his own. He threw perhaps the most powerful right hand of his career — defying those who had mocked his punch — and landed it flush on Braddock's jaw. For a moment it seemed that Braddock was going down. His body went slack. All the exhaustion he was feeling seemed to overtake him. But he stayed on his feet, the round ended, and he gathered himself in his corner.

The rest of the fight was fairly uneventful. Loughran was simply too elusive. As Braddock slowly realized that his title shot was evaporating into the night sky, he started talking to Loughran, egging him on, challenging him to stand firm and exchange blows. Of course Loughran was too smart to be baited into a brawl.

"He couldn't hit me to save his life," Loughran said years later, "and, poor Jimmy, he started to curse me. I walked into him, I said, 'Do you talk like this to your mother?' 'What the hell do you mean?' I said, 'Exactly what I'm saying. I'm as good as your mother and you don't use that kind of language.' I hit him with a left hook, I split his tongue wide open, he grabbed hold of me, he said, 'All right.' I said, 'You better keep quiet.' I was carrying him along, no point in knocking him out, because he was a young fellow, he had a lot pulling for him and I couldn't see any point."

At one moment during the fight, a Braddock partisan seated at ringside screamed out, "Hit him with your right hand!" Braddock turned to him and said, "You come up here and hit him with *your* right hand."

James P. Dawson of the *Times* was among those disappointed in Braddock's showing. "In the fourteenth, Braddock, sensing that his foe was weary, heeded the entreaties of his handlers and waded in recklessly, desperately," he wrote. "He pounded the body with both hands and twice grazed the jaw with his right, forcing Loughran to clinch. And always Braddock dared Loughran in vain to discard his wonderful boxing."

Damon Runyon was among the few observers who focused more on Loughran's artistry than on Braddock's incompetence. "The way Loughran boxed last night," he wrote in the *New York American*, "he would probably have licked anybody around right now."

To see both of the boxers in their shabby dressing rooms after the fight, you would have thought they had both lost. "Jimmy looked like he had been run through a gristmill," the future Mae Braddock said. "That left jab of Tommy's had just sheared all that flesh off the side of his face." Loughran's face was also temporarily disfigured, by the cuts above his eye and on his forehead.

Burris Jenkins, a full-time cartoonist and part-time reporter for the *New York Evening World*, interviewed Loughran after the fight. He wanted to know just what it felt like to be hit by Braddock's right. "He didn't land his right solidly once on anything except my shoulder," Loughran said. Then, pointing to his wounds, he continued, "These were the result of left hands. The kid has a good left hand. If he could only learn to box."

Braddock could not have known it then, but he had peaked as a light heavyweight. The loss to Loughran, suffered at the age of twenty-four, was the beginning of his decline. He had lost before, but he had never before been overmatched. "It was a very bad night for Jim and it did something to him," Frank Graham later wrote. The Philadelphia Phantom had certainly spooked him. Outclassed in his first fight against a world champion, Braddock wondered whether he had a future in the sport to which he had dedicated everything.

Gould probably didn't question his decision to match Braddock against a consummate boxer, but he should have. His stewardship of Braddock's career is often hailed as the apex of managing genius. "No fighter ever had a better or more faithful manager," Graham wrote, "and never was there a stronger bond of affection between fighter and manager than there is between Braddock and Gould."

However, Joe Williams, the *World-Telegram*'s columnist, disagreed. "It always seemed to me that if Gould had been a good manager," Williams wrote, "Braddock's career would have been less difficult and spotty."

But it is quite possible that no other manager would have pleaded Braddock's case so loyally with promoters and the press long after it seemed the fighter was finished.

In any event, Braddock was devastated by the loss. His confidence was shattered. He was embarrassed. He sulked around the house for a few days, avoiding human contact. Everyone he saw wanted to offer him words of encouragement; he didn't want to hear it.

Before the fight, he had been a man with a future. If he had won the championship, his fortune would have been made. By losing in the way that he did, he had become a laughingstock. In the *New York Times*, John Kieran wrote that Braddock's performance was one of the funniest things he had ever seen in the ring:

> That was a comedy interlude that left the laughing crowd gasping for breath. For ten rounds, James J. went peering around the ring, trying to locate that fellow Loughran. His vision was somehow bothered by the fact that Loughran's left glove was covering his eyes about half the time. But, even so, James lashed out north, south, east, and west, hoping to find and hit Loughran if only by accident. It was no go. In his bewilderment James let a left hook go at the referee and took a right swing at a ringpost. The spectators tried to be helpful. They shouted directions to James. "He's over here. Take the next turn left. Over your shoulder, Braddock. Look out, Braddock, he's coming up on the other side." It was fine fun for everybody except James J. from Jersey.

6

The Great White Way

··

New York City: Fall 1930

After Frankie Campbell died, Ancil Hoffman decided that Max Baer needed a change of scene. Baer agreed. "What I wanted was to get away from California, go somewhere else and try to forget," he said.

At that time Baer owned only two thirds of himself — the other third he had sold to Lorimer. Now Lorimer told him that if he wanted to make some quick cash, he should sell more of himself to Hoffman, which he did. For $5,000, Hoffman secured one sixth of Baer's stake in himself.

Baer took the money and headed to Reno, Nevada, which was a bacchanalian paradise a generation before Las Vegas rose from the desert. "This was a way of temporary escape from my troubles," he said. But in Reno he found other trouble. "That dough lasted me just one week," he explained, "and then I came back to California."

He returned to California in love. Most of the money he had spent in Reno was showered on a sophisticated and beautiful woman named Dorothy Dunbar, who was seven years his senior. "She was a type of magnetic womanhood such as he had never known before," Nat Fleischer wrote. Few men had. Elegant, worldly, and talented, Dunbar was a heroine worthy of Hemingway. She was feisty and independent. She was clearly not from Livermore. Unlike all the waitresses Baer had known, Dunbar had options; she rejected his proposal of marriage. This was a reasonable decision, considering that they had met only a few days earlier and that she had just gotten married to a man named Jaime S. De Gerson y Baretto.

In the space of just a few months, the *New York Times* described Baretto variously as a Spanish diplomat, a South American millionaire, and a French diplomat attached to the embassy in London. Maybe he was all three. Dorothy married him in London after the death of her previous husband, the Minneapolis millionaire Bucklin Wells II, in 1928. Wells had contracted malaria while he and Dorothy were living in Liberia, in West Africa, operating a rubber plantation; he died in her arms on the ship bearing them home.

Before she married Wells, Dorothy had starred in several silent films, including *The Amateur Gentleman*, *The Flaming Crisis*, and *The Masquerade Bandit*. She was best known, however, as Jane, Tarzan's girlfriend, the role she played in 1926 in *Tarzan and the Golden Lion*. Johnny Weissmuller had not yet been fitted for his loincloth; James Pierce played the lord of the jungle. Pierce, incidentally, married the daughter of Tarzan's creator, Edgar Rice Burroughs, and somehow avoided marrying Dorothy Dunbar. But seven other men did.

When Baer and Dunbar met, Dunbar — who had been born Edith Augusta Dunbar in Cripple Creek, Colorado, on May 28, 1902 — had been famous, had lived abroad, and had made men weak with desire. Max Baer never knew what hit him. It was a mismatch from the beginning. Ancil Hoffman took one look at Dunbar and knew his fighter had no chance against such a formidable opponent. She toyed with men the way Baer toyed with outgunned fighters. She kept him at a distance but close enough. Her coolness, of course, only made him more determined to have her.

Consumed by his passion for the actress and still feeling guilty about Campbell, Baer was not eager to return to California. The trip home convinced him that it was time to say farewell to the Bay Area and the ugliness of the postfight witch-hunt. So he and Hoffman went east — all the way east, to New York.

When he left California, Baer was clearly not the same spirited young man Hoffman had met before the Campbell fight, the young man whose enthusiasm for boxing was always so palpable, who wanted to show everyone just how hard he could punch. Now he had trouble falling asleep and was prone to sullenness. He had started smoking, a bad habit he never gave up. When Hoffman talked encouragingly about his future as a fighter, Baer surprised him by saying he wasn't sure he wanted to fight anymore. Sometimes he was still the lively character he had always been, clowning, laughing, quipping. But then his thoughts would return to the night of August 25 and the fight at Recreation Park. In midsentence he would drift off, staring and nodding. Frankie Campbell haunted him.

It took a while, but over the course of several weeks Hoffman finally managed to persuade Baer that Campbell's death had not been his fault. "It could have been you," Hoffman said. "You were just doing what you were supposed to do." He tried to make Baer believe that fighting was his true calling, that God would not have blessed him with such talent if He didn't intend for him to use it.

Riding the rails over the Rockies, over the plains, and then across the Midwest, Baer slowly started to feel better. The guilt and the sadness lifted slightly. Hoffman was encouraged, too, by Baer's newfound fame. As the man who had killed Frankie Campbell, Baer's stature as a fighter and a drawing card had grown. A man-killer was an attraction, especially one like Baer, who looked the part, with his dark features and chiseled muscles. Suddenly everyone wanted to see the Livermore Butcher Boy fight.

Newspapers everywhere had covered Campbell's death and

the investigation it had sparked. In most accounts Baer was portrayed as a dark-countenanced villain with a devastating punch, a lawless brawler from beyond the frontier. As a rule, western heavyweights such as Dempsey and Baer were given a mystique by the eastern writers, who liked to portray them as gunslingers rather than fighters. By killing Campbell, Baer had piqued their interest more than anyone since Dempsey, and now they were clamoring for a chance to see him fight in person.

The irony of the situation was not lost on Baer. The worst thing he had ever done had turned into an unintended blessing. To ease the anguish he still felt, he promised himself that when he made it big, he would arrange a fight to benefit Frankie Campbell's widow and son.

When Baer's train pulled into Pennsylvania Station on Manhattan's West Side in November 1930, the city, only thirteen months removed from the stock market crash and descending into the Depression, was desperately in need of a good laugh. Eager for a fresh start himself, Baer intended to oblige.

With the money he had made by selling himself to more than a dozen investors just before leaving California, Baer checked into the Plaza on Central Park South, then, as now, one of the city's premier hotels. He was accompanied by ten trunks of clothes, filled with thirty custom-tailored suits, among other items. Of course, off-the-rack wouldn't have fit Baer, whose shoulders were so wide he instinctively walked sideways through doors, but even if they had, he would have bought only bespoke.

His conspicuous consumption contrasted starkly with the situation on the streets, where the soup lines were lengthening every day. In December 1930, an average of 50,000 free meals were distributed every day in New York City, mostly to homeless men. In fact, the federal government asserted that the situation was giving visitors to the city "an erroneous impression regarding the extent of human suffering throughout the country," and it moved to register those who were eating the free soup and bread. The national unemployment rate was swelling to 25 percent, but Baer was living like the Astors and the Vanderbilts. Shuttling from fancy restaurants to swank nightclubs in evening clothes, he was totally oblivious of the worsening condition of his fellow Americans. To him, it seemed there had never been a crash.

It was no coincidence that New York happened to be where Dorothy Dunbar had taken up residence. Still under her spell, Baer tried to elevate himself to her level in matters of culture and etiquette. He employed an appointments secretary, who was charged with teaching him the meaning of two fifty-cent words every day. He worked overtime, not on the speed bag but at the elbows of waiters and sommeliers, learning which fork to use with which course and which spoon to dig into a quivering mound of aspic. He tried hard to be a gentleman in the Old World sense. (By nature he really was a gentleman.) He tried hard to impress Dorothy. Every morning he would run in Central Park, far enough to disappear from Hoffman's sight, then plant himself under a tree, remove Emily Post's manual on etiquette from his trousers, and read. (At other times, it should be noted, he eschewed Emily Post for comic books.)

Chauffeured around town in an enormous Cadillac, attended by secretaries and footmen, and accompanied by the elegant Dorothy Dunbar, Baer was an instant sensation. His nightly exploits were duly noted in the gossip columns, which never failed to mention the fact that he had killed a man in the ring.

In Baer, New York's sports writers discovered an inexhaustible source of colorful quotations and anecdotes. One was so grateful that he wrote a double limerick to honor Madcap Maxie:

> There was a young scrapper named Baer
> Who had the most beautiful hair
> He could flirt, he could fight,
> He could dance all the night

> That fantastic fast puncher, Max Baer!
> That frivolous fighter named Baer
> Had the ladies all up in the air,
> He would love 'em and leave 'em,
> And blithely deceive 'em,
> That bewitching young biffer, Max Baer!

The day after Baer arrived in New York, Hoffman and Lorimer took him to Madison Square Garden to meet the press. Together they climbed the stairs to the second floor and Francis Albertanti's office. Baer sat down in one of Albertanti's rickety chairs, which gave way immediately under the force of his two-hundred-plus pounds. A replacement was located, and Baer sat down again.

"What's your full name?" one of the writers asked Baer.

"Max Adelbert Baer," Baer said.

"Not Maximilian, is it?"

"Not yet — I still have the million to get."

Baer was, in the parlance of the era, a wisecracker. It seemed to the writers that the man haunted by his last, deadly foray into the ring had disappeared.

"I figure the fight game like this," Baer went on. "I am a puncher. I can knock 'em over with either hand. I figure the smartest of them will get careless once in ten rounds. That's all I ask. Let him slip up once and I've got him. I can take it, too. My knees have sagged more than once, but they always came up again."

In his white tie and tails, Baer cut a dashing figure in New York society. Everyone loved him — except Dorothy Dunbar, who continued to reject his daily proposals.

"They were a handsome, eye-fetching couple," Fleischer wrote, "a spectacle Broadway grew accustomed to as they rolled along the Great White Way in Max's sixteen-cylinder car, the owner in evening clothes and a silk hat, his lady-friend a vision of beauty expertly gowned and be-diamonded."

Although Max's affection for Dorothy was genuine, fidelity was not his strong suit. Not many men could have resisted the temptations offered him. Nor could Max Baer. He was handsome, wealthy, famous, charming, physically powerful, and twenty-one years old. The women of New York responded accordingly. He was linked with showgirls and debutantes, waitresses and actresses. Like Harry Greb, the great middleweight champion of the previous decade, Max Baer spent much more time finding, courting, and bedding women than training. On the loose in the world's biggest playground, he rarely caught his breath.

No one knows whether this was his way of dealing with the sorrow he felt after killing Frankie Campbell. He certainly didn't appear to be in mourning. But Baer was a showman. He knew how to promote himself. He wanted to be a star. The smile the public saw was mostly a mask. The clowning was a defense mechanism. He was telling the world, "See how much fun I'm having?" In fact, he was deeply conflicted.

Before heading east, Hoffman had tried to line up a fight for Baer in New York. Rather than throwing him into the ring against a top contender, he wanted Baer to experience live combat against a less challenging opponent in his first fight after the death of Frankie Campbell. He wanted him to fight James J. Braddock, in fact. But the papers reported that the New York State athletic commission had ruled Braddock an unfit opponent for Baer.

So instead of fighting Braddock, Baer would make his New York debut against Ernie Schaaf, a solid left-handed heavyweight who had been the all-services champion while serving in the navy. Schaaf's two most impressive wins had both come at the expense of Tommy Loughran, who, like Schaaf, was left-handed and more boxer than puncher. Schaaf was a six-to-five favorite against Baer, whom he outweighed by three pounds, 203 to 200.

The fight took place on December 19, 1930, at Madison Square Garden. The estimable W. O. McGeehan was among the reporters and columnists who joined Baer in his dressing room before the fight. Baer told McGeehan that he had never been seriously injured in a fight, and to demonstrate the thickness of his skull, he slammed his head into the radiator.

Whatever point he was trying to make, it was lost on Schaaf, who shredded him. In the *New York Times*, James P. Dawson wrote, "Ernie Schaaf, Elizabeth (N.J.) heavyweight, shattered the illusion that Max Baer, California youngster, is a heavyweight title threat or prospect last night in Madison Square Garden, where, in a ten-round struggle that bristled with action, he battered the Coast invader as thoroughly as ever a boxer has been pounded to win a decision in as exciting a heavyweight encounter as has been seen here in some time." In one sentence, Dawson buried Max Baer.

All night Baer had stormed around the ring, chasing Schaaf, throwing right hands that rarely connected. Patiently, Schaaf snapped left after left into Baer's face, which was unrecognizable by the eighth round. Still, Baer was game. He stayed on his feet and kept fighting to the end — there was no way he was going to quit with Dorothy seated at ringside. The crowd of 10,000 admired his spirit if not his artistry. New York's fight fans, knowledgeable and usually ungenerous with their praise, cheered him, even if the writers did not. They liked his unusual style, which was both flashy and ferocious. His East Coast debut was a loss but a success.

Hoffman's fears were allayed. Baer had not lost his will to fight. True, he did no damage whatsoever, but he fought hard and appeared to be focused. Hoffman's goal now was to line up another fight as quickly as possible — it was the only way to keep Baer out of the nightclubs and out of Dorothy's bediamonded grasp. The good news was that Baer did not drink very much. For a teetotaler, though, he certainly enjoyed the nightlife.

Hoffman had no trouble securing another fight for his crowd-pleasing heavyweight at the Garden, four weeks later, against Tom Heeney, the New Zealander best remembered as Gene Tunney's final opponent. Unlike Schaaf, he was far from artistic. He was a straight-ahead puncher. When he went straight at Max Baer — who this time actually bothered to train for the bout — he got knocked out, in the third round.

Now Hoffman was encouraged — not excited, but encouraged. Tom Heeney was a legitimate, albeit aged, opponent. In two years Baer had come a long way from Chief Caribou. "Keep him active" was the mantra.

But Baer was still emotionally unhinged — and bewitched. On January 27, 1931, two weeks after the win against Heeney, the *New York Times* reported that Dorothy Dunbar had flown the previous day from Newark Airport to Reno "to prosecute divorce proceedings against her present husband." Everyone who read the papers knew why Dunbar was getting divorced from De Gerson y Baretto.

Dorothy was back in New York by the night of February 6, when Baer stepped into the ring at Madison Square Garden for a third time — to face Tommy Loughran. Hoffman saw the fight as a no-lose proposition. It would be great if Baer somehow managed to win, but if he lost, he would learn a valuable lesson at the hands of one of the most skilled fighters in the game.

Loughran, by now competing as a heavyweight, wasn't quite the fighter he had been nineteen months earlier, when he had humiliated James J. Braddock. In fact, the sports writers who liked him so much were urging him to retire before their memories of him tarnished. Still, he was much too clever for Baer.

Baer was not convinced that a man he outweighed by fifteen pounds, whom the papers were calling over the hill, could possibly withstand the fury of his assault. He was less focused on his opponent than on the referee — his hero, Jack Dempsey. To the dismay of his seconds, Baer tried to outbox Loughran. "Round after round I pleaded with Baer to quit boxing, to get in close and bang away, telling him it was his only chance," the veteran trainer Gus Wilson said. "Along toward the end of the fight he finally promised to do what I asked. He went out and gave Loughran a good pounding. 'That's the stuff, Max,' I told him when he came back to his corner. 'You just keep fighting him that way and you'll knock him out the next round.' What do you think he did? He laughed and took a playful poke at me as he sat on his stool. 'You don't want me to knock him out, do you, Gus?' he said, and laughed. And the next round he went back to boxing."

Just as Loughran had frustrated Braddock, he frustrated Baer. "It was like trying to box a shadow," Baer said. Loughran danced, jabbed, flitted in and out of Baer's reach, and avoided a lucky punch at all costs.

"We boxed ten rounds and Max didn't hit me with one punch," Loughran once said. Then, reconsidering, he said, "Yes, he did. He hit me one punch in the second round. I thought he broke all my ribs. He had a terrific punch."

Baer's experience fighting the Philadelphia Phantom perfectly paralleled Jim Braddock's. But his reaction to the loss was markedly different and influenced the course of the rest of his career. After Braddock's loss to Loughran, Braddock had sulked. After *his* loss to Loughran, Baer walked into Loughran's dressing room.

"Tommy," Baer said, "I know you don't owe me anything, but I want to succeed in this sport and I want you to tell me what I'm doing wrong."

"Sure, Max, I'd love to help."

Loughran and Baer, victor and vanquished, made plans to have lunch the next day. Baer then went home to the Plaza and Dorothy.

The next morning Baer walked out of the Plaza, turned right and walked west on 58th Street, turned left on Sixth Avenue, and walked four blocks south to the Warwick Hotel. He was meeting Jack Dempsey and the columnist Grantland Rice for breakfast. His face was puffy but still pretty.

"I've been looking at left jabs all night," Baer said, sipping his coffee, eager to hear what Dempsey and Rice had to say. "Lefts . . . lefts . . . lefts . . . that's all I've seen!"

"The funny part," Dempsey said, "is that you could have stopped that lefty in the first round."

"How?" said Baer.

"Take off your coat," Dempsey said. Baer threw off his coat, stood up, and faced Dempsey, who had also risen. Now everyone in the restaurant was watching.

"Now lead with a left, just as Loughran did," Dempsey said. Baer did as he was told, and as he shot out his left arm, Dempsey fired his right fist into Baer's left biceps.

Baer cried out in pain. "You broke my arm," he said.

Rice had started scribbling in his notepad.

"I'll show you another punch," Dempsey then said. He twisted Baer around as if they were dancing and then punched him in the side.

"You can't do that," Baer said. "It's illegal."

"They'll only warn you the first time," Dempsey said, grinning. Then Baer sat down and finished his coffee.

A few hours later, at a coffee shop near the Garden, Baer was treated to another lesson. To the surprise of their fellow diners — some of whom had seen them pounding each other the previous night — Tommy Loughran was buying Baer lunch. Chatting amiably, Baer told Loughran that Bob McAllister had tried to teach him to jab effectively, but it just wasn't working.

"One reason he failed," Loughran said, "was that you really weren't interested. You had been winning in your own style and couldn't see the use in changing. Now you know you can't tag everybody with that right, so it's up to you to acquire a straight left delivery. You'll get it okay sometime. If you keep on practicing, it will suddenly become just as natural as swinging is for you today. And since you've asked my opinion, you might try shortening your punches. Your technique is faulty there, for you telegraph your blows. And, as I said before, practice is the only thing. It's the old slogan — 'Keep punching' — hard work, but it'll be worth your while."

From the lunch table, Baer and Loughran headed to the gym. There the old(er) master demonstrated for Baer what he had talked about at lunch. Baer proved to be an apt student. From that day on he was a more scientific and artful fighter. As Hoffman had anticipated, losing to Tommy Loughran would be a win.

7

The Crash and the Jinx

....

North Bergen: October 1929

On October 29, 1929, the stock market crashed.

The previous year, in the summer of 1928, as former secretary of commerce Herbert Hoover was barnstorming around the country campaigning for the presidency, he said, "We in America today are nearer to the final triumph over poverty than ever before in the history of any land. The poorhouse is vanishing from among us. We have not yet reached the goal, but, given the chance to go forward with the policies of the last eight years, we shall soon, with the help of God, be in sight of the day when poverty will be banished from this nation." Hoover won the election in a landslide, defeating the Democratic candidate, former governor Al Smith of New York, with 58 percent of the vote. Smith, the first major-party Catholic candidate for the office and an opponent of Prohibition, received only 41 percent.

Hoover campaigned on the continued promise of prosperity — the prosperity that had flourished in the Roaring Twenties. In 1923 the volume traded on the New York Stock Exchange was 236 million shares. By 1929 it was more than a billion. In the weeks just before the crash, many of the nation's most highly respected financial minds, including the financiers Charles E. Mitchell and Bernard M. Baruch, were predicting unrestrained growth. The forecaster Roger W. Babson was one of the few who could see that the bubble was about to burst. "Sooner or later a crash is coming, and it may be terrific," he wrote. "Factories will shut down . . . men will be thrown out of work . . . and the result will be a serious business depression." Wall Street considered Babson a crackpot.

On October 29, after nearly two months of small declines, the value of the stock market plunged 11.5 percent. The day came to be known as Black Tuesday. Still the blinders stayed on. The next day, around the country, newspapers — Americans' primary source of news — assured their readers that there was no reason to panic. "What can be said, and what very much needs to be said," the *New York World* said in its editions on October 30, "is that, however sour things may look to individuals at the moment, the country has not suffered a catastrophe. There will be many cases of individual hardship, but no hardship like that which is almost normal in other countries." The *Daily News* was even more upbeat: "The sagging of the stocks has not destroyed a single factory, wiped out a single farm or city lot or real estate development, or decreased the productive powers of a single workman or machine in the United States. All those things are still there, and when they are essentially sound, as this country is, the more magnificently they recover." The *Baltimore Sun* was equally sunny: "The stock market crash obviously is the result of many forces, most of them transitory and all of them combined incapable of upsetting the firm base of prosperity." Similarly, the *Chicago Herald and Examiner* urged readers to buy, buy, buy: "The Stock Exchange has become the bargain counter of the world. It is difficult to believe that financial shoppers in this country and abroad will not take advantage of the low prices at which the very best of securities are selling."

Millions of Americans, most of them optimistic by nature and because of the experiences of the previous decade, made the mistake of believing what they read in the papers. Jim Braddock was one of them. Having grown up in poverty, he didn't like bankers. He never trusted the Wall Street brokers he met. He knew that if he weren't a boxer, they would have no use for him, an Irish-American who had never graduated from high school. He had no social aspirations — unlike, for instance, Gene Tunney, a New York Irishman who married into society, moved to Greenwich, Connecticut, and lived the life of a white Anglo-Saxon Protestant aristocrat. But Braddock had money. In only three years as a professional, he had managed to make nearly $30,000 — a significant sum in the late 1920s, the equivalent of about $500,000 in 2004 dollars. His friend Owney Madden, the notorious gangland boss of Hell's Kitchen, was probably the man who encouraged him to invest a large portion of his savings in a taxicab company. In addition to his bootlegging and nightclub interests, Madden controlled the taxi business. So Braddock invested in taxis after his savings in the Bank of the United States had been lost.

In the months leading up to the crash, after losing to Tommy Loughran, Braddock had started focusing his energies on his business interests while Gould struggled to get him into the gym. "Jim, you've got to put this behind you," Gould told him one day in the summer of 1929. "You can't beat yourself up anymore. You've got to get back in the gym. I'll get you another shot."

Braddock had heard Gould's pep talk before. "Joe," he said, "I don't know. Once Mae and I get married, I think I'm going to quit. I gave it my best shot, and it wasn't good enough."

Braddock had proposed to Mae Fox just after the Loughran fight, and she had accepted without hesitation. They planned to get married in January 1930.

"Listen, Jim, trust me," Gould said. "Loughran won't be able to make the weight much longer. He's through as a light heavyweight. When he moves up, you're going to get a shot at the title." The title would mean what it always meant — more money than Braddock would ever need, security, and respect. Braddock said he would think about it.

While he mulled over his future in the ring, he opened a nightclub at 33rd Street and Hudson Boulevard in North Bergen. "It was a nice club in a nice spot," Mae Braddock would later say. But Braddock broke the cardinal rule of saloon keeping: he extended credit. In a matter of months the club was boarded up. Even before it failed, however, he was back in the ring.

In August, just a few weeks after losing to Loughran, Braddock fought for the first time outside the New York area. He and Gould took a train all the way to Los Angeles for a fight against Yale Okun, a Jewish light heavyweight from the Lower East Side. Their stay in California was short and unproductive. Okun won the decision from Braddock in ten rounds. Once again Braddock looked slow and awkward. It was apparent that the loss to Loughran had robbed him of much of his confidence. Gould spent a long time on the train ride home trying to figure out what he and his fighter should do next. Braddock was uncharacteristically indifferent. He had almost given up trying to figure out why he was so inconsistent. They would take a break, Gould decided, to give him some time to work things out in the gym, to regain his focus, and then they would get back to work in the fall.

Gould had been right: Loughran was finished as a light heavyweight — he simply couldn't keep his weight anywhere near 175 pounds any longer — and the division was wide open. One of the top contenders to win the vacated title, along with Braddock, Lomski, and Slattery, was Maxie Rosenbloom, the Harlem Harlequin.

With the possible exception of Max Baer, Rosenbloom was the most colorful fighter of his era. Like Baer, he spent as much time in the ring playing to the fans as he did trading punches with his opponent. He had been discovered by the film star George Raft, who was famously friendly with the men of Murder Incorporated, the Jewish and Sicilian gang. Raft was walking through East Harlem one day and happened upon a street fight. Tall, slender Maxie Rosenbloom was in the midst of a dispute with one of his neighbors. Quick and strong, he stopped his opponent with a few fast, flashy punches. Legend has it that Raft said to him, "Hey, kid, you can handle yourself with your fists. Have you thought about boxing as a career?" With Raft behind him, Rosenbloom quickly established himself as one of the best fighters in the city, and therefore the world. Not since Benny Leonard had Jewish Harlem produced such a compelling fighter.

On October 21, 1929, Rosenbloom was a headliner at an extraordinary event at Madison Square Garden. In what the papers called one of the greatest cards ever promoted in the name of charity, ten fighters fought five five-round fights to benefit "the stricken Jews of Palestine." Each fight featured one Jewish fighter — Al Singer, Jack Berg, Ruby Goldstein, Yale Okun (fresh from his win against Braddock), and Rosenbloom. The event raised more than $100,000, with $75,000 going to the Palestine Emergency Fund. The man behind the evening was Samuel Rosoff, who had made a fortune building New York City's subways, which first started running in 1904. Mayor Jimmy Walker and Chairman James A. Farley of the boxing commission also served on the committee that organized the card. The event was attended by hundreds of politicians, most of them Irish, all of them conspicuously supporting a Jewish cause and at the same time sticking it to the British, who occupied the Holy Land at the time.

Of course Joe Gould was there, in evening wear, shaking hands and talking fast. He worked his way into his old friend Maxie Rosenbloom's dressing room. They exchanged a few pleasantries about mutual acquaintances from the old neighborhood, agreed that it was a swell cause they were raising money for, and then got down to business.

Gould and Rosenbloom decided it would be a good idea if Maxie fought Jim Braddock on November 15 at the Garden.

Braddock had put on several pounds in the two months since he had fought Okun and would not be able to make the light heavyweight limit — he was "a late-maturing Irishman," as he described himself, and was finally filling out. Maxie said no problem; they would fight as heavyweights. Gould wished Rosenbloom good luck — just not enough to defeat Braddock.

Gould announced the fight to the writers at ringside. "This will be Jimmy's first heavyweight fight," he said. "Next year he'll be fighting for the title." Gould had suddenly decided that Braddock was too good — and too big — to fight as a light heavyweight. His plan now was for Braddock first to win the light heavyweight title from Loughran and then to grab the vacant heavyweight title.

His boast was met with rolled eyes and deep skepticism. In one of his occasional assaults on Braddock, John Kieran wrote:

That's another point about Braddock. He can't make up his mind whether he wants to be a light heavyweight or a heavyweight champion. On late reports, he won't be either. He fancies he's a heavyweight now, but the only thing that supports him in that claim is the scales. On what he has shown to date, he isn't entitled to push himself into the picture with Jack Sharkey or Max Schmeling. But Braddock is young and he can hit. He has a chance to improve and get ahead. The chance is all the bigger because there is so much room for improvement.

Kieran was the king of the backhanded compliment.

Two weeks after the crash, Braddock, weighing 182 pounds, mostly because he had been training only sporadically, stepped into the ring to fight Maxie Rosenbloom, all 172 pounds of him. Braddock was a two-and-a-half-to-one underdog. He fought like a ten-to-one underdog. Rosenbloom dominated him, losing only one round, the fifth. Braddock didn't just lose; fighting against a masterful boxer, he again looked silly. At ringside, Lud Shabazian watched in disbelief. He had been pleased to see Braddock fighting again. But that didn't last long. The beating Braddock took was so thorough, it seemed to Shabazian he should quit. Braddock looked appallingly awkward and unbearably slow. As Shabazian prepared to file his fight story, he was certain that the men sitting around him were busy writing Braddock's "fistic obituary," as he put it.

Mae was at the fight, and Shabazian said she was so distraught at the sight of her fiancé's terrible beating that she "fled from the building long before the final round came around."

"As soon as they started trading punches, I got sick at my stomach," Mae said. "I just couldn't stand to see Jim — my sweetheart then — pummeled around."

Gould told Braddock to ignore the attacks of the newspapermen, but Braddock was truly wounded. Twice in four months he had looked foolish in the ring, and the critics were pouncing. He was wondering if they were right. Forced again to reassess his worth as a boxer, he found himself wanting. It was a stabbing realization. "I'm disgusted with it all," Braddock told Mae a few days after the fight. "Let's get married and I'll settle down. I'll devote all my time to the taxicab business."

The wedding was set for Saturday, January 18, 1930. But Gould had other plans for Braddock. About ten days before the event, he told Braddock that he had scheduled a rematch against Leo Lomski for January 17 in Chicago. Jack Dempsey was offering Braddock $6,000 for a night's work. "The money's too good to turn down," Gould said, stating the obvious. "You can fly home right after the fight. You don't even have to move the wedding back."

"Okay, okay, I'll see what Mae says," Braddock said.

He knew that a win over Lomski would put him right back in line for another shot at the title. Still, breaking the news to Mae was not something he was looking forward to. When he finally mustered the courage and suggested that he would fly back after the fight, she started shaking her head. "Nothing doing," she said. "Suppose you get a black eye? Do you think I want to walk up the aisle with a bridegroom who has a black eye?" The wedding was postponed a week — which was fine with Gould, who wanted Braddock focusing on the fight.

In Chicago, Braddock fared better than he had in his first fight with the Aberdeen Assassin. He didn't lose, but he didn't win. The fight was a draw. The crowd, however, disagreed. Most felt that Lomski had won, and for several minutes after the draw was announced they booed lustily. Braddock and Gould went home the next day — by train, not airplane — $6,000 richer but with another stain on Braddock's record.

Braddock, usually hard on himself after a disappointing performance, managed to dispel the draw from his thoughts as the wedding approached. Gould resisted the urge to schedule another fight for the night before the ceremony. On January 26, James J. Braddock married Mae Fox. Shortly after the priest blessed the union, Jim and Mae were on a train for Miami Beach.

In the days before jet travel, a trip to Miami was for northeasterners like a trip to the far side of the solar system. Mae had never before seen palm trees. The art deco hotels and the stucco houses painted in pastels were very different from the drabness of north Jersey. The newlyweds were just getting acclimated when the Illinois Boxing Commission made a surprise announcement. Disturbed by the draw that it felt had robbed Lomski of a clear win, the commission reviewed the scoring of the fight and concluded that the referee, Dave Miller, had added up the scores incorrectly. "While the action of the commission was nothing more than a routine matter," the *New York Times* noted dryly, "it caused great consternation among the gambling element." Miller refused to accept the blame for the miscalculation, instead pinning it on the ring announcer, Al Smith (not the presidential candidate). "Announcer Smith grabbed my score card before I had a chance to review the tally," he said.

By changing the result of the fight, the Illinois commission made itself an easy target for the ridicule of the eastern establishment, which was still paying close attention to Jim Braddock's fights. In the *Times*, Kieran dedicated a full column to the Illinois follies: "Any time now the general public can expect bulletins like this: 'Appomattox Court House — The estate of Gen. Robert E. Lee, C.S.A., is herewith informed that a recount of the point total indicates that Gen. Lee won the decision over Gen. U.S. Grant. Official papers signed under a mistaken impression are herewith recalled, and every effort will be made to right the error.'"

Gould was justifiably furious. His written response to the commission was equal parts righteous indignation and biting sarcasm: "I have received from you today a letter notifying me that Lomski has been declared the winner over Braddock ten days after the fight. May I and Braddock, who has just been married, thank you for the wedding present? We expect to hear any day now that Gene Tunney has at last been counted out in his fight with Jack Dempsey."

The last line was a low blow. The Long Count had taken place in Chicago, under the auspices of the Illinois Boxing Commission. Gould's pen was as sharp as his tongue.

Try as it might, the commission couldn't ruin Braddock's honeymoon. The heat soothed him, even as the sun turned him into a giant welt. For the first time in his adult life, boxing just didn't matter so much. "Everything looked rosy, ever so rosy, right after our marriage," Mae Braddock told the *Daily Mirror* in 1935. "Jim had about twenty thousand dollars in the bank, his purse from the losing ends of his bouts with Leo Lomski and Maxie Rosenbloom. Well, with all that money in the bank, Jim had made up his mind to give up fighting. Believe me, I was thoroughly agreeable. And to me — the biggest money I had ever seen was my twenty-five dollars a week earned as a telephone operator — twenty thousand dollars looked like a billion."

Braddock had had it with boxing. With plenty of money to invest, he decided he would make a little money in the stock market, fight a few more fights, then quit to focus on business. By this time, when it had become apparent that the crash was not anomalous, most Americans were wary of the stock market. But Braddock overcame his wariness and on the advice of a friend invested heavily. He soon lost most of his savings again. What he didn't lose in the stock market, he poured into his failing taxicab company. All the money he had earned was disappearing.

Braddock fought for the first time as a married man on April 7, 1930, in Philadelphia, against Billy Jones, a fighter of little distinction. Braddock weighed 183 pounds and fought hard for ten rounds, but the decision went to Jones. This time the crowd booed because it thought that Braddock deserved at least a draw. The defeat was crushing. It eliminated Braddock as a contender in the light heavyweight division. He had now lost five of his last six fights. He was washed up. Still, Gould continued to find him opponents.

The crash had hit Gould hard too. The money he had earned managing Braddock in several big fights was gone, most of it contributed to the general funds of various bars, restaurants, and haberdashers. But Gould kept up appearances. He continued to dress well. He lived on Central Park West. He ate steaks and oysters. He knew how to enjoy life, and nothing as trivial as a global depression was going to interfere with that enjoyment. Like most men who know how to work the angles, he never expected that he'd be broke for long.

To boost Braddock's confidence, Gould arranged for him to fight Harold Mays on June 5 in West New York. Braddock needed a win — Mays was supposed to be nothing more than "an opponent" — but all he got for ten rounds of work was a no-decision. Four weeks later, Braddock and Gould took the train to Boston, the city where Braddock would fight his next three bouts. On July 2 he fought Joe Monte for the third time, now on Monte's home turf. Instead of drawing, as they had done the first two times they met, Braddock won an easy decision, dominating the fight from the first round through the tenth. He seemed to be back on track. A month later he returned to Boston to fight Babe Hunt. It was a "sensational ten-round battle," as the Associated Press put it. Braddock lost the decision.

Again he was disgusted with the fight game. Nothing makes a fighter angrier than losing a close decision. By this time Braddock had lost several. He would have liked to follow through on his plan to quit the sport, but the United States in 1930 was not a place where men willingly gave up their livelihoods. So he kept fighting, in part because Mae was now pregnant with their first child. But he was at best a reluctant pugilist. For the first time the sacrifices he had made as a fighter seemed to him pointless. As an up-and-comer, he had found in boxing something ennobling. Now he wasn't so sure. "There is no profession as dangerous as boxing, and there is no profession which forces so much denial," he told Francis Albertanti of the *Ring*.

> It is not a game for weaklings, and those who survive deserve whatever they earn. They have paid for it with lost youth that was wasted away in stuffy gyms and sweat rooms. They have paid for it in parties they could not attend, sweets they could not eat, water they could not drink. It is a hard game. When you go to Madison Square Garden and see it jammed to the roof, you think to yourself that the fighters in the main event are pretty lucky stiffs. The next time that thought hits you, just remember that a fighter doesn't break into the Garden overnight. He has traveled a long, hard, unattractive path. The fan only sees the end of that path, but they are too far away to see the hills that we had to climb on our way to a main bout in a big club.

A few years later, Gould summed up Braddock's malaise more succinctly in a conversation with Frank Graham of the *Sun:* "He got married in 1930 and got lazy and he began to blow fights he should have won. He would make a good fight and then a bad one and everybody thought he was washed up."

Only Gould — and the Depression — kept Braddock from quitting boxing in 1930. "We're gonna pull through this slump," Gould said one day as he and Braddock were sharing a sandwich at Stillman's. "And when you start winning, you're gonna keep winning."

"I know," Braddock said. "Just get me the fights."

Slowly Braddock reembraced the sport. Training and fighting were his therapy as well as his profession. He found solace and comfort in the rhythms of the gym, its easy camaraderie and familiar rituals. Here he knew what was expected of him and how to deliver it. It was outside, where the ropes disappeared, that he had trouble making sense of things and finding his footing.

On September 19, in Boston, Braddock knocked out Phil Mercurio in the second round. It was a solid win — not enough to make everyone forget the recent losses, but a solid win nevertheless. Gould now saw an opportunity where before he had seen none. A fighter from California named Max Baer was about to make his New York debut. All that Gould knew about Baer was that he had killed his last opponent, a pretty good fighter named Frankie Campbell, in the ring. Gould, though, didn't scare easily — at least not when Braddock was fighting. He thought that Braddock would welcome Baer to New York the way he had welcomed Tuffy Griffiths, another knockout artist from beyond the Alleghenies. Despite Braddock's recent mediocrity, Gould, like a proud parent, was almost blind to his weaknesses. He believed in him to a fault — especially when he was fighting powerful punchers rather than artful boxers.

But the boxing commission — the same body whose William Muldoon had two years earlier predicted that Braddock would one day win the world heavyweight championship — wouldn't let Braddock fight Baer. According to the papers, the commission ruled that Braddock was an unfit opponent. The commission, it was reported, feared for his safety in a fight against the proven man-killer Baer. Joe Gould pleaded Braddock's case at a special hearing, to no avail. The commission stuck to its decision.

In fact, the minutes of the boxing commission's meeting on November 18, 1930, stated,

Tom McArdle, matchmaker, appeared relative to the proposed Max Baer–Jimmy Braddock bout at his club December 19, 1930. He was informed that this match will not be approved by the Commission in view of the alleged entangling alliances existing between the Eastern representatives of Baer and the present recognized and unrecognized managers of Braddock. It was suggested to McArdle that he return Friday, November 21, and submit another opponent for Baer. In giving this information to McArdle, the Commission desired to emphasize to him that it meant no reflection on the honesty of either Braddock or Baer.

Three days later, McArdle returned to the commission's offices on Lafayette Street. In the minutes, Bert Stand, the commission secretary, wrote, "Tom McArdle, matchmaker of Madison Square Garden S.C., appeared requesting permission to stage a match at his club between Ernie Schaff [sic] and Max Baer December 19. Approved."

Gould was incensed, but there was nothing he could do except find Braddock another opponent. One month after Ernie Schaaf defeated Baer — soundly — he would be that fighter. Braddock was coming off a four-month hiatus and Schaaf outweighed him by nearly thirty pounds, yet Braddock was not deemed unfit to fight Schaaf, which strongly suggests that his fitness was not the real issue when the commission refused to allow him to fight Baer.

The prospect of fighting in Madison Square Garden again, against anyone, emboldened Braddock. It had been more than a year since he had fought in New York City; the bouts against Lomski, Jones, Mays, Monte, Hunt, and Mercurio had all been elsewhere. The idea of fighting again on his home turf, of experiencing the cauldron of sound produced by a big crowd at the Garden, reignited his desire to fight.

In spite of this, Braddock, looking typically flat-footed, lost the fight, a ten-round split decision, though James P. Dawson wrote in the *New York Times* that Schaaf "failed again to impress onlookers as a prospect who will develop proportions as a serious contender for heavyweight title consideration." Considering that Schaaf had defeated Baer and Braddock, two future champions, in the space of a few weeks, it is reasonable to question the intelligence of the onlookers who were so unimpressed. Once again Braddock was the victim of a questionable decision. "A majority of the slim crowd disagreed with the award, a divided one," Dawson wrote, "and voiced this disagreement in no uncertain manner when the New Englander [Schaaf was from Boston] was declared the winner. Objection to the decision, however, was unjustified, for Schaaf established his right to the honors by winning six rounds against four for Braddock."

Once again John Kieran of the *Times* unsheathed his saber to prick Braddock: "After watching James J. Braddock in his bout with Ernie Schaaf, the impression is stronger than ever that James J. would make a great chess player. He has all the necessary speed for that game." There was more. "Braddock has a willing disposition and a durable chin," Kieran continued, "but like the big clock in the Metropolitan Tower, he strikes every quarter of an hour, which isn't often enough for pugilistic purposes."

Incredibly, five days later, in the January 30 edition of the *Times*, Braddock was again the butt of Kieran's column. "James J. Braddock is an exponent of the delayed-attack style," Kieran wrote. "He aims his most deadly punches at a spot occupied by his opponent's chin or ribs some thirty seconds previously. He rarely misses by more than five or six feet. Braddock would be a great fighter to watch on a warm Summer [sic] night. He stirs up a fine breeze with his swings."

It was certainly true that at this time Braddock was struggling to find his form, but Kieran's attacks were beyond the pale and indicative of just how cavalierly the press could mock and denigrate easy targets, which is exactly what Braddock had become in the eighteen months since he had lost to Tommy Loughran. Still, in 1931, at least people were still talking about Braddock. In December, Kieran made fun of him again — "It was pathetic the way bewildered James J. stood there and wondered where the blows were coming from and what invisible miscreant was assaulting him": a reference to the Loughran fight — but even Kieran was above kicking a man who fell as far as Braddock fell in 1932 and 1933. Kieran didn't mention his name again until 1935.

The loss to Schaaf would prove to be the highlight of Braddock's year in the ring in 1931. In March he won two fights, against Jack Roper in Miami and Jack Kelly in New Haven, Connecticut, but neither win meant much because the opponents were relatively obscure. Braddock's financial situation took yet another turn for the worse. The taxicab company went out of business — people simply couldn't afford to take taxis anymore — and Braddock, who had failed to carry enough insurance to protect his investment, went into debt.

Braddock took the misfortune hard, but Mae was despondent. "I wept and wept until it seemed my eyes would burn out," she later said.

"Never mind, baby," Braddock said to her shortly after the business failed. "I'm going to go back in the ring and we'll get it all back with interest. Don't you worry. And we'll know what to do with it the next time we get a bankroll." Of course, he had no way of knowing that it would be years before he built up another sizable bankroll.

In October, Braddock fought Joe Sekyra at Madison Square Garden. Only four thousand people were there to see him fight listlessly for nine of the ten rounds. He lost another decision.

In November, feeling the financial pinch, he went all the way to Minneapolis to fight Maxie Rosenbloom for a second time. Rosenbloom was now the light heavyweight champion, but this was not a title fight; James J. Braddock's days as a light heavyweight were over. He was now fighting at 180 to 185 pounds. Braddock and Rosenbloom got along well and were probably less than eager to exert themselves fully in what amounted to little more than an exhibition in a minor-league boxing town. For the better part of two rounds, they pawed and circled each other. Braddock later said that his hands were hurt in the fight, which by this time was usually the case. The crowd, though, was disgusted by the amateurish display. So was the referee. In the second round, he threw up his hands and kicked both fighters out of the ring. He declared the fight "no contest," on the grounds that neither Braddock nor Rosenbloom was willing to throw a punch. The commission gave each of them $350 to cover their expenses but donated Rosenbloom's $1,195 share of the purse and Braddock's $996 share to charity. "In return for pledges not to bring legal action to recover the full purse, the commission agreed not to suspend them nor to ask their suspension in other states," the Associated Press reported. Braddock and Gould could barely afford the train ride home.

Now Braddock, who had more than a little superstition coursing through his veins, began to think he was jinxed. The strange manner in which he had been losing fights, the close calls, the questionable decisions, the Lomski reversal, the Rosenbloom no-contest — they all confounded him. The only explanation he could muster was that he was jinxed, which he told Mae.

Still, he kept training and fighting. He haunted Stillman's, along with Gould, trying to rediscover whatever it was that had vanished on the night he lost to Tommy Loughran. On the days that Braddock looked bad against even the amateurs, Gould would encourage him. At lunch they would share a plate of beans or a hamburger; they were always hungry. Braddock often told Gould that he would understand if Gould dropped him and concentrated on finding another fighter to manage. Gould, though, continued to believe in Braddock. He saw in him the same fighter who had made Harry Galfund look bad, the same fighter who had knocked out the great Tuffy Griffiths. Gould knew that somewhere deep inside Braddock there was a champion — and even though most people thought Braddock was finished, Gould treated him with as much respect as ever.

Gould often thought that if only Braddock's right hand would heal properly, he would be a fighter to be reckoned with. But the hand was chronically injured — like most fighters' hands, only more so. (At the time boxers wore six-ounce gloves, which were little more than dress gloves, really, and it was not uncommon for them to break their hands frequently. The gloves did not have chambers, so a fighter could push what little padding there was — usually horsehair — away from the knuckles to maximize the impact of each punch. The result was more damage to both the fighter getting punched and the fighter throwing the punch. Today gloves are heavier — eight or ten ounces — and chambered, to assure even padding.) Every time Braddock hit the punching bag, he winced. Every time he landed a punch, a wave of pain shot up his spine.

Gould continued to plead Braddock's case with Jimmy Johnston, who had replaced Tom McArdle at Madison Square Garden, and more often than not Johnston would relent, giving Braddock a fight that he probably didn't deserve based on his recent ring record. Often, though, Gould and Braddock were forced to go outside New York to find fights. On March 18, 1932, in Chicago, a relative nobody named Baxter Calmes from Oklahoma City easily outpointed Braddock, who was unlucky even the day after St. Patrick's Day.

Three months later, at the Madison Square Garden Bowl — where he usually fought well — Braddock appeared on the undercard of the heavyweight championship fight between Max Schmeling and the challenger, Jack Sharkey, and outpointed

Vincent Parrille of Argentina. Parrille, who outweighed him 203 pounds to 179, had a decent reputation, and Braddock's victory should have given him some momentum. At the very least, it impressed Johnston, who booked him for another fight five weeks later.

Braddock hit the gym hard — sparring constantly, working diligently on his footwork and timing. Gould and Doc Robb were convinced he was back, despite the pain in his right hand. But early on the morning of July 7, Braddock hurt his hand again — not in the ring but at North Bergen police headquarters.

Braddock's younger brother, Alfred, who worked on the ferries that crossed the Hudson, spent the night of July 6 drinking with his friends Jeff Bostwick and Henry Werner. The morning too. At about 4 A.M., Al Braddock and Bostwick decided that it would be a wonderful idea to visit their friend Anna Quinlan. They knocked on her door, but she refused, quite sensibly, to admit them. Al and Jeff then proceeded to break several of her windows with rocks. Quinlan called the police. Captain Louis Bachman, Sergeant Thomas Neggia, and two patrolmen responded, listened to Quinlan's story, and, suspecting that the perpetrators had not yet decided to call it a night, arrived shortly thereafter at a bar on Fisher Avenue. The policemen's instincts were correct. They arrested Braddock, Bostwick, and Werner, even though Werner had not been to Quinlan's house, and hauled them down to police headquarters, where Quinlan identified Braddock and Bostwick as the rock throwers. Just as they were being booked on charges of disorderly conduct, Jim Braddock arrived, hoping to obtain their release (a desk sergeant had called him to tell him that Al had been arrested).

According to that afternoon's edition of the *Jersey Journal*, Jim then insulted a man who had accompanied Quinlan to police headquarters. Captain Bachman told him to knock it off and added that Al was a good-for-nothing so-and-so. Braddock did what he always did when either he or his relatives were insulted. He threw a punch — right at Bachman's nose, breaking it and knocking the man unconscious. It was Braddock's first knockout in months. Punching a police captain was stupid enough. Punching him in his own station house was an act of almost transcendent stupidity. In an instant Braddock was laid upon by three sergeants, a detective, three patrolmen, and the patrol wagon driver. Braddock fought back, with token assistance from his brother, Werner, and Bostwick. For a few seconds it appeared that Braddock might knock out the entire North Bergen police department. Then one of the sergeants got a nightstick around his neck, another grabbed him by the legs, and the melee was over. Jim Braddock and Werner, who needed four stitches to close a gash on his forehead, were arrested on a charge of assault and battery and held on $2,000 bail. Two policemen, apparently sympathetic to the Braddocks' cause, were investigated for failing to assist their comrades.

The *Jersey Journal*'s story was splashed across its front page. More embarrassing for Braddock, the writer described, more or less accurately, the state of his boxing career. "Braddock was ranked among the leading light heavyweights in the country a few years ago," he wrote, "but of late has been more or less inactive. He engaged in numerous local bouts and was finally rewarded in September, 1929 [it was actually July], with a chance at the world's light heavyweight title, then held by Tommy Loughran. The Philadelphian's masterful boxing was too much for the North Hudsonite and he was soundly beaten. Since then his ring engagements have been far and few between. He never again attained the heights he had reached prior to his bout with Loughran."

His hometown paper literally wrote him off.

Even before Gould found his way to the station house late that afternoon, Braddock's friends had arranged his release. Harry Buesser, one of the town's five commissioners and its chief of public safety, was the man who a decade earlier had promoted Jim Braddock's first pro fight, when he fought as Jimmy Ryan. Buesser had made a smooth transition from promoting to politics, which tells you all you need to know about north Jersey politics. In some towns, assaulting a police captain could get you killed. In North Bergen, when the assailant was Jim Braddock — even a washed-up Jim Braddock — the dustup was treated for the most part as a case of boys being boys. Although Braddock was eventually sentenced to ninety days in jail for using profane language in court, the sentence was suspended and the charges were reduced from felonies to misdemeanors. Still, Captain Bachman's nose had rather inconsiderately damaged Braddock's right hand, which was not what Gould wanted to hear.

"Are you insane?" Gould said, staring at the bandages on Braddock's hand. "Who punches a police captain? Couldn't you have at least used your left?"

To Braddock, the explanation was simple. "He insulted Al," he said.

Two weeks later, Braddock — who was free on bail — and his ailing right hand were back at the Madison Square Garden Bowl, to fight Tony Shucco on the undercard of the Ernie Schaaf–Paulino Uzcudan fight. Schaaf won, and so did Shucco, easily. Braddock had won forty-three of his first forty-six pro fights, from 1926 to 1929; his subsequent record, beginning with the Loughran fight, was seven wins, eleven losses, one draw, and one no-contest. For three years he had been close to awful. Finally, even with Gould sniffing them out, there were no more fights to be found in New York. No one wanted to pay to see Jim Braddock in the ring.

Braddock had no choice. Leaving behind Mae and his infant sons — Mae had given birth to Jay in January 1931 and to Howard the following December — he went west with Gould, to California again. The Pacific breezes did nothing to change his luck. In August he won a ten-round decision in San Diego against Dynamite Jackson. But in September, in San Francisco, he suffered another reversal, this time against a promising young black light heavyweight named John Henry Lewis, who would eventually capture the world championship. A month later, in Los Angeles, Braddock lost again, to Tom Patrick, who opened a deep gash over his eye.

Less than three weeks later, dead broke and in desperate need of the train fare he would need to get home for the holidays, Braddock went back to San Francisco to fight Lou Scozza. As he and Gould made their way up the California coast on November 8 — the match was made suddenly, when Scozza's original opponent pulled out — the nation was at the polls. Governor Franklin D. Roosevelt of New York trounced the incumbent, Herbert Hoover, winning forty-two of the forty-eight states. At about the time Braddock and Gould pulled into Union Station in San Francisco, Hoover, only thirty miles away at his home in Palo Alto, conceded the election. The next night Braddock fought Scozza, who almost immediately reopened the cut over his eye, temporarily blinding him. In the sixth round, the referee stopped the fight and declared Scozza the winner by technical knockout. Never before had Braddock been knocked out.

Finally, after almost four months on the West Coast, Braddock and Gould went home. On the train ride, they spent hours together watching the country roll by. It didn't look good. The land had been blighted by drought and dust. Whenever the train pulled into a station, they would get off to stretch their legs. The people they encountered were hungry and ragged. Some begged for change, others for food. Braddock's thoughts drifted back to the days when he rode the rails to Chicago. Then, ten years earlier, every whistle stop had held out the promise of adventure and potential prosperity. Now Braddock realized that that had been a mirage. To his mind, he was powerless against the Fates, who had treated him roughly for the past three years. The poor were a constant reminder of what might happen to him. He had no education to fall back on, no trade outside box-ing. If he and Gould had to spend the foreseeable future riding the rails in search of fights in order to survive, then that's what they would do. There was no such thing as relief or welfare; the New Deal was still just an idea. Together, Braddock and Gould had only a few dollars in their pockets. They mostly subsisted on cheese sandwiches and apples. The ride home was long.

Back in North Bergen, Braddock spent the holiday quietly with Mae and the babies. His eye had healed, but his hand was still painfully sore. He went to the gym every day, though, because boxing was all that stood between the Braddocks and poverty. He had to fight to feed his family. Almost every morning he took the ferry into Manhattan and walked to Stillman's, where Gould would be waiting. Sometimes with a trainer, usually alone, the two spent hours together as Braddock punched and sweated. The writers came and went every day. Before his bigger fights — against Griffiths, Lomski, and Loughran, for instance — they had sought out Braddock and Gould. Now they didn't ignore them; it was just that Braddock and Gould had become invisi-ble. They were alive, but their careers were dead. Shabazian dropped by once every few weeks, and the three of them would share a few execrable sandwiches from the Stillman's conces-sionaires. But mostly Braddock and Gould were together and virtually alone. They strategized and dreamed, of big fights and big paydays. Gould lifted Braddock's spirits, and Brad-dock lifted Gould's. Meanwhile, they watched as the stars of the sport filtered in and out of Stillman's with their entou-rages. Sharkey, Schmeling, Carnera, Baer, Ross, Rosenbloom, and Loughran led the procession. None of them, Braddock and Gould noticed, looked hungry. They all looked like they had just returned from Miami Beach.

Just before Christmas, Gould came to Braddock with a fight — in Chicago on January 13. Once again Braddock was being offered up as a trial horse for a promising young knockout artist, Martin Levandowski of Grand Rapids, Michigan. Naturally, the Illinois Boxing Commission — the same commission that had, in Braddock's eyes, cheated him out of the draw with Lomski — feared for Braddock's safety against a terror like Levandowski, and before it would license him for the fight, it demanded that he prove his fitness. Braddock would have to spar a few rounds under the gaze of the commissioners at a Chicago gym. Subjected to yet another humiliation, he overcame the throbbing pain in his right hand — Gould wanted him to take a shot of Novocain, but Braddock preferred pain to numbness — and subjected his two sparring partners to terrible beatings. The commissioners had no choice. They cleared him to fight.

Like Tuffy Griffiths before him, Martin Levandowski had built up a fearsome reputation by knocking out virtually every man he had fought. Like Tuffy Griffiths, at the opening bell he sprang from his corner like a bull from a chute. He swung wildly at Braddock's head. Braddock waited for him to lose his balance. When he did, Braddock stuck his right in Levandowski's face. Wincing as his hand absorbed the force of the blow, he watched as Levandowski dropped to the canvas with a dull thud. Slowly Levandowski got up. Then he went down again. By the end of the ten-round fight, Braddock had knocked Levandowski down five times. He won a unanimous decision.

As Gould iced his hand, Braddock, who in victory was oblivious of the pain, said, "Them knockout sensations are my meat."

Just seven days later he was in the ring again, fighting at Madison Square Garden for the first time since October 1931. His opponent, Hans Birkie of Germany, who outweighed him 200 pounds to 182, had fought just four days earlier, at St. Nicholas Arena on the West Side. (It was not unusual for boxers to fight more than once a week in the 1930s. Even pro athletes near the top of their sport were forced to work more often for less money during the Depression.) The smallest crowd in the history of the new or old Garden, about 3,500 weak, watched Braddock and Birkie fight like two men who were fighting for the second time in less than a week. That wasn't a good enough excuse for James P. Dawson, who called the bout "a slow-motion picture of a ring struggle between two mediocre heavyweights." Braddock was more mediocre than Birkie, winning only two of ten rounds and losing the fight by decision. He wouldn't fight again in New York City for seventeen months.

A few days after losing to Birkie, Braddock was driving through North Bergen with some friends when they collided with another car. No one was seriously hurt except Braddock, who broke several ribs. Again he couldn't believe his bad luck; the jinx, he believed, was real. There was further proof to come. He was scheduled to fight Al Ettore on March 1 in Philadelphia, and neither he nor Gould could afford a postponement. At Stillman's, Gould made sure that Braddock's ribs were properly taped. But when Braddock entered the ring to fight Ettore, his ribs and his right hand were aching. First Ettore struck him in the ribs, and then Braddock hit Ettore with his right hand, nearly shattering it. After that he was useless. He stumbled around the ring. The crowd jeered him relentlessly as he awkwardly ducked Ettore's punches and pawed at him with his weak left hand. By this time Braddock should have been accustomed to looking foolish, but it infuriated him that he was embarrassing himself. He could have found a way to quit, but instead he tried to get through the fight honorably. In the ring, Braddock still clung desperately to honor. By the fourth round, however, the referee, Joe McGuigan, had had enough. Unaware of Braddock's splintered ribs and cracked hand, he kicked him out of the ring and declared the fight no contest. Adding insult to ignominy, the Pennsylvania boxing commission suspended Braddock and Gould for what it considered an unprofessional performance.

Braddock and Gould were undeterred. Twenty days after that debacle, despite Braddock's injuries, they were in St. Louis for a fight against Al Stillman, another puncher in the tradition of Tuffy Griffiths and Martin Levandowski. Braddock knocked him out in the tenth round. Braddock liked St. Louis. He fought there again two weeks later, against Levandowski, who this time defeated him in a ten-round decision. Six weeks later, adhering to the now familiar pattern, Braddock met Stillman in a rematch and lost a ten-round decision, again in St. Louis. Having exhausted his drawing potential on the East and West Coasts, he was now equally unwanted in the Midwest. In three time zones he was washed up — and there were no big arenas in the fourth. For the first time since 1927, his second year as a pro, Braddock would have to fight in small-time clubs and medium-sized arenas.

In the 1920s, Braddock had made thousands of dollars a fight. Now he was making a couple of hundred or less. The situation at home was getting worse. He was struggling to pay the rent and utilities. But he kept training and fighting. His hopes of one day winning the championship had long ago been dashed; in the space of just a few years, he had become a professional opponent.

Yet he still found satisfaction in the simple rituals of boxing. When people saw him at the gym, they were always impressed by the quality of the effort he put into his workouts and by the seriousness with which he approached his profession. Braddock could easily have grown cynical about boxing, which at times had treated him cruelly. Even when he had believed that he wanted out of the fight game three years earlier, he could not have stayed away for long. Fighting was as essential to him as breathing. When the sport seemed unfair, he maintained an abiding respect for it, and he was determined to acquit himself honorably regardless of the bad decisions and chronic injuries he had suffered.

In the late summer of 1933, Braddock and Gould were still spending their days on West 57th Street, at Stillman's. Braddock was getting thicker as he aged. His frame carried his 185 pounds easily, without any fat. If anything, he was getting stronger. His right hand, though, was always a problem and impeded his training. The extra weight he was carrying also affected his foot speed, which went from bad to very bad.

The Depression had changed the mood at Stillman's. Its rings, once drenched with the sweat of the ambitious, were now darkened by the sweat of the desperate and defeated. Boxing was their only hope; there were no good jobs to be had anywhere. In the 1920s, boxers fought because they liked it or were good at it. In the 1930s, they fought because they had to. Braddock had to fight. On September 25, he would fight Abe Feldman at Memorial Stadium in Mount Vernon, just north of the Bronx.

At twenty, Feldman was eight years younger than Braddock, but he had already fought twenty times as a professional, compiling a 19–1 record. In August he had defeated Hans Birkie, whom Braddock had lost to in January. Earlier in September he had defeated Pietro Corri. Feldman was thought to have a future; Braddock was considered finished. Still, Gould thought that Braddock would easily defeat Feldman and that a win would get him back into Madison Square Garden and out of arenas in Jersey City, West New York, and Mount Vernon.

Braddock, Gould, and Robb drove to the fight together in Gould's beat-up Ford. Getting dressed before the bout, Braddock was unusually sullen. He was behind with the rent and utilities. His hand hurt, which meant he could not fight at his best. He was depressed by the surroundings — the bush-league dressing room, the small crowd, the high school ambience of the suburbs. He thought to himself, *How did I end up here, fighting in the sticks, against some kid who was in grade school when I was fighting for championships?* But there were no alternatives. No one was clamoring for another Braddock fight at the Garden. No promoters in Chicago or Los Angeles wanted Jim Braddock on their cards. More than four years after his only title fight, he was just hanging on. The papers were filled with stories about Primo Carnera, the new heavyweight champion, and Max Baer, the top contender. Braddock was forgotten.

It was a cool early-fall evening, and only a few hundred people were sitting in the bleachers at the stadium. In the first round, Braddock and Feldman established their rhythms — a few flurries here, a few combinations there. They were just getting to know each other. Between rounds Braddock felt good; throwing a few punches had helped lift his mood. He told Gould not to worry, they were going home winners. In the second round, he found an opening when Feldman dropped his guard. Braddock, among the most accurate punchers ever, nailed the twenty-year-old squarely on the jaw. But it was Braddock who was in agony from the punch. His right hand was broken in three places, the knuckle crushed beneath his skin. Feldman now advanced with impunity. Despite all his right-hand troubles, Braddock still hadn't learned to use his left. In the third, fourth, and fifth rounds, he tried to mount some kind of attack, to stay on his feet, as he had against Al Ettore in Philadelphia.

In the ring, quitting was never an option for Braddock, who through eighty pro fights had never been knocked out, except by Lou Scozza on a technicality. But the futility of his effort against Feldman was greeted with loud derision from the crowd, which had no way of knowing that he was fighting with a broken hand.

In the sixth round, Braddock kept slugging, to no avail. He was now lurching around the ring, too slow to catch up with Feldman, too proud to throw in the towel. Finally, as the jeering reached a crescendo, the referee waved his hands over his head and ended the fight. Again it was no contest. One no-contest on a fighter's record was enough to end a career; three were almost unforgivable.

Braddock went back to his dressing room and cried, he later said. Then he made up his mind that he was quitting.

On the ride back to New Jersey, he broke the news to Gould.

"I guess I'm all washed up," he said as they drove south out of Mount Vernon. "I think I should quit. I don't want to embarrass myself."

Gould, reflexively, tried to talk him out of it. "Listen, Jim, once your hand heals, you'll be better than ever," he said. "You've just had some bad luck. You can still earn."

"No one wants to see me fight anymore. Why should they?"

"What else are you going to do?" Gould said. "It's not like we've got a lot of options." But even as the words formed, Gould was wondering if Braddock should fight again. Even he was beginning to think that Braddock needed to retire. After all, he was twenty-eight and losing more fights than he won. His hand was chronically sore. Jimmy Johnston admired his gameness, but there were at least two dozen heavyweights who were more promising and more bankable. Braddock's future as a fighter would probably be filled with nights in neighborhood clubs and small-town Elks lodges. Gould didn't want to see him diminished any further. But Braddock's career was the only thing keeping them from the soup lines.

"Let's get a cast on that right hand, let it heal up, then we'll talk," Gould said as they sped through the darkness. The rest of the ride passed in unfamiliar silence.

Imitating their counterparts in Pennsylvania, the state boxing commissioners ordered Braddock's purse withheld until they could determine why he had fought so badly against Feldman. On October 3, at the hearing, the commissioners heard the report of Dr. Vincent Nardiello, who had examined Braddock after the fight and determined that he had in fact broken his hand. Nardiello's report proved that Braddock had fought bravely, not indifferently. The purse, $250, was handed over.

Braddock and Gould walked out onto Lafayette Street and made plans to see each other later in the week to discuss their next move, if there was to be a move.

"It's gonna take months to get this hand fixed," Braddock said as they crossed the street.

"Just let it heal," Gould said.

Somewhere deep inside, though, they were both thinking that after more than seven years together, their partnership was over. Without boxing, Braddock would have to find another line of work. Without Braddock, Gould would have to find another fighter.

They parted at the subway station, each carrying $125. Neither would see that much money again for a long time.

8

The Lord of the Jungle

....

Reno, Nevada: Spring 1931

Even as Jim Braddock was struggling to get back to New York as a headliner, Baer and Hoffman had had enough of the city — at least for the time being. Their East Coast experiment had been only a partial success. By late February 1931, Baer had experienced much of what New York had to offer, and he had lost two out of three fights, to Schaaf and Loughran. He had boned up on Emily Post. He knew which fork to use for salad and which to use for dessert, and under the tutelage of two world champions, he had come to understand that there were many ways in which he could improve as a boxer. As he paced the decks of the ship that took him through the Panama Canal and back to the West Coast, he was satisfied, and in love. Despite his losses, New York's fight fans had embraced him for his showmanship, and Dorothy was about to get divorced. The city, Baer thought, loved him. He would return. Only occasionally now did his mind wander back to Frankie Campbell.

Hoffman knew that he was dealing with a fragile psyche and that idleness was poison. It was important to get Baer back in the ring against an opponent he could dominate. On April 7, in Portland, Oregon, Baer fought Ernie Owens. He knocked him out in the second round.

Hoffman then matched Baer with Johnny Risko in Cleveland.

Known as the Rubber Man because he was constantly jumping up on his toes as he circled the ring, Risko had his greatest moment when he upset Jack Sharkey on March 12, 1928, at a time when Sharkey was being groomed by Tex Rickard to succeed Gene Tunney as the heavyweight champion. Rickard called Risko "the spoiler of championship ambitions." With Max Schmeling, the reigning champion, among the crowd of more than 7,000 attending the fight, Risko won an easy ten-round decision after Baer inexplicably stopped fighting and started posing. Playing to the crowd, he wound up his punches from far behind his head, then checked himself. He pretended he had been hurt by a punch, then sprang back into action. Hitching up his trunks every few seconds, he preened more than he punched.

"What were you trying to prove out there?" Hoffman asked him when it was over.

"I wanted to keep them entertained," Baer said.

Sulking because he had disappointed Hoffman and thrown away the fight, Baer went back to his hotel room and called Dorothy, who was in Oakland. Later the *Oakland Post-Enquirer* reported that the call cost $132.

Baer had now lost three of his five fights since the death of Frankie Campbell — he was only two or three bad performances from washed up, even though he had just turned twenty-two. Clearly, he was still struggling to absorb the lessons Dempsey and Loughran had taught him.

In mid-May, Baer and Hoffman returned to Oakland. To Hoffman's considerable chagrin, Dorothy Dunbar was waiting. Hoffman would have presented Baer with an ultimatum — "me or her" — if he hadn't thought that Baer would choose her. Once he realized that Dunbar wasn't going away, he encouraged Baer to marry her. Hoffman reasoned that the only way to kill infatuation was matrimony. But when Baer proposed again, Dorothy refused again. Now he was truly confused.

By the summer of 1931, Jack Dempsey was trying hard to establish himself as a promoter. He wanted to break Madison

Square Garden's monopoly, but even after Rickard's death, in 1929, the Garden was a formidable foe. He decided to stage a big fight in Reno on July 4, with Max Baer in the main event, which would be scheduled for twenty rounds — a nod to those who longed for the days before fights went no more than fifteen rounds. In the few months that he and Baer had known each other, Dempsey had grown tremendously fond of the young fighter, in whom he must have seen so much of himself. Like so many people who met Baer, Dempsey took one look at his shoulders, hands, and chest and saw a championship in his future. He had felt the power of Baer's right hand. But Dempsey, who was one of the fiercest competitors ever, could not understand Baer's softness. He hated the younger man's reluctance to fight hard all the time. He wanted Baer to be more like him — a perpetual fighting machine who always kept punching until his opponent was felled.

A large part of Baer must have wanted to please Dempsey, his hero. But he also must have resented the older fighter, who was like a father who could never be pleased. In the end, Dempsey had no more luck influencing him than anyone else; no one could tell Baer what to do.

"You can never tell what Max is going to do next," Dempsey said in 1933. "If you take him out for a walk, the only way to be certain he will not get into some sort of a jam is to put a chain around his neck and lead him around like a performing bear. And even then he will stir up some kind of trouble if you are not careful."

Superficially, Dempsey and Baer had a lot in common. They were both westerners. They were both charismatic. They were both one-quarter Jewish. They were both built like Adonis. They both punched with legendary power. They were both feared. But in fact they could not have been more different. Dempsey was tough; Baer was soft. Dempsey was relentless; Baer was lackadaisical. Dempsey liked to play the role of the baddest man on the planet; Baer just wanted to play the clown.

Dempsey was a man's man; Baer was a ladies' man. Like Machiavelli's prince, Dempsey wanted to be feared rather than loved. Baer wanted love, which is what he got from Dempsey, if not from Dorothy Dunbar.

Like most managers, Ancil Hoffman would have preferred his fighters to be celibate. According to the conventional wisdom, women were only slightly less perilous to a fighter's future than firearms. Sam Langford, the gifted early-twentieth-century heavyweight, summed it up best: "You can sweat out beer and you can sweat out whiskey. But you can't sweat out women." And the ghost of Langford's one-time opponent Stanley Ketchel haunted all boxing romances. Ketchel, the legendary middleweight champion of the first decade of the century, who bested Langford in Philadelphia on April 27, 1910, paid the ultimate price for his amours. "Stanley Ketchel was twenty-four years old," John Lardner wrote in an immortal lead, "when he was fatally shot in the back by the common-law husband of the lady who was cooking his breakfast."

Resigned now to the presence of Dunbar in Baer's life, Hoffman and Lorimer — who still had an interest in Baer but was slowly being pushed aside — accepted the fight in Reno. Hoffman was hoping that a trip back to their frequent refuge in the Sierra Nevadas might clear Baer's head and that Dempsey's presence would force him away from his bad habits. Instead, Dunbar tagged along. Together, she and Baer hit the town every night, dancing if not drinking, and stayed up far too late.

Exasperated, Dempsey had the transmission on Baer's car sealed. For good measure, he locked the car — a limousine, of course — away in a Reno garage. But Baer could always get a taxi.

Dunbar returned to Oakland, but Baer pined for her. When it seemed that he might get his way and she would return to Nevada, Dempsey and Lorimer wrote her a letter asking her to stay away so that he could concentrate on his training. She did not.

One night not long before the fight, Baer tried once more to get her to marry him. In a crowded restaurant, with the band blaring behind them, he got down on one knee, produced a diamond, and said, "Dorothy, will you marry me?" This time, to his considerable surprise, she said yes. Baer celebrated by buying champagne for everyone in the restaurant.

Tarzan had his Jane.

Displaying uncharacteristic level-headedness, Max and Dorothy agreed that it would be impetuous to have the ceremony before the fight. Max would defeat Paulino Uzcudan in Reno and then they would exchange vows.

Uzcudan, known as the Battling Basque, was a very clever boxer and the best heavyweight ever produced on the Iberian peninsula. He fought out of an exaggerated crouch, affording his opponents the smallest possible target. Despite his other nickname — the Spanish Woodchopper — he wasn't a great puncher, but he was good enough to fight almost everyone in the heavyweight division in the 1920s and 1930s. For a promoter like Dempsey, Uzcudan gave good value. Everyone knew who he was, but at the same time he wasn't as expensive as Schmeling, Sharkey, and Carnera.

With his impending marriage occupying most of his thoughts, Baer fought well, but not brilliantly, against Uzcudan. After twenty rounds, the Livermore Larruper and the Battling Basque were still on their feet, so the decision was in the hands of the referee — Jack Dempsey. Despite his affection for Baer, Dempsey called it as he saw it — for Uzcudan. Four days later, on July 8, 1931, Max Baer married Dorothy Dunbar in Reno, "while a fashionable audience looked on and the wrath of the fighter's manager subsided," according to the Associated Press reporter who witnessed the exchange of vows.

Back in Livermore, Baer's mother complained bitterly to the press that her son was making an enormous mistake.

*   *   *

Over the next six months, until the end of 1931, as Jim Brad-dock was plunging into the depths of the Depression on the other coast, Baer was on a prolonged honeymoon. He and Dorothy set up house in Oakland, and by most accounts they left the bedroom only when necessary. Baer was also learning some new tricks in the gym. The loss to Uzcudan had been his fourth defeat in six fights following the death of Frankie Camp-bell. But beginning with his victory on September 23 against Jack Van Noy in Oakland, he went on one of the most spectac-ular winning streaks ever, a streak that lasted almost four years.

Fighting exclusively in the Bay Area, Baer defeated Van Noy, Jose Santa, Johnny Risko (evening their series at one win apiece), Les Kennedy (evening their series at one win apiece also), and Arthur DeKuh, all in a three-month span at the end of 1931. Victories in the ring and bliss at home — it was an odd feeling for Baer.

In January, Baer and Hoffman decided to give New York an-other try. The city greeted Baer with open arms and open wal-lets. Bored by the champion, Max Schmeling, and the man about to succeed him, Jack Sharkey, fight fans were eager for some entertainment. It had been nearly a year since they had last seen Max Baer, but they knew that win or lose, he would put on a good show. "Hence, loathed Melancholy," John Kieran wrote in the *Times*. "The fight game has been conducted in too solemn a manner. Now there is to be an allegro interlude. Max of the California bounding Baers is to due to clash in the ring with Harry Levinsky, called the Kingfish of Chicago."

Kingfish Levinsky, a former Maxwell Street fishmonger, was one of the more eccentric fighters of the era. Among his many peculiarities, he was known to sing to the crowd as an oppo-nent was being counted out. He and Max Baer did not get along especially well, perhaps because they both reveled in the adu-lation of the fans and did not like to share it.

It was just about at the time of his visit to New York to fight

Levinsky that Baer's marriage started to sour. After six months — after Max and Dorothy had sated themselves sexually — the couple looked at each other and realized that there was nothing solid underpinning their relationship, which is another way of saying that Max wasn't prepared to limit himself to the bed of one woman. He was realizing that everything Dorothy had taught him and everything he had learned to make himself more attractive to her also made him more attractive to other women. More than ever, women flocked to him.

For the first but not the last time, Max and Dorothy separated.

For a twenty-two-year-old man of means, Manhattan in 1932 was a wonderful playground — if you were able to ignore the beggars. In the waning days of Prohibition, the city was still feeling the aftereffects of the Roaring Twenties. Speakeasies and nightclubs still required their patrons to turn out in evening wear. Women consorted more freely with the opposite sex than they would in the 1940s and 1950s. And many women did consort with Baer, including the beautiful starlet June Knight. Their affair was fodder for all the gossip columnists.

But Baer's return to New York was a success with more than the showgirls, actresses, cocktail waitresses, and socialites. He dominated Levinsky, winning seven of the ten rounds they fought. His strength was the story of the fight. Baer pounded Levinsky's body with shot after shot, not even bothering to attack his head. The bell ending each round usually failed to stop the fighters from hitting each other. More than 11,000 people saw the fight at Madison Square Garden, and it was apparent to most of them that Max Baer was much improved from the fighter who had left New York after losing to Tommy Loughran in the same arena.

On the Fourth of July, Baer was back in Reno for another twenty-round Dempsey promotion. This time he would fight a rematch with Levinsky. Levinsky thought Baer was sloppy and told the press that he was a dog. "I'll make Baer jump over the ropes to get away from me," the Kingfish reportedly said. That comment got back to Baer, who replied, "Just for that I'll give him the worst beating of his life."

Levinsky rattled Baer early in the fight with a solid right to the jaw. From then on, though, Baer dominated. It looked as if he were heading to an easy knockout, but in the fifth round, in a clinch, he told Levinsky, "Don't worry, I'm not going to let you off so easy as to knock you out now. I'm going to make you stick around and then knock you out in the twentieth round." For the next fifteen rounds he toyed with the Chicagoan, pawing him with his big right hand but never exploding it in Levinsky's face. With Tom Mix and Wallace Beery among the film stars in attendance, Baer fought much better than he had against Uzcudan a year earlier. He fought better than he had against Levinsky the first time. He couldn't deliver the knockout he had promised in the twentieth round, but he won the decision easily.

By this time Baer's self-confidence was surging. Levinsky was one of the four or five best heavyweights in the world, and Baer was confident enough, or crazy enough, to allow him to stay on his feet — and potentially land a knockout punch — just to punish him. If Baer was still thinking about Frankie Campbell, it didn't show. He enjoyed hurting Levinsky.

The next month Baer went to Chicago to fight Ernie Schaaf again. It had been almost two years since the night at the Garden when Schaaf withstood an early Baer onslaught and won a decision. As Baer had improved, Schaaf had plateaued. He was still a skilled boxer and only twenty-three years old, but Baer had leaped past him. Baer dominated the fight, and as the tenth and final round was about to end, he unleashed a furious assault in an attempt to knock Schaaf out. Just before the bell signaling the end of the fight, he landed a powerful right hand that sent Schaaf to the canvas. Schaaf was saved by the bell but remained unconscious for several minutes. Everyone agreed that he had taken a vicious beating.

Slowly it dawned on Baer that he had nearly killed a man — again. He was sickened by the thought of what he had done. When Schaaf revived, Baer sighed in relief. So did Hoffman and Mike Cantwell, his trainer. They didn't think Baer was strong enough emotionally to handle another death at his hands. As blithely as Baer took the sport, this was one of those moments when the reality of boxing — its murderous potential — came crashing down on him. This time he couldn't muster any laughter, which was so often a mask anyway.

Schaaf was never the same fighter after that night. He fought a few weeks later and won a lackluster decision. Then, on February 10, 1933 — almost six months after he fought Baer — he faced Primo Carnera, who was just tuning up for his shot at Sharkey's title. In the eleventh round, Carnera landed what was described as no more than a passing blow on Schaaf's chin. Still, it sent the New Englander to the canvas. He was unconscious, and this time he never woke up.

In the ensuing coverage of his death, the entire press corps came to the conclusion, which was never medically substantiated, that Schaaf had been killed by Baer. The beating he absorbed from Baer, it was reasoned, had done permanent though undiagnosed damage to his brain. How else could Carnera's powerless punch have ended his life? Baer was again vilified — for beating Schaaf senseless when the fight was already won — and caricatured as a killer. And again another man's death only improved his standing in the fight game.

Baer had been seated beside the ring at the Schaaf-Carnera fight. He saw Schaaf go down and knew that Carnera's punch could not have killed him. He read the columns that blamed him for Schaaf's death, and part of him believed them. More than ever, boxing revolted him.

After defeating Schaaf in August, Baer fought only once more before the end of the year. On September 26, in Chicago, he knocked out Tuffy Griffiths, who was still considered a dangerous opponent four years after James J. Braddock had knocked him out.

After the Griffiths bout, Baer was positioned to fight one of the top heavyweight contenders, if not Sharkey himself. What he got was a shot at Max Schmeling, the Black Uhlan, the former champion and probably the most dangerous fighter in the world.

Star of David

....

New York City: Spring 1933

That Max Schmeling became a universal symbol of Nazi ideology is one of the enduring ironies of boxing in the twentieth century. Although he was held up by the Nazis as a Superman and exploited for propaganda purposes, especially after he knocked out Joe Louis in 1936, Schmeling was never a Nazi. He was, on the contrary, defiantly anti-Nazi. When he was pressured to discard his manager, Joe Jacobs, a Jew, he refused. In 1938, during the German action known as Kristallnacht, during which hundreds of synagogues, homes, and businesses were destroyed and thousands of Jews were killed, beaten, and terrorized, Schmeling, who was in Berlin at the time, hid two Jewish teenagers in his hotel room. He never joined the Nazi party. And he often spoke witheringly, but usually quietly, of the Nazi leadership.

But in 1933, just after Hitler assumed power, Schmeling was being paraded by the Nazis as the embodiment of their Teutonic virtues. For Ancil Hoffman, who was Jewish, and Max Baer, who was trying to be Jewish, that was enough. To J. Edgar Hoover and his G-men, John Dillinger might have been public enemy number one. To Hoffman and Baer, it was Schmeling.

The extent of Baer's Jewishness has been debated for more

than seventy years. Those who denied that he was descended from Moses claimed that Hoffman circumcised him, at least metaphorically, to appeal to the Jewish fight fans in New York and to make the fight against Schmeling more compelling. In a country that at the time resembled less a melting pot than an aggregation of distinct ethnicities, the question was on many minds: if Baer eventually won the title, would he be the first Jewish heavyweight champion?

Paul Gallico attempted an answer in *The New Yorker:* "He was supposed to be but a synthetic Jew, a Hebrew ordained overnight for box-office appeal; he has been rated Irish, Bohemian, and Litvak. Baer's mother, a six-foot, 230-pound Scotch-Irish woman, was born Dora Bales in the town of Abel, Iowa. Jacob Baer, the father, was born in Michigan, but Jacob's father was a Jew from Alsace-Lorraine." Thus, it seemed, was the question of Baer's Hebraic bona fides answered — but not to the satisfaction of the skeptics.

Nat Fleischer, the king of boxing writers and the founder and longtime editor of the *Ring*, did not accept Baer as a Jew. (Perhaps he employed a strictly Talmudic interpretation, under which Jewishness is determined through one's mother's line.) But the skepticism of the Eastern writing establishment disturbed Dora Baer. "You can tell those people in New York," she said, "that Maxie has got a Jewish father, and if that doesn't make him Jewish enough for them, I don't know what will."

For his part, Ray Arcel, the Hall of Fame trainer who knew Baer well, sided firmly with the nay-sayers. He insisted that as part of the not-so-elaborate deception, Hoffman had taught Baer some Yiddish expressions — *Oy vey* and *schmuck*, among other pearls — and encouraged him to attend synagogue.

Arcel's anecdotes don't prove that Baer was not Jewish. Raised in a gentile community, Baer might have known little of Jewish customs even if he had been 100 percent Jewish. What is clear is that while Fleischer, Arcel, and others did not accept him as one of the chosen people, the Nazis certainly did. To preserve the honor of the German race, they needed a victory for Schmeling over Baer.

Schmeling had achieved pugilistic prominence long before the Nazis came to power, as a citizen of the Weimar Republic. Sandwiched between the reign of Kaiser Wilhelm II and Hitler's Third Reich, Weimar has been romanticized as a haven for the artistic and the debauched; in fact, under Weimar, Germany was a grim, poor, extraordinarily violent place, a petri dish in which all the bacteria that would grow into Nazism were allowed to fester. It was also the place where Max Schmeling learned to box.

Max Siegfried Adolf Otto Schmeling, the first world heavyweight champion whose native tongue was not English, was born on September 28, 1905. In 1919, the year after the Treaty of Versailles ended World War I, Schmeling, who was a few months younger than Jim Braddock, dropped out of school to find work. He tramped around the devastated country, working as a farmhand, typist, stonemason, steelworker, and miner, all before turning seventeen. Finally he settled in Cologne, where he worked a few menial jobs and somehow gravitated to the Sports Club Colonia. In 1925, just as he was about to turn twenty, he had his Dempsey moment — just as Braddock had had his in 1919, listening to the reenactment of the Willard fight on the streets of Union City.

The Manassa Mauler was in Europe collecting easy paychecks, sparring here and there with the locals, dispensing good will and a few less-than-solid punches. One day in Cologne he appeared at a local arena and gave the fans a chance to admire his muscles. It had been two years since he had last defended his title — against Firpo. He was just biding his time until Rickard and Kearns could locate a challenger who would make it worth their while to risk the belt. The Germans certainly didn't worship Dempsey as most of America did at the time, but he was admired. It didn't hurt that the Germans thought he had avoided service in the war. In Germany, if nowhere else, Dempsey's alleged draft dodging was actually a selling point.

As Dempsey was waiting to get into the ring, he watched the club fighters wade into each other, most of them eager to show off in front of the world's toughest man. When Max Schmeling climbed through the ropes, Dempsey was taken aback. Virtually the same height and weight as Dempsey, Schmeling, blessed with a shock of jet-black hair and black eyebrows, was a dead ringer for the world champion. Years later, a story in the *New York Times* began, "Max Schmeling's most popular characteristic is his striking resemblance to Jack Dempsey, retired former heavyweight champion of the world." Schmeling fought like Dempsey, too — not as savagely, not as brilliantly, but just as determinedly. Dempsey couldn't fail to notice the similarities. He turned to the reporters who had traveled with him to Europe and said, "That kid can fight."

When Schmeling finished off his opponent, Dempsey gestured to him. "What do you say we spar for a couple of rounds?" he said through his interpreter. When their session was through, Dempsey told Schmeling, "Listen, kid, don't let anyone tell you that you can't fight. Keep at it. Practice all you can, and someday you may be the world's heavyweight champion."

Those words, Schmeling later said, were sometimes all that kept him from quitting the sport. Three years later, in the spring of 1928, he sailed for New York (on the steamship *New York*). He had already won Germany's heavyweight championship, but he was greeted with no fanfare upon his arrival in the United States. Training in solitude in New Jersey for six months, he didn't fight until the fall. Then, in rapid succession, he defeated Joe Monte, Joe Sekyra, Pietro Corri, and Johnny Risko. By knocking out Risko, the Cleveland Rubber Man, who had already upset Sharkey, and Paulino Uzcudan, the Battling Basque, Schmeling positioned himself for a shot at the heavyweight title Tunney had vacated.

In 1930, Schmeling and Sharkey fought for the championship. In the fourth round, Schmeling went down. His manager, Joe Jacobs, protested that Sharkey had landed a low blow, not for the first time. After several minutes of confusion — the referee did not see the punch — Sharkey was disqualified, and Schmeling became the only man ever to claim the heavyweight championship on a foul.

Everywhere except Germany, he was not a very popular champion. The manner in which he won the title stained his achievement. In the United States he became known as the Black Uhlan of the Rhine, for his features and his perceived seriousness. (Uhlans were lancers in the German army; colloquially, *uhlan* simply came to mean any German soldier.) In 1931 he successfully defended his title against the veteran Young Stribling. The following year he and Sharkey met again, at the Madison Square Garden Bowl. Schmeling pounded Sharkey all night, methodically dissecting the Mad Balt, as Sharkey, who was of Lithuanian extraction, had been dubbed. But he failed to score a knockout, and only a knockout would have allowed him to retain the championship. This was the decision that caused Jacobs to exclaim, "We wuz robbed!" Sharkey had indeed stolen the title, but in defeat Schmeling was a bigger star than he had ever been before. When Max Baer signed to fight him, he assumed he was fighting the best heavyweight in the world.

Early on the evening of April 18, 1933, Baer, his trainer, Mike Cantwell, and Sam Taub, Jack Dempsey's publicist, walked into the offices of the *New York Sun* and headed straight for the desk of Wilbur Wood, the *Sun*'s veteran sports editor. Wood hadn't seen a stunt like this in years. To drum up interest in his forthcoming fight against Schmeling, Baer was making the rounds at all of New York's daily newspapers — about a dozen

— demonstrating his fighting style, dispensing printable and unprintable quotes, and ingratiating himself as best he could. Meanwhile, Dempsey and Schmeling were in Pittsburgh, doing their utmost to promote the fight, which would be Dempsey's first promotion in New York, breaking Madison Square Garden's monopoly. The hard work of selling the fight in New York, though, was left to Baer, whose name was still being linked to Ernie Schaaf's death. By the time they arrived at the *Sun*, Baer, Cantwell, and Taub had been to nine or ten papers; poor Taub was already a beaten man. Baer, whose mood had swung from glumness to childish euphoria, had been using him all day as a punching bag — and worse.

"For the amusement of the onlookers," Wood wrote for the next day's paper, "Baer would pick up Taub and toss him over half a dozen desks into a wastebasket, or demonstrate headlocks and arm locks as well as left hooks and right crosses upon him. At a late hour, Taub was still removing bits of broken cigars, pencils, and whatnot from his pockets and applying soothing lotions to various parts of his anatomy."

But when Baer pulled back his left arm to strike Cantwell, the old trainer gave him a shot to the stomach. "That'll teach you not to leave yourself wide open when you start a punch, even if you're only going to take a shot at a guy like me," Cantwell said.

"I'll beat that Hun to the punch, don't worry," Baer replied. To motivate him, Hoffman had convinced Baer that Schmeling was the personification of Nazi evil. He had told Baer repeatedly that Schmeling was a Jew-hater and that a Schmeling victory would be used by the Nazis as propaganda against Germany's Jewish population.

While Hoffman worked on Baer's brain, Cantwell trained his body. His biggest concern heading into the fight was Baer's habit of loading up too much on his punches. The German's blows were quick and short, and Cantwell thought he might have an easy time beating Baer to the punch.

Wilbur Wood liked Baer very much, but like almost everyone else, he thought he was too undisciplined to stand a chance against the Black Uhlan, a young man who had been hardened by suffering. Schmeling, Wood knew, took fighting as seriously as Baer took carousing. Wood's preconceptions were reinforced when Baer spent most of their meeting jumping up from his chair, chattering constantly, and assaulting Cantwell. "He is as playful as a half-grown pup," Wood wrote. No pup, he might have added, could beat Schmeling.

On June 8, the day Jim Braddock turned twenty-eight, the twenty-four-year-old Max Baer got in a cab at the Park Central Hotel on Seventh Avenue and headed for Yankee Stadium to fight Max Schmeling. Just a year earlier, Schmeling had been the heavyweight champion of the world. He had lost the title to Jack Sharkey even though he had thoroughly beaten the Mad Balt. In the minds of millions, Schmeling was still the champion and Baer was just another overhyped contender. Baer was anywhere from a two-to-one to a four-to-one underdog.

But the Max Baer who fought Max Schmeling that night was Max Baer at his best. He could have beaten Jack Johnson, Jack Dempsey, and Muhammad Ali. He was game, he was savage, and he was in great shape. With 60,000 people packing the stadium, including four governors and scores of less exalted politicians, movie stars, and Broadway figures, Baer marched to the ring confident that it would be his night. In his mind he wasn't just fighting Schmeling; he was fighting the new dictator of Germany, Adolf Hitler, and all his minions. For the first time in his four-year career, Baer, who was still only one-quarter Jewish, was wearing trunks that featured a giant Star of David, which covered virtually the entire right leg. Joe Jacobs took one look at the six-pointed star and shook his head. He had predicted that it would be a tough fight but that Schmeling would win when Baer got tired or bored; now he was worried. He had been expecting to see Max Baer the clown; instead he was confronted with Max Baer the avenger. When Baer stepped into the ring, he was scowling.

The fight was scheduled to go fifteen rounds. Baer wanted to end it quickly. He came out in a fury. Whatever demons still lurked from the deaths of Ernie Schaaf and Frankie Campbell had been exorcised, at least for the purpose of destroying the Black Uhlan. Baer dominated the first round, but Schmeling landed a right that made his head swim. In his corner after the round, Baer told Dempsey, who was acting as one of his seconds, "I see three of him." "Hit the one in the middle," Dempsey famously responded. Baer took Dempsey's advice.

After wounding Schmeling badly in the opening rounds, Baer, curiously, let up. Maybe it was fatigue. Maybe it was frustration. Maybe it was pacing. Maybe all the hatred he had built up for the German had dissipated. Maybe he was still reluctant to fight all-out. As he dallied, Schmeling started piling up points, winning round after round in his methodical, unspectacular fashion. "Baer started out like a human tornado," James P. Dawson wrote in the *New York Times*, "and petered out, as if the intense heat from the overhead ring lights, the plodding yet burning pace of Schmeling, and the latter's short, powerful punches were all exacting their toll."

After the ninth round, Hoffman and Cantwell told Baer, who now seemed typically detached from the proceedings, exactly where he stood. "You're losing," Hoffman said as he doused Baer with a sponge. "Now go out there and end this."

"No problem," Baer replied, muttering through his mouthpiece. He finally snapped out of his malaise and fought the tenth round as if it were the first. Disregarding his defense, he reared back and delivered a devastating right hand to Schmeling's jaw. The blow knocked Schmeling's head violently to the right, and then the rest of his body followed, toppling to the canvas. Somehow he staggered to his feet at the count of nine. Baer went after him again, pummeling him mercilessly. "That one's for Hitler," he said theatrically to Schmeling, who was now stumbling around the ring, helpless. Finally, one minute and fifty-one seconds into the round, Arthur Donovan, the referee, stopped the fight.

Standing in Baer's corner, Jack Dempsey was beaming. Not since he had eviscerated Firpo in 1923 at the Polo Grounds had anyone seen such a pure display of punching power. Another of Baer's biggest fans was at ringside: June Knight, with whom he had been having an affair. The blond beauty had been handpicked by Florenz Ziegfeld to appear in his follies and had starred in such Broadway fare as *Take a Chance*, with Jack Haley and Ethel Merman. When Max knocked out Max, she was conspicuously delighted. Mrs. Dorothy Baer was not at the fight.

Even while he was showering in his dressing room, Baer received well-wishers. Rubbing his swollen nose but otherwise unmarked, he shook hands with some reporters and friends and seemed to them completely unfazed by the magnitude of his achievement. "I'm gonna win that championship," he said as he soaped himself. "How did I do it? When I hit Schmeling with a right to the jaw in the first round, I knew that I could do it again."

Knocking out Schmeling made Baer a full-fledged star. Previously, he had been better known for his flamboyance than his fistic achievements. But now he had claimed a victory over the man who many believed was still the true heavyweight champion.

For once, his notices were almost all positive. Dawson wrote, "A new star is in the pugilistic firmament today and his name is Max Baer, a larruping thumper from Livermore." Before knocking out Schmeling, Baer had been a question mark. After, with his looks and charm, he was too big to be merely a boxer. Hollywood came calling.

The moguls of the film industry, many of whom were Jewish, loved Baer for wearing a Star of David on his trunks against

Schmeling. While they almost religiously suppressed their Jew-ishness to protect the industry from anti-Semitic attacks, they lived vicariously through the muscular young boxer who liter-ally wore his religion on his clothing. Louis B. Mayer had met Baer at a few parties in Los Angeles and figured he would make a great actor, or at least a movie star. He immediately com-missioned a project to feature Baer and a beautiful young ac-tress who had not yet become famous, Myrna Loy. The film was called *The Prizefighter and the Lady*.

Over the course of ten weeks in the summer and fall of 1933, Baer shot *The Prizefighter and the Lady*. He wasn't just win-dow dressing, either. Unlike so many fighters who have ap-peared on film, he was truly the star of the project. He was paid $30,000 to make the movie, a handsome sum for anyone, espe-cially a twenty-four-year-old making his acting debut.

Baer had thought the nightlife of Manhattan was a paradise of temptations. By comparison, on any given day the MGM lot made New York look like Livermore on a slow night. Hundreds of starlets were working on the lot, many of them just about Max's age. And he wasn't just another actor — he was a famous boxer, he was good-looking, he was rich, and he was amusing. His marriage was a technicality.

Baer took naturally to film; he enjoyed acting much more than he enjoyed fighting. The movie was a fairly typical melo-drama — fighter falls in love with gangster's moll, marries her, cheats on her, promises her he won't stray again, strays again, eventually redeems himself in the ring. In the film's big musical number, Baer sings "Lucky Fella," an original song written by Jimmy McHugh and Dorothy Fields. The great character actor Walter Huston (the director John Huston's father) costarred as the Professor, Baer's character's trainer.

Jack Dempsey, Jess Willard, and James J. Jeffries had sup-porting roles in *The Prizefighter and the Lady*, as did the reign-ing heavyweight champion of the world, Primo Carnera, the man Baer was expected to fight the following June. Carnera agreed to appear as himself and, incredibly, to lose by knockout to Baer's character, Steve Morgan. Today it is inconceivable that the world heavyweight champion would agree to lose to the number-one contender, even if only on film, especially if the contender was already scheduled to be his next opponent. Eventually Carnera's handlers changed their minds; they wouldn't let Primo get knocked out by Baer. But for an additional $20,000, they agreed to allow Baer to knock Carnera down twice en route to winning the fight by decision.

Choreographing their big scene, Carnera and Baer spent two weeks rehearsing with each other under the direction of W. S. Van Dyke. Shy and awkward around women and strangers — and just about everyone else — Carnera was terribly uncomfortable on the set. It must have pained him to watch Baer act, and interact with the crew, so easily. Side by side, the six-foot-seven Carnera must have appeared to be almost a Frankenstein's monster — he did resemble Boris Karloff's screen creature — while Baer was very much the dashing young man. Poor Carnera was forced to endure Baer's relentless practical jokes, which the crew helped him carry out. As Baer mocked Carnera's accented, broken English and belittled him to amuse the rest of the people on the set, Carnera simmered with resentment. Finally one day he snapped and charged after Baer. Somehow the fighters were separated before anyone was hurt. Meanwhile, as they were rehearsing and filming in the ring, Baer was carefully measuring Carnera, who he thought couldn't fight at all.

Baer's antics — which included the time-honored hazing ritual known as the hotfoot, in which the hazee's shoe is discreetly set on fire — masked his real intent: to develop a strategy to defeat Carnera. That Carnera's handlers allowed their man to be so thoroughly dissected is a testament to both their stupidity and their crookedness. Not only was Baer given a primer on how to beat Carnera, but he also went to work on the Venetian's psyche, calling him "champ" facetiously and toying with him in their scenes in the ring. For all his sensitivity and gentleness with others, he showed real cruelty in his dealings with Carnera, as he had with Schmeling. It was almost as if he reserved all his hostility for world champions. No one else was worthy of his enmity.

Meanwhile, Baer's marriage was going from bad to irreconcilable. He and Dorothy were separated more often than they were together. At a time when sports writers as a rule protected star athletes and ignored their personal peccadilloes, Baer was so indiscreet that his flings were considered fair game. Jean Harlow and Greta Garbo, perhaps the most desired women on the planet, were among his noteworthy conquests, though Harlow was apparently more aggressive than Baer. She eventually made herself a nuisance, showing up at the house he had bought in Los Angeles late in the evening, unannounced and uninvited. Sometimes Baer would hear her limo approaching, throw on a pair of pants, and run out the back door.

Dorothy Dunbar Baer didn't need to read the papers to know what was going on. By the time *The Lady and the Prizefighter* was wrapping up production, after slightly more than two years of marriage, she had had enough of her mostly estranged husband.

HOLLYWOOD, Sept. 27 (AP) — Separated and reconciled on numerous occasions heretofore, Max Baer, leading contender for the world's heavyweight boxing title, and his wife, the former Dorothy Dunbar, were headed toward the divorce courts again today. Mrs. Baer said she had consulted her attorney, W. W. Davis, with a view of seeking an absolute divorce this time.

A week later, it was official:

HOLLYWOOD, Oct. 4 (AP) — Mrs. Dorothy Baer, formerly Dorothy Dunbar, screen actress, has received a divorce from Max Baer, heavyweight boxer, her attorney, Wallace W. Davis, was advised today from Juarez, Mexico, where the suit was filed. He said the divorce was obtained by mutual consent. The couple separated shortly after Baer made his debut as a motion picture actor several weeks ago.

Baer lost a wife but soon gained something more valuable to him: good reviews. *The Prizefighter and the Lady* opened on November 11 to unanimous acclaim. "Max Baer may have astonished many pugilistic enthusiasts by his defeat of Max Schmeling last June," the *New York Times* film critic Mordaunt Hall wrote, "but the chances are that many more persons will be surprised by his extraordinarily capable portrayal in the picture "The Prizefighter and the Lady" . . . This California giant has such an ingratiating personality and an easy way of talking that one forgets signs of fistic encounters on his physiognomy."

At the end of the year, Richard Watts, the film critic of the *New York Herald-Tribune*, rated *The Prizefighter and the Lady* one of the top ten films of 1933. "It is reliably reported," the *Ring* reported — unreliably, as it turned out — "that Baer will receive one million dollars for his next motion picture."

Baer was sui generis — a fighter who could act, a movie star who could fight. There was nothing new about fighters turned thespians, but Baer's abilities put him in rare company. Among the heavyweight champions — virtually all of whom, from Sullivan to Ali, performed either onstage or on film or both — perhaps the only better actor was Gentleman Jim Corbett, who starred on Broadway in several plays, including the original New York production of George Bernard Shaw's *Cashel Byron's Profession* (his profession was boxing).

But Baer's solid notices did not impress Dr. Paul Joseph Goebbels, Germany's minister of propaganda and public enlightenment. On March 16, 1934, three months before Baer was to enter the ring to fight Carnera for the championship, *The Prizefighter and the Lady* opened at the Capitol Theater in Berlin, despite Dr. Goebbels's opposition. Goebbels had recently banned the English film *Catherine the Great*, which starred Elisabeth Bergner, an Austrian Jew. Officially, *Catherine the Great* was banned because Bergner was an émigré. It was all but acknowledged, however, that her Jewishness was the only thing Goebbels found objectionable about the film. In the case of *The Prizefighter and the Lady*, George Messersmith, the American consul in Berlin, warned the Germans that there would be serious consequences if the film were banned. Foreign Minister Konstantin von Neurath, not yet a member of the Nazi party but eventually convicted as a war criminal, asked Goebbels to let the film open, which he did, reluctantly.

But Goebbels had not forgotten what Baer had said after he knocked out Schmeling: that every punch he threw that night was aimed at Adolf Hitler. On March 29, when the Propaganda Ministry was asked for permission to allow the film to open in its dubbed, German-language version, Goebbels balked. One of his lieutenants was quoted by the American press as saying that he had "scruples against the film as not being in harmony with the purpose of the new Germany because the chief character is a Jewish boxer."

Six thousand miles from Berlin, in Lake Tahoe, Max Baer was just returning from a five-mile run when Hoffman told him that *The Prizefighter and the Lady* had been banned in Germany. Baer was, as always, very quotable, not to mention immodest. "They didn't ban the picture because I have Jewish blood," he said. "They banned it because I knocked out Max Schmeling. It doesn't make much difference to me, but I'm sure sorry for the women and children of Germany. Too bad they won't get a chance to see the world's greatest lover and the world's greatest fighter in action."

10

On the Waterfront

....

Weehawken and Hoboken:
Winter 1933–1934

For more than a month after the Feldman fight, Braddock sat at home with his right hand in a cast. The dirty white plaster reminded him constantly of that night in Mount Vernon when his career seemed to have ended in ignominy. Mae had just given birth to their daughter, Rose Marie, but Braddock could find little joy in her arrival. Another mouth to feed, and the winter was coming soon. For the first time in his life, Jim Braddock was bad company.

"After the fight, I tried to comfort him," Mae Braddock would later say, "but it was no use. His heart was broken. Despite the fact that he knew he couldn't have done better; despite the fact that he had actually gone ahead fighting, standing the agonies of that stabbing hand, when any other man would have quit, meant nothing to him. He was morose for weeks." Even though Braddock knew he had displayed uncommon courage by continuing to fight after breaking his hand, he was despondent. His honor meant a great deal to him, yet retaining it was no solace in the face of the harsh realities of his situation. He was perilously close to the poorhouse.

When the cast came off, Braddock started looking for work.

With no high school diploma and no skills outside the ring, he had limited options. Some friends worked down on the docks in Weehawken and Hoboken, and he thought they might help him find some paydays. They did. But the work was sporadic. And without a car or any money for public transportation, Braddock had to walk the three miles from his home in Woodcliff to the waterfront, uncertain if there would be work.

Exhausted physically and emotionally, he would walk in the early morning darkness to 69th Street in Guttenberg, to the long set of stairs that led to the docks of Weehawken and Hoboken, and descend to the place where the railroad tracks nearly met the deep-water port. He would ask if there was any work. When the answer was yes, he would spend the day unloading railroad ties from the enormous ships that brought them up from the steel mills in the South. Laboring shoulder to shoulder with hardened stevedores and others who were down and nearly out, Braddock never suggested, in words or deeds, that he was too good for such work. If the other guys insisted, he would tell them about some of his fights. But he didn't like talking, and he especially didn't like talking about himself.

Braddock's status as a former contender did not shield him from the grim facts of working on the docks. Like everyone else, he was subjected to the elements and the casual cruelty of the foremen, who tended to treat the dock wallopers, as they were sometimes called, like cattle. The work was hard, and made even harder by the knowledge that the wages were miserably low because the economics of the place were skewed by kickbacks and no-show jobs. Dissent was not an option. Mobbed up and lawless, the International Longshoremen's Association, the union that controlled the docks, was notoriously corrupt. It was not uncommon for those who made waves to disappear beneath them.

Braddock often worked within a few hundred yards of the Fifth Street Pier in Hoboken, where the big ships of the Holland-America line docked and where his father was a night watchman. Tourists and immigrants made their way down the gangways of the *Statendam*, *Veendam*, and *Volendam*. He would watch them and wonder just how bad things had to be in Europe for them to want to come to America. Hoboken, though, was relatively quiet compared to Weehawken, where hundreds of men were beginning a new public works project. Eventually the Lincoln Tunnel would link Weehawken and West 39th Street in midtown Manhattan. It was in the shadow of the bulldozers and cranes that Braddock quietly labored.

With his bum right hand, he had to do all the heavy lifting with his left. Sometimes he operated a hand truck, again without benefit of his right hand. He would work until the ships were unloaded. There was no overtime, just an expectation that he would work until he was done. Then he would get four dollars — and sometimes he would have to kick some of that back to the hiring boss.

Even during the Depression, there was work on the docks — the constant flow of commerce was never interrupted. Most of the men there were comfortable with manual labor, and Braddock fit right in. He developed a reputation as someone who was willing, indeed eager, to do his share and more. He never looked for an easy way out; he never let the guy on the other end of the load take the brunt of it. He never expected to be treated any differently from anyone else merely because he was Jim Braddock, former contender for the light heavyweight title.

When the day's work had been completed, Braddock would sometimes treat himself to a nickel beer at one of the pubs frequented by seafaring men and longshoremen for a century. He celebrated the end of Prohibition on December 5, 1933, with two beers. Usually, though, he was too exhausted and depressed for camaraderie. He would simply walk home — another three miles — and climb into bed with Mae.

Those were the good days, when there was work in Weehawken or Hoboken. On the days when the answer was "No, champ," he would climb the stairs back up to 69th Street, then turn north for the docks of West New York, walking another two miles. Sometimes there would be work there. Usually there wasn't. If no work was to be found anywhere on the docks or in the railroad yards, he would trudge back to North Bergen, looking for something to do. He would offer to clean basements, sweep floors, shovel snow. He was a familiar and sad sight in his faded green sweater, threadbare pants, and battered shoes. Once in a while he would tend bar at the North Bergen Social and Athletic Club, serving the same men who for years had crossed the river to Manhattan to watch him fight. They were the men he had grown up with, who had proudly watched his rise as a fighter; now he was pouring drafts for them. Each day it seemed he was further humbled.

As the new year dawned, Gould delivered some encouraging news. He had managed to locate an opponent — a good opponent, the big German Walter Neusel. On December 30, 1933, Neusel defeated Ray Impellittiere at Madison Square Garden. To secure Impellittiere as an opponent, Neusel had guaranteed him $5,000. When the gate receipts were tallied, the total purse for the main event was $5,025. After his managers' and trainers' fees were deducted, Neusel received $3.19 for his ten-round effort. Hoping to make more against Braddock, he agreed to fight him on January 21. But the New York boxing commission would not sanction the fight. With the Feldman fight still fresh in their memories, the commissioners did to Braddock what they had done in 1930 when he was scheduled to fight Max Baer. They were genuinely concerned that he might get seriously hurt, though he had never been seriously hurt in the ring.

With the fight off, the Braddocks lived on bread and potatoes. Potato stew and potato hash were the staples of their table. For several months they couldn't pay the rent. Finally they were forced to move from their cramped apartment to an even smaller basement apartment in the same building, which they could barely afford. The milk bill went unpaid; so did the gas and electric bill.

Braddock knew he was jinxed when the winter of his misery developed in February into the coldest winter on record in the Northeast. Lake Ontario froze for the first time since 1874. Ice a foot thick formed in Long Island Sound. John D. Rockefeller, who was ill, employed three shifts of firemen to keep his mansion in Tarrytown, New York, at 72 degrees Fahrenheit. After one bitingly cold day on the docks — temperatures in north Jersey in February dipped to minus ten degrees, at the time the coldest temperature ever recorded in the state — Braddock walked home to his apartment, opened the door, and said, "Mae, what's going on? Why are the lights off?" "Jim, they shut off the electricity," she said. Braddock cursed the electric company and himself. At least the apartment still had heat, but he knew that it would soon be turned off too, and then his family might die. He spent the night considering what his options might be. There was only one.

In the morning he walked from his apartment to the ferry in West New York. He had exactly one dime in his pocket. The fare to cross to Manhattan was four cents. With six cents left, he crossed the Hudson, walked more than a mile to Madison Square Garden, and tried to find Joe Gould.

Gould's friends at the Garden were kind enough to accept his mail and take his messages. By this time Gould was working as a door-to-door salesman, hawking gadgets and radios. Every day, though, he would check in at the Garden to see who was looking for him. Usually it was no one. His old friend Francis Albertanti, the Garden's publicist, made sure that he was kept in the loop and made to feel as if he still mattered, which in fact he didn't. When Albertanti saw Braddock walk through his office door — gaunter than ever, his eyes made moist by the cold and his hat literally in his hands — he told him that Joe was out but would be in soon. Albertanti had known Braddock since 1928 and had profiled him for the *Ring*. He tried to make conversation but avoided asking how things were going, because he knew how things were going. Still, he could see in Braddock's face a desperation that he had never seen there before. He wanted to tell Braddock not to worry, but he knew that he had every reason to worry.

Finally Gould walked through the door. "Jim, what are you doing here?" he said. "Is everything all right?"

"Joe, I know you're broke, but I don't know where else to go," Braddock said. "I need thirty-five dollars. Rose Marie needs milk and we need the heat."

"Wait right here," Gould said.

He scurried away, leaving Braddock to his thoughts. Here he was, it occurred to him, back at the Garden, where he had once fought for the championship. For years he had hoped to return to this building to fight in another main event. Now he was back, pleading for what amounted to little more than chump change.

"Here's thirty-five dollars. Pay your bills. I'll get you more when I can," Gould said.

"I'll pay you back soon."

"I know."

Gould had borrowed the money from Jimmy Johnston, who never expected to see it again.

Braddock walked back to 42nd Street and west to the river, handed the ferryman four cents, and crossed back to New Jersey. On his way home he stopped to pay the milkman and the utility company. When he got back to the apartment, he paid the rent.

Within days he was broke again, and now he had nowhere to turn. In those days, Lud Shabazian would see him occasionally on the streets of Union City and North Bergen. He noticed, he later wrote, how the well-wishers of Braddock's youth now crossed to the other side of the street when they saw him coming. As Joe E. Lewis would later say, a friend in need is a pest.

The guilt and the anxiety he was feeling turned Braddock into an insomniac. Most nights, at about 2 A.M., he climbed from his sleepless bed, got dressed, went out into the cold, and walked for miles. Mae feared that he might kill himself. On the rare occasions when sleep came, he tossed and turned, mumbling to Mae. He would say the same things over and over. "Mae, please believe me," he would say, "I'm doing everything I can. I'm so sorry, darling. I'm sorry, so sorry."

Finally Braddock made the most difficult decision he had ever made. With nowhere else to turn, he decided to apply for relief from the county.

Today millionaires unashamedly accept benefits from the state when they are unemployed. Millions of people of lesser means survive because of the welfare programs that were conceived during the Depression. That a man might be embarrassed to apply for money from the government is almost laughably anachronistic. But in 1933, Jim Braddock applied for relief only when all his other options had been exhausted — only when he was desperate. He was too ashamed to tell his parents.

"Darling, I can't stand this any longer," he said to Mae. "It just tears my heart into little bits to see you and the babies suffering for want of food and clothing. I'm going over to the relief bureau and see if they can't make us a loan until I can get something to do."

Braddock went to see his old friend Harry Buesser, the promoter turned politician who had made the assault charge against Captain Bachman go away. As one of the commissioners of the township of North Bergen, Buesser oversaw the municipal relief office, which happened to employ the brothers Joe and Jimmy Kelly. Joe Kelly had worked for Lud Shabazian in the sports department of the *Hudson Dispatch;* Jimmy Kelly was in charge of case #2796, Braddock's case. Eventually questions would be raised about the legitimacy of Braddock's application and the decision to grant him relief. But in early 1934, when Jim Braddock was just another young man down on his luck, no one seemed to pay much attention. If people had been paying attention, they would almost certainly have come to the conclusion that despite the appearance of impropriety, Braddock was a worthy candidate for relief.

When Jim and Mae were on relief, receiving twenty-four dollars a month for ten months, they reached a point when they could no longer care for their children. For a brief time the children were sent to live with their grandparents, who were also barely surviving. All this time Braddock was trudging to and from the docks. Sometimes, when there were no ships to unload, he worked as a furniture mover. He also worked in a coal yard.

The one constant was the manual nature of his labor, except when he was tending bar. On the docks he operated a tie hook, which he had to attach to each railroad tie with a swift punching motion. Once it was attached, he would lift the tie and haul it to a flatbed railroad car. When Braddock first used a tie hook, he tried using his right hand, but the pain was too great. For no other reason than the fact that he had no choice, he made himself ambidextrous; for a while, actually, he was unidextrous, using only his left hand.

Finally, by April, when the weather broke, Braddock's right hand had healed. Soon he was feeling stronger than he had ever felt. But he was still on the docks, staring across the Hudson at the Manhattan skyline. The Garden, where he had once starred, could almost be discerned. Never, though, had it felt farther away.

11

Last One Up's a Sissy

....

New York: Spring 1934

In the late fall of 1933, Max Baer told Harry Cross, one of his writer friends, that making *The Prizefighter and the Lady* had convinced him that Primo Carnera was no tougher an opponent than Chief Caribou. "It was all I could do to hold myself back," Baer said, "when we were rehearsing for the bout in the pictures. Say, I'd like nothing better than to get rough with that fellow. Do I think I can beat him? I should say I could. I said I was going to knock out Schmeling, didn't I? Well, I tell you the same thing about Carnera. He's so big that it's a cinch to hit him. I'd like to take one good smack at him."

By this time the public was clamoring for a Baer-Carnera showdown. Baer was attracting an enormous following among Jewish fight fans, who were accustomed to seeing their fellow Jews excel in the ring but not in the heavyweight division. At their peak, in the 1920s and 1930s, Jewish fighters were champions in several other weight classifications. The lightweight champion Benny Leonard, Joe Gould's childhood friend, was probably the greatest Jewish fighter ever. But Barney Ross was also brilliant. So were King Levinsky, Maxie Rosenbloom, and Joe Choynski. Bob Olin, Art Lasky, Ted "Kid" Lewis, Harry Lewis, Lew Tendler, Jackie "Kid" Berg, Leo Lomski, Yale Okun, and Louis "Kid" Kaplan also made an impact on the sport.

At one point during boxing's golden age, Jews simultaneously held world titles in four weight classifications. Still, no Jewish fighter had ever captured the heavyweight championship, unless you include Daniel Mendoza. A Spanish-English Jew, Mendoza claimed the English bare-knuckle championship on November 12, 1794, when he defeated Bill Warr on Bexley Common. Unlike the fifteen men who had previously held the title, Mendoza used tactics similar to those employed by modern fighters. He ducked. He weaved. He counterpunched. "He was much above the intellectual level of his contemporaries," Nat Fleischer once wrote.

There is a relatively little known addendum to the subject of Jewish heavyweights. Jack Dempsey's paternal grandmother, born Rachel Solomon, was 100 percent Jewish, which by Talmudic standards made Dempsey's father a Jew. Technically, one Jewish grandmother trumps one Jewish grandfather, and therefore Jack Dempsey could be considered more Jewish than Max Baer.

In early March 1934, after nine months of inactivity, Baer finally signed a contract to fight Carnera for the title. To train for the bout, he crossed the Hudson in early May and pitched camp in Asbury Park, on the Jersey shore. He was perhaps the least motivated challenger for the heavyweight championship ever. He was infinitely more interested in the women sauntering on the boardwalk than he was in sparring and shadowboxing. Despite the entreaties of Hoffman (who had completely displaced Lorimer) and Cantwell, Baer somehow managed to train even less for Carnera than he had for Schmeling. He had measured Carnera during the filming of *The Prizefighter and the Lady*. He knew the champion's weaknesses. When he visualized climbing into the ring on June 14, he saw no way that he could lose. Consequently, he could not think of a single good reason to exert himself.

"Ancil," he said one day as Hoffman was begging him to take

the fight more seriously, "that big monster couldn't beat me once in a thousand fights. I know him better than I know myself."

"Max, he's a huge man," Hoffman countered desperately. "One punch, just one punch — that's all it takes."

"Well, training isn't going to change that," Baer said.

Finally Hoffman concluded that it was hopeless. He stopped arguing and let Baer turn the camp into a circus. Once again Baer wrestled when he should have sparred and quipped when he should have been running. Many of the fight fans who turned up to witness the proceedings were genuinely amused. Bill Brown was not.

Of the several men who served as boxing commissioners in the state of New York in the 1920s and 1930s, none took his duties more seriously than William J. Brown. William Muldoon, James A. Farley, John J. Phelan, and D. Walker Wear were dedicated men too, but Brown was fanatical. Born in County Cork, Ireland, in 1874, he immigrated to the United States with his widowed mother in 1888, making landfall in New York just as the great blizzard was about to strike. A true incarnation of the spirit of Horatio Alger, he had amassed a fortune by his mid-thirties as a professional wrestler, physical fitness guru, boxing trainer, and promoter. He never smoked or drank and considered those who did mentally and physically inferior. His success was built on the notion that achievement is the product of hard work and single-minded dedication. As a trainer he was known, even in relation to his peers, as an extreme disciplinarian.

It was only a matter of time before Max Baer ran afoul of Bill Brown.

As Baer dallied, Brown scanned the papers every day for news of his latest antics. A year earlier, he had been appalled by Baer's lack of preparation for the Schmeling fight. When Baer won, it made him angry. So on May 7, when Baer and Hoffman arrived late for a meeting with the commission in downtown

Manhattan, they were informed that they had been suspended for tardiness.

Eventually Brown went down to Asbury Park to see for himself how Baer was training. Hoffman tried again to get his fighter to spar seriously, if only out of politeness to Brown. "Nothing doing," Baer said. "I'm not going to change my routine to impress that old man." What Brown saw sickened him. The newspapers were right: Baer was making a mockery of his preparations. Instead of trading punches with his sparring partners, he hammed it up for the audience. He interrupted his shadowboxing sessions to tell one-liners. He was about to fight for the world heavyweight championship and he was behaving like . . . well, a clown.

Brown told the reporters covering the camp that if it were up to him, the fight would be canceled, to spare the paying customers the sight of a drubbing. To emphasize his disgust, he also said, loudly, "Baer is a bum."

He wasn't alone in his assessment of Baer's state of readiness. In the *Sun*, Edward Van Every wrote, "There must be something radically wrong with the condition of Max Baer." Baer's old friend from San Francisco, Harry Smith, told the other writers, "The trouble with Max is that he is trying to do in three weeks the work that called for three months' diligent application after the way he had been conducting himself since he defeated Max Schmeling last summer." Dempsey, especially, was concerned about Baer's preparedness. After he voiced his doubts to the writers, Hoffman and Cantwell told him to keep them to himself. "The newspapermen are friends of mine," Dempsey responded, "and if they ask me a question, they are entitled to the truth. Max isn't ready, and that's all there is to that."

Baer's only genuine concern as the fight approached was Carnera's awkwardness. He thought that the champion's enormous feet might crush his own, disabling him as they had disabled Tommy Loughran when Loughran and Carnera had fought in February. In Asbury Park, sparring partners were encouraged to use their feet as weapons. On May 31, Ceil Harris planted his size thirteen feet on Baer's, and Baer responded with a kick to the ankle. As the papers feverishly noted, though, Baer's kick looked more devastating than his punch.

But Baer deflected the writers' doubts about his readiness. "I'm not like Carnera," he said. "I'm not a gymnasium fighter. I'll admit I looked bad today, but I feel strong and I know I can hit."

A few days later, on June 4, Baer was rounding into form. For the first time in Asbury Park, he was sharp, staggering his sparring partners with crisp right hands. The former light heavyweight champion Philadelphia Jack O'Brien watched him work out and told the writers, "He is at just the right peak for this stage of his training. With a week more, he'll be in the best shape possible, and will be strong enough to go fifteen rounds easily."

For his part, Baer was curious about Carnera's conditioning. Standing in a corner of the outdoor ring, he asked the writers assembled outside the ropes what they had seen in Pompton Lakes, where Carnera was training.

"He looks pretty good, Max, watch out," John Kieran said. Kieran did not mention Corn Griffin, the sparring partner who was the talk of Carnera's camp.

"Carnera looks good? That's fine," Baer said, hitching up his trunks. "I give him credit. I guess he has improved. So there'll be all the more credit for me when I lick him." Then he slid on his robe. "Listen, if it wasn't meant for me to be world's heavyweight champion, I wouldn't be here. No kidding. I don't like fighting."

It was a strange confession for a fighter to make. Kieran and the others pressed closer to the ring. Baer continued. "But just as sure as there's water in that ocean, I'm going to be champion," he said. "I'm going to lick Carnera. Can't miss. It's meant to be. I know it. Why not? He can't hurt me and I can hurt him.

I don't care a lick for fancy boxing. The idea is to go out there and knock the other guy down, isn't it? Well, I can do that."

Baer wasn't finished, but he wanted to shower. He told the writers to wait for him to get cleaned up. When he returned thirty minutes later, he was wearing gray slacks, white shoes, and a short-sleeved blue shirt with a zippered front. John Kieran wrote, "With his bronzed features and his curly black hair, he was a fetching picture in that costume." Then Baer picked up his monologue where he had left off.

"You know that movie we made together?" he said. "Say, if I had hauled off and taken a swipe at Carnera's chin, think I'd have had a chance to get this bout? Don't be crazy. No, sir. I had to play dumb. You think he's strong? Well, I'll bet I'm stronger, now or any other time. I'll get by his left. Don't worry. I know I'll beat him."

But two days later he again looked awful. And Dempsey again criticized his conditioning. "The boy's not right," he said. "He needs plenty of work. I doubt that he can be made ready for the fight."

Hoffman had shaken off Dempsey's earlier criticism, dismissing it as uninformed grandstanding, but this time he was worried too. Mike Cantwell spent most of his time shaking his head, watching his fighter clown and struggle with his sparring partners. Cantwell's doubts were rubbing off on Hoffman, who decided that Dempsey and Brown might be right. He announced that he would ask the commission for a one-week postponement. "Baer's timing is way off," he said on June 6, eight days before the fight was scheduled to take place. "I'd rather have him at his peak when he faces Carnera. He doesn't fear the Italian man mountain. But I agree with Dempsey that he needs plenty more hard work. He might get himself into shape the next four days, but I doubt it. The public is entitled to a fair shake, hence my last-minute request. I hope they grant it. Then the customers will surely get a great fight."

Hoffman's interest in the public's viewing pleasure was, the newspapermen felt, heartwarming — and completely insincere. Simply put, his fighter was a bum, just as Brown had said.

Now, strangely, the Baer camp was in agreement with Brown, its most persistent critic. "On what Baer showed me in his burlesque workout yesterday in his training camp," Brown told the press on June 7, "on what my eyes tell me today on looking the man over, he is not physically fit for his match now, nor would he be after ten days' training. For the good of the boxing game I hope Baer will acquit himself satisfactorily in the ring next Thursday."

But Jimmy Johnston scoffed at the idea of a delay. "Baer has had plenty of time to get into shape for the fight," he said, "and any postponement would be unfair to Carnera and to the public. When I made the match, I suggested June 28 for the date, but both Carnera and Baer insisted on June 14 instead, each asserting that he would be physically fit by that time."

Carnera was equally dismissive of the postponement proposal. "I will not stand for any change," he was quoted as saying. "If there is no fight on the fourteenth, there will not be any fight at all. Why should I agree? Baer has had enough time to train. If he is not in shape, is that my fault? I wouldn't mind if he asked me for a postponement because of a broken leg or some such legitimate reason. But he hasn't, and no matter what anybody says I won't favor any delay."

On Friday, June 8, Baer, Carnera, and all their seconds came together at the commission's offices. First both fighters would undergo physical examinations. Then the commission would decide whether it would grant Hoffman's wish and postpone the fight.

Baer was led to a room filled with newspapermen, where he and Carnera would be examined by Dr. William H. Walker (the brother of former mayor Jimmy Walker), Dr. Morris Beyer, and Dr. Vincent Nardiello, the commission's physicians, who would determine whether they were fit to fight. An imposing specimen at 260 pounds, Carnera, well proportioned and chiseled, was stripped to the waist and already sitting on the examining table when Baer walked in. Baer, dressed in white linens, took off his shirt and, like a young lady taking her seat on a park bench next to her beau, sat down right next to Carnera on the table. In the same mocking tone he had used when they were making the movie, he said, "Hello, *champ!*"

Carnera nodded and grunted.

Dempsey, standing a few feet away, turned to Nat Fleischer and said, "Here comes the stunt business."

With Carnera looking away, Baer put a finger to his lips to indicate to the newspapermen that he wanted them to keep quiet. His eyes alight with mischief, he reached for Carnera's hairy chest with his thumb and forefinger, plucked a hair, and said, "He loves me!" Before Carnera realized what was happening, Baer plucked another hair and said, "He loves me not!"

According to the assembled media, which regularly mocked Carnera's accent, Carnera sprang from the examining table and said, "You maka me a damn fool — you wise guy, hey?"

The newspapermen and photographers erupted in laughter. Baer had indeed succeeded in making Carnera look like a fool. Certainly no previous challenger for the heavyweight championship had ever shown less respect for the title-holder, a clear indication to the press that Baer was completely unfazed by the significance of the event or the enormous size of his opponent.

At this point, to prevent any real damage, Dempsey leaped between the champion and the challenger. Then Baer directed his jokes at Louis Soresi, Carnera's manager, who announced that Baer would get his comeuppance in the ring.

The doctors pulled out their stethoscopes and blood pressure monitors and went to work. When they were finished, they wrote an official report to the boxing commissioners. "Our opinion on both these boxers, which we have reached unanimously," they wrote, "is that they are both in splendid physical condition, and we fully believe that they are physically able to engage in this contest of fifteen rounds of boxing. From every test we are able to make, we fail to find any reason why either one of them should not be allowed to box on June 14, 1934."

At the subsequent meeting, Brigadier General John J. Phelan, who had succeeded James A. Farley as the chairman of the commission, vetoed the proposal to postpone the fight. "The contestants having been found physically fit, we could not afford to take any action that might lay us open to legal action on the part of the promoters," he said.

Baer was beaming. He was squarely situated at the center of attention and loving it. "Look at all the excitement I stirred up," he said, standing in the hallway outside the commission's offices. He sounded nothing like a man who wanted the fight postponed. "Believe me, I certainly am one colorful fighter. Fellows like Jack Sharkey never stirred up such a fuss. I'm going to knock him out early," he added, "I have to. I'm getting ten thousand dollars to act as master of ceremonies at a nightclub later in the night."

"You can't convince me that Baer is in shape," Brown said, defying Phelan's request that he keep his opinions to himself. "Although I do not mean to show any disrespect to the medical profession, I think the challenger would do better in a circus ring than against Carnera."

Perhaps because it was true that he was out of shape, Baer ignored the slings, then motored back to Asbury Park. Carnera also returned to New Jersey.

The negative assessments of Baer's state of readiness and Hoffman's attempt to postpone the fight scared off some potential customers. A special train had been chartered in San Francisco to speed fans across the continent. On June 6, two days before it was scheduled to begin its journey, the train was put back in a shed. Some people thought the fight might be delayed, but most thought Baer was not in good enough shape to make it competitive. A week before the bout, the odds against him were two to one, even though no one thought especially highly of Carnera.

Still, the giant from Sequals had a few natural advantages. He was five inches taller and fifty pounds heavier than Baer. His reach was longer, and his chest, wrists, ankles, thighs, waist, forearms, and neck were bigger. Only his biceps were smaller than Baer's. The greatest advantage Carnera enjoyed, at least in the collective assessment of the public, was his relative dependability. Max Baer, in contrast, was considered — despite his dominating performance a year earlier against Schmeling — a flake of the highest order. No one knew whether the Livermore Butcher Boy, the man who had killed with his punches, was going to show up, or whether instead it would be the Fistic Harlequin, who refused to train properly.

On Saturday, June 9, the day after he was declared fit to fight, Carnera started to experience some throat pain. His condition wasn't serious — hardly more than a sore throat — but the betting public, searching for any weakness in the champion, began to have doubts. Quickly the odds against Baer diminished, eventually falling to six to five. (Although betting on boxing — and other sports — was illegal, the newspapers in those days paid close attention to the unofficial odds. Stories about boxing in particular, regardless of their length, uniformly included the betting odds — the information readers craved most. It was also common at the time for odds to fluctuate wildly in the days leading up to a fight, mostly because of the influence of organized crime.) Baer was still the underdog, but barely. The media had fun with Carnera's pharyngitis, as the doctors called it. John Kieran's take was typical: "Max wore down all the listeners in Asbury Park and Primo bobbed up with a sore throat."

Meanwhile, in Asbury Park, Baer was putting on a show. He wrestled his younger brother, Buddy, who already weighed 244 pounds, for a round. At one point he picked Buddy up, spun him over his head, then put him down, without even breathing hard. "See, I'm a wrestler," he said to a man standing ringside. "Oh," the man responded, "that's what you are."

The press contingent covering Baer's camp was surprised by the gentleness he displayed with his sparring partners. Baer consistently had one of them, Dynamite Jackson, on the ropes, but even though Mike Cantwell urged him to keep punching, Baer would drop his hands and walk away to let Jackson catch his breath. After a sparring session on June 9, Joseph C. Nichols of the *New York Times* wrote, "It was plain to see that Baer lacks viciousness — the 'tiger instinct' that is so necessarily a part of the equipment of a heavyweight champion."

Baer rejected that theory and predicted victory. "I licked Carnera in the office of the commission on Friday," he said. "I got his goat plenty while we were being examined, and he looked like a scared rabbit after I got through with him. I am going to be the new world's champion, and don't say I didn't tell you. I'll knock him out in eight rounds, or maybe with a single punch. I feel great. I'm no gymnasium fighter — and don't want to hurt my sparring partners. But I'll go after Carnera. He doesn't know what it's all about. And I'm going to be a fighting champion."

Carnera spoke English the way he fought — awkwardly — but in his public statements he made it clear that he thought he would retain the title. "I am in good shape," he told the reporters, who on this occasion were gracious enough to clean up his broken English in their stories, "and I will retain my title. I will not predict a knockout, because that will depend entirely on the kind of a fight Baer puts up. If he wants to box, I'll box, and get the decision, but if he slugs, I'll slug too, and knock him out. I will do my best, and will try to give the fans a run for their money."

Meanwhile, a woman named Amelia Tersini was giving Carnera a run for *his* money. Described as a "London waitress," she won a judgment of $15,000 against the champion for breach of promise. (Apparently Baer wasn't the only heavyweight who had a habit of making engagements he wouldn't keep.) Consequently, Carnera's 37 percent share of the purse was attached by the New York State Supreme Court on June 12. Baer's purse was also attached, because of his contractual dispute with J. Hamilton Lorimer, who claimed that Baer still owed him money. Never before in boxing history had two fighters entered a world championship bout with both of their earnings held up by the courts.

From Chicago, the triple champion Barney Ross displayed solidarity with Baer by predicting that he would defeat Carnera. "Baer can hit harder than Carnera, and I think he's every bit as good a boxer," Ross said two days before the fight. "If he'd just take training a little more seriously, there would not be any doubt about the outcome."

On June 13, Baer broke camp and drove into the city with Hoffman, Mike Cantwell, his brother, Buddy, and his father, Jacob. To prevent fatigue, fighters generally prefer not to travel on fight days. The group checked into the Park Central, on Seventh Avenue. A few of Baer's newspaper friends stopped by. They were looking for quotes and tidbits, any way to paint a picture of the Livermore Larruper on the eve of the biggest fight of his career. Baer, though, was uncharacteristically subdued.

He and his seconds spent the night quietly. No nightclubs. No girls. No booze. Baer slept soundly, undisturbed by memories of Frankie Campbell and Ernie Schaaf. He dreamed instead of winning the championship, and this time knocking Carnera out.

On Thursday, June 14, Max Baer woke up early (for him), at around ten. He took breakfast in his room and mapped out his fight plan with Hoffman and Cantwell.

"Max," Cantwell said, "you don't have the stamina to fight fifteen rounds straight. You've got to take it in bursts."

"Pick your spots," Hoffman said.

Baer would be best served, his seconds thought, by exerting

himself fully for a few flurries, then intentionally slowing down to build up strength for another attack. He was not to exhaust himself trying to hammer the champion. He would thrust, then parry, thrust, then parry. If one lucky punch ended it, so be it; if not, then surely Carnera would eventually succumb to the cumulative effect of Baer's assaults.

By the afternoon of the bout, the odds of the previous week had reversed — Baer was a seven-to-five favorite, thanks to the last-minute influx of bettors from California. While he was in his dressing room before the fight, a security guard came in to tell him that a blonde was waiting outside. "Only one?" Baer said.

Outside, the Madison Square Garden Bowl was rapidly filling up. Shortly before the main event — just after James J. Braddock disappointed Johnston by knocking out Corn Griffin — Mayor Fiorello La Guardia entered the arena with a cadre of police officers. An enormous cheer rose from the crowd when it recognized him. A diligent usher, however, demanded La Guardia's ticket. Flustered for a moment, the mayor dug into his pocket and produced the ticket. The usher punched it and escorted him to his seat. Again the crowd cheered.

Meanwhile, as Baer was getting a rubdown next door to his dressing room, two well-dressed men with bulges in their jackets walked into his room unannounced. They told Hoffman that they were representing Owney Madden's interests and Madden was interested in seeing Carnera win. The men were seeking Hoffman's assurance that Baer would choose not to win the fight, and implicitly threatening his life. Before Hoffman could respond, Jerry "Iron Neck" Cassall, Baer's bodyguard, stood up from the chair in which he was sitting, unfurled himself to his full height, and opened his jacket, revealing a pistol in his waistband. "Get out," he said.

Unprepared for a gunfight, Madden's minions turned and left. Hoffman decided it would be best not to tell Baer what had happened until after the fight.

To emphasize his versatility and remind people that he was also a movie star — and perhaps to refresh Carnera's memory as well — Baer climbed through the ropes wearing a silk robe that bore on its back not the embroidered name Max Baer but instead the name Steve Morgan, his character in *The Prizefighter and the Lady*. When he disrobed, his trunks bore a black Star of David aligned with the bottom edge of the left leg.

When the bell finally rang, Baer did not stalk after the champion, as many had expected. First he felt out Carnera for about a minute, measuring him and acclimating himself to his surroundings. Suddenly, in Baer's mind, they were back on the soundstage in Hollywood and the champion was his plaything. Only then did he commence a vicious assault, startling Carnera with a left to the stomach. Even as his left hand protected his head, Baer's right hand was levitating at his waist, waiting to strike. He fired it at the champion with stunning swiftness, landing it flush against his jaw, and the giant went down in an instant.

Stunned by the power and precision of the punch, Carnera leaped to his feet without waiting to gather himself. Baer, snarling, was on him again quickly and chased him around the ring like a leopard attacking an elephant. Carnera stumbled from one corner to another, clutching at the ropes. Then Baer nailed him again and he went down again. A moment later, he went down for a third time. Three knockdowns in the first round. Then three more in the second. Another in the third. Several times Baer and Carnera were entangled and fell together to the canvas. Baer was always quicker getting up and once turned to Carnera and said, "Last one up's a sissy." He was surprised that he had been unable to produce a knockout, but he was not flustered. He kidded with his friends at ringside and mugged for the crowd as Carnera flailed around, sometimes almost falling through the ropes, his incompetent seconds utterly at a loss to advise him. Carnera lurched after Baer comically; Baer, like a matador, waved him to the side.

Careful not to wear himself out, Baer eased back for a few rounds and relaxed, as he had planned to do. When his friend Harry Smith had a heart attack and was carried away on a stretcher, Baer called out to the other writers, "Don't worry about me. Take care of Harry." Never before or since in a heavyweight championship fight has one of the combatants displayed so much interest in the welfare of someone in the crowd. Rarely has a challenger so thoroughly dominated a champion. The fight was just as easy as Baer had thought it would be. (Smith, incidentally, recovered.)

When the fighters were next to each other in the ring, the disparity in size and height between them disappeared. Baer fought standing straight, on his toes, constantly hitching up his trunks, preening for the crowd. Carnera slouched, which made it easier for Baer to reach his chin.

Carnera actually won the fourth, seventh, eighth, and ninth rounds, but only because Baer was waiting for an opening. In the tenth round, he found it. He knocked Carnera down three more times. Then he turned to Arthur Donovan, the referee. "Art," he said evenly, "stop the fight. Carnera's helpless." At that moment Donovan stepped in to separate the boxers. Baer's corner thought that Donovan had stopped the fight. He had not. The bell sounded, and it took a few moments for Baer to understand that there would be another round. In the eleventh round, Carnera was toppled for the eleventh time, but he got up again. Finally, two minutes and six seconds into the round, Baer knocked down Carnera one more time. At the count of two, Donovan finally stepped in and ended the fight.

Seconds later, Dempsey was in the middle of the ring, giving his protégé an enormous bear hug. Then the ring announcer, Joe Humphreys, faced the crowd, took Baer's right hand in his left, and lifted their arms together, officially signaling that the world's heavyweight championship had passed into the possession of twenty-five-year-old Maximilian Adelbert Baer. With his left hand still gloved, Baer hitched up his trunks and let out a

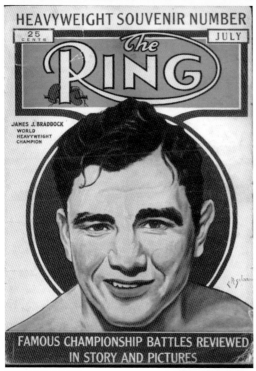

Courtesy of *Ring Magazine*

In this cover portrait, if nowhere else, Braddock's smile isn't crooked.

Bettman/CORBIS

Jimmy Braddock a few months before his fight with Tommy Loughran in 1929.

More than 80,000
people crowded into
Boyle's Thirty Acres
to watch Jack Dempsey
fight Georges Carpentier
on July 2, 1921.
It was boxing's first
million-dollar gate.

Leonard McCombe/Time-Life Pictures/Getty Images

Stillman's gym,
the University
of Eighth Avenue.

The sports writers who helped immortalize Braddock (clockwise from top left): Frank Graham, Grantland Rice, John Kieran, Lud Shabazian, and Damon Runyon.

Tex Rickard (left) and Jack Dempsey. Rickard promoted five million-dollar gates. Dempsey fought in all of them.

"They looked like Mutt and Jeff and behaved like Damon and Pythias": Braddock and Joe Gould.

In 177 professional fights, Tommy Loughran was knocked out exactly twice. He defeated both Braddock and Baer, soundly.

Braddock working the speed bag at "Homicide Hall," his training camp on the grounds of the Hotel Evans.

Yankees center fielder Joe DiMaggio planting a kiss on Braddock after Braddock's final fight in 1938.

Mae Fox Braddock and her husband the week before he fought Max Baer.

Above left: "I got a million-dollar body and a ten-cent brain": Max Baer showing off for the camera.

Above right: Frankie Campbell (second from left) and Max Baer (second from right) moments before the opening bell of their fight on August 25, 1930.

Dorothy Dunbar with her third husband, heavyweight contender Max Baer, in 1933.

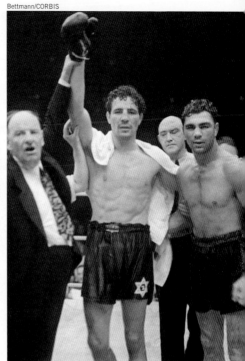

Above left: Baer hamming it up with Myrna Loy in a publicity shot for *The Prizefighter and the Lady*.

Above right: The Jew smites the German: Baer after his greatest triumph, over Max Schmeling, who appears somewhat dazed after the knockout.

Jack Dempsey (left) contemplating Max Baer's legendary right hand.

At the weigh-in a few hours before their fight, Braddock gave Baer a good look at his left.

Braddock (left) and Baer trading left hands at the Madison Square Garden Bowl.

Braddock moments after he upset Baer to win the world heavyweight championship. Jimmy Johnston sports a straw hat.

triumphant yelp. Hoffman kissed him on the cheek. "How's Harry?" were Baer's first words to his manager. Assured that Smith was okay, he turned his attention to Bill Brown, who was on the other side of the ropes. "What do you think of me now, commissioner?" he said. "You're still a bum," Brown said, then hastily added, "and so's Carnera."

Donovan told the newspapermen that Carnera had asked him to end the fight while he was lying on the canvas after the twelfth knockdown. But in his dressing room, between sobbing fits, Carnera said otherwise. "I lose, don't you see? I lose the championship, that's all," he said. "But I didn't ask Donovan to stop it. I didn't quit. I'd have fought until I couldn't move, but I'd never give up." Then, his face grotesquely swollen by Baer's punches, Carnera burst into tears again. The reporters had never seen a defeated champion weep, and the pathetic sight of the enormous fighter breaking down stayed with many of them for the rest of their lives.

In Baer's dressing room, the new champion was peppered with questions from dozens of reporters. Finally, in frustration, Baer said, "Will you fellows let *me* talk?

"Primo's a nice chap," he said when the floor was finally his, "and he's got lots of heart, a lot more than I thought he had. But I could not hit him near the end of the tenth round. Donovan pushed me away while Carnera was still on his feet, and he stood there with his hands down. I pleaded with Donovan to stop the fight. Primo was such a dead cinch to wallop that I was afraid I might crack something back here." Baer pointed to the back of his skull. "Donovan was trying hard enough, but I guess he just got excited. I'll bet he never refereed a fight with so many knockdowns in it before." No one had refereed a fight with so many knockdowns. Dempsey-Firpo and Dempsey-Willard, the wildest heavyweight championship fights up to that time, were almost tame affairs compared to Baer-Carnera.

Baer couldn't resist a well-deserved parting shot at Bill Brown. "I guess Primo found me in better condition than Commissioner Brown," he said. "I'm glad I wasn't up to the commissioner's idea of top form, or there might have been a tragedy."

In the streets of New York and elsewhere, thousands of Jews exulted in Baer's triumph. They collected their winnings from their Italian friends and neighbors and went to bed elated and indescribably proud.

Back at the Park Central that night, Baer celebrated by signing several contracts to make appearances and endorse products. There was nothing the public would not want to know about the new heavyweight champion. There was nothing he endorsed that people wouldn't buy. He signed a contract to serialize the story of his life in thirty-six parts. He signed another contract for a series that would be titled "My Life and Loves," to appear in the *Journal*.

"How about Marian Norton, the screen star?" Jeannette Smits asked Baer that night, in her first interview for the *Journal* series.

"A nice girl," Baer said, "a charming girl, in fact, but nothing to me personally."

"Yeah, well, what about Jean Harlow?"

"A nice girl, a charming girl, in fact, but nothing to me." Baer was wearing a fawn gabardine suit, a brown-and-white-striped shirt, a brown-and-white-striped necktie, and shiny tan shoes.

"How about Bee Star and Shirley La Belle?" Smits asked. Those women had both sued Baer for breach of promise.

"Nice girls," Baer said. Then, struggling for the right words, he added, "What I mean is, I don't know them and they don't know me. They've dropped the suits. Just wanted some publicity, I guess."

"No sweetheart now?"

"Only my mother," Baer said. "And what a sweetheart she is. Wouldn't think of suing me for breach of promise. And boy, what an advantage that is. Women to date have cost me a hundred thousand bucks."

Smits then asked Baer about his relationship with his ex-wife, with whom it was rumored he might reunite. "We've been separated seven times," he said. "Isn't that enough? Besides, I'm too young to get married again."

In fact, Baer was still seeing June Knight, the actress, and had also initiated a relationship with Mary Ellen Sullivan, the manager of a coffee shop in Washington. After his win, though, he was not terribly interested in commitment.

Uptown at the Cotton Club, in midtown at the Stork Club, and everywhere in between, Baer celebrated his victory. Tens of thousands of glasses of champagne were raised in his honor. At the Park Central, management was forced to hire an extra telephone operator to handle all the incoming calls for the new world heavyweight champion. Joan Brewster, Baer's personal secretary, was inundated with letters from lovesick women and admiring men. "If Max Baer tried to keep all the appointments various persons desire to make with him since he became champion," she told Edward Van Every of the *New York Sun*, "the days would have to be at least fifty hours long, and even then he would have to dispense with eating, sleeping, and the business of making a living."

One of the thousands of women who sent Baer letters proclaiming their love wrote a poem that included this stanza:

> For I'm fed up with musicians
> And clerks with poor positions
> With doubtful politicians
> And silly electricians

She finally declared that she was "starving for a curly-headed Baer."

Something about Baer brought out the poet in many women. Another wrote these lines:

Max Baer, My Heart,
Many nights in my sleep
You come to me as Sir Galahad;
But in the morning I wake up to
Find
You were only a dream I had.
Oh, but for an hour with you
To fill my soul with honey pure,
Oh, for a picture from you
To put above my bed for you —
I remain your own.

A latter-day Elizabeth Barrett Browning, the lovestruck young lady might not have gotten her picture. By early July, Brewster had exhausted her reservoir of Baer publicity stills — some two thousand prints, most of which had been mailed to the adoring public. It's quite possible that in the late spring and early summer of 1934, Max Baer received more love letters from more women than any other man ever received. Another began, "My dear Max: Am deeply in love with you; am penning this missive with violet ink, as I think that is the color of your dear eyes."

A recent graduate of the University of Michigan, Brewster was disgusted by the love letters, as anyone would be after reading thousands of them. Each declaration of undying love prompted her to shake her head in disapproval.

Day after day, the newspapers were filled with accounts of Baer's life and loves. Pictures of Dorothy Dunbar and June Knight were dug out of the photo archives to illustrate stories about the champion's escapades. The *Journal* ran a multipart series under Baer's byline and promoted it with an advertisement that read: "Don't miss the give-it-the-works story of how the new heavyweight champion breaks jaws and hearts! It will bowl you over with its thrills, drama and torrid romance! It's terrific — it's a knockout — and it's true!"

The headlines focused on his amorous pursuits:

BAER NEVER LEARNED WHAT GREAT PALS GIRLS COULD BE
UNTIL HE WAS 20

UNKISSED AND 'YELLOW' AT 19, 'BASHFUL' CHAMP ADMITS

(In the accompanying story, Baer confessed that "if there
was a yellower fellow in the whole state than I was up to the
time I was nineteen, he must have been a Chinaman.")

FLOOD OF MASH NOTES FLOWS TO NEW CHAMP

LOVING LETTERS OVERWHELM BAER

TOO BAD, GIRLS! MAX BARS CUPID

MA BAER NOT READING MASH NOTES TO MAX!

Dorothy Dunbar kept silent when Baer won the title. She refused to comment on his accession to the high throne of fist-
iana, as Fleischer might have said. While she took the high
road, Baer couldn't help insulting her new boyfriend, the de-
posed playboy prince of the Caucasus, Serge Mdivani, of the
royal house of Georgia. "I've got more royal blood in my right
hand than he has in his whole body," Baer said on September 8.

Responding to this jibe, Dunbar said while attending a polo
tournament with Prince Serge, "That's absurd, petty, and mean
of Max. Please overlook his statement." The United Press reporter of course did not. Every aspect of the new champion's
life was fair game, and everything he said was duly recorded
and printed.

By defeating Schmeling and Carnera so convincingly, Baer
had not only ascended to the championship, he had captured
the imagination of tens of millions of people around the world,
who assumed he would reign at the top of the heavyweight division for a decade. His punching power, the solidity of his chin,
and his charisma made him the most popular champion since
Dempsey, who had lost the title eight years earlier. But mentally
Baer was not prepared to have greatness thrust upon him. He
had not lost any hard fights. He had never even been knocked

down, much less knocked out. His career might have benefited from a loss to Schmeling or Carnera, which would have forced him to regroup and rededicate himself, and eventually he might have been psychologically stronger and a more complete fighter. Instead he was a champion with no real grounding in the game. Everything was so easy for him — but great champions usually are fashioned by adversity.

12

Another Upset

....

New Jersey and New York: 1934

When Joe Gould finally found Jim Braddock on the docks on June 12, 1934, Braddock had not fought in almost nine months. It was his longest layoff ever. Yet he was in remarkable shape. A little skinny, yes, but more muscled than ever before. His arms had always been powerful; now they looked like weapons. He weighed only about 180 pounds, 8 fewer than when he fought Abe Feldman the previous September. But he was lean and sinewy, and his legs were stronger than they had ever been. When Gould told him that he was matched to fight Corn Griffin two days later and asked, "Are you in shape?" Braddock replied, "Look at me." It signaled the beginning of a remarkable 366 days.

Having already spent his twenty-four-dollar monthly relief stipend on several bills, Braddock needed money badly. He asked Gould for an advance on their $250 purse. Gould was able to squeeze $100 out of Johnston, and they split it. Fifty dollars was the most money Braddock had seen since the day the commission had handed over the purse from the Feldman fight. For the first time in months, he felt he could breathe — not breathe easy, just breathe. Still, he had only forty-eight hours to prepare for a fight against the great Corn Griffin. Even Braddock, who had stopped buying the papers, had heard of him.

"How'd you get us Corn?" he asked Gould.

"Jimmy owes us," Gould replied, referring to Johnston, who in fact owed them nothing. "I told you we'd get a break." It was true that Gould had always *said* they would get a break; there were times, though, when he had been far from sure that they actually *would* get a break.

Working out at Stillman's the day before the fight, Braddock thought about how much was at stake at the Madison Square Garden Bowl. If he could just beat Griffin, the toast of the boxing writers and trainers, he would set himself up for a bigger payday against one of the top challengers, Steve Hamas or Art Lasky or Ray Impellittiere. None of them scared him at all. For a fighter who had lost sixteen of twenty-six fights in the previous four years, he had very little doubt about his abilities. He did question his luck, but not his ability. After all, despite all the losses and humiliations, he had never truly been outclassed as a fighter. He had been outclassed as a boxer, by Loughran, but no one but Scozza had ever managed to knock him out, and that was a technical knockout. He had been battered in the ring on several occasions, but he had never come close to being counted out.

These were his thoughts as he prepared to fight Corn Griffin, who was, after all, another knockout artist — in his mind "more meat," the kind of boxer he always seemed to fight his best against. Braddock thought about the day five and a half years earlier when he had been at Stillman's preparing to fight Tuffy Griffiths. He could see the old-timers gasping as Griffiths flattened one sparring partner after another. He remembered with satisfaction the disappointment etched on the faces of Rickard and Tom McArdle when he sent Griffiths to the canvas. He would do the same to Corn Griffin.

Almost in a trance, Braddock threw hundreds of punches at the heavy bag, and the names melted together in his thoughts. Griffiths. Griffin. Griffiths. Griffin. Couldn't be a coincidence.

Twenty-four hours earlier, he had considered himself retired. Now he was a warrior again. He would show everyone. He would show the writers who mocked him. He would show the fair-weather friends who avoided him in the street. He would show the gas and electric company. He would show himself that he was, at twenty-nine, still a fighter. There was only one problem: all the walking had helped his foot speed and his stamina, and all the dockwork had made his left hand newly powerful, but nothing he had done in the previous nine months had prepared him for the rigors of the ring, the quick bursts of energy and explosiveness required of fighters. With Gould and Doc Robb, Braddock formulated a plan — he would knock out Griffin before he, Braddock, had a chance to get winded. Easy enough. Knock him out. Make it quick.

The habitués of Stillman's were consumed with the Baer-Carnera championship bout. Was Baer in shape? Had Carnera recovered from his sore throat? Braddock tried to filter out all the voices competing to be heard through the fetid air. He wasn't going to spend one second thinking about Baer or Carnera. Corn was all that was on his mind. If he could only beat Corn. Then he'd get another payday, a payday that would carry him through the next winter. He could escape from the docks. He could feed the kids. It was almost too much to consider. So he focused on the mitts that Robb held up in front of his face.

On the night of the fight, June 14, Braddock didn't even notice the extent to which he had become an afterthought — the tiny dressing room, the lack of interest from the writers and the fans. He focused instead on how good it felt to be back in a big arena on a big night. And how strong he felt. After Griffin knocked him down in the second round, he turned into a fighter he had never before been. The knockout in the third round was so sudden that Braddock could barely describe it afterward. The feeling was completely unfamiliar — not knocking someone out, he had done that dozens of times, but knocking him out with his right after softening him up with his left. The left hand that had only pawed at Abe Feldman, the left hand that had been useless against Al Ettore, now moved weightlessly and at the same time forcefully, like a greased piston. *This is what I should have been doing years ago*, Braddock thought. *This hand is a bludgeon.*

But if Braddock was expecting a ticker-tape parade after knocking out the great Corn Griffin, what he got was indifference. Since the entire sporting public was infatuated with Max Baer, the new Dempsey, there was little room to consider anyone else. The fights Braddock thought would materialize did not. And even in 1934, his share of the purse, $125, including his $50 advance, did not go far. It went, of course, to pay the rent and the milkman and the gas and electric company. Even after scoring a decisive knockout on the undercard of the world heavyweight championship fight, with 56,000 people in the stands, he still needed relief.

Gould was trying to make another match. He continued to haunt the Garden's executive offices. But Johnston was more disgusted with Griffin than impressed by Braddock. Griffin's reputation had been built up by sparring well against Carnera. When Baer made Carnera look foolish, Griffin's prefight notices were rapidly devalued, which in turn devalued Braddock's victory. Four months after knocking out Griffin, Braddock was still laboring on the docks, in the coal yard, and on a moving van. Understandably, his spirits were low. But he went to Stillman's whenever he could, training hard for fights that were only figments of his imagination.

It was at this time, in the fall of 1934, that Frank Graham, the newly promoted sports columnist for the *New York Sun*, happened to find himself watching Braddock work out at the gym. Graham, a future giant of press row, was describing the atmosphere, the attitude of the fighters, and concluded his column — one of his first — with a paragraph about Braddock:

Over there, for instance, is a heavyweight whose punch almost took him to the top of the division. Hurled back into the rut, he plods along with neither hope nor inspiration, training doggedly, fighting where he can. He would quit the ring and take a job somewhere at $25 a week if he could get it, but jobs are scarce, especially for a fellow approaching 30 who has had no training in any other business. So he goes on fighting because he has a wife and three children who must eat, too.

Braddock couldn't understand why his victory over Griffin had done so little to change his fortunes. But he kept training, spending more time in the gym than the heavyweight champion, who was busy performing in vaudeville and on radio. Gould had been out of touch for weeks.

Then Braddock was approached by a north Jersey promoter who wanted him to fight an up-and-comer from the neighborhood named Steve Dudas. (Dudas would eventually fight a memorable trilogy against Abe Feldman.) Arrangements were made. Posters were printed. Purses were promised. It was only about $750, but it would get Braddock through the winter and off relief. After nearly ten months, he had told no one other than Gould and a few close friends that he was on the dole. He wouldn't even tell his parents, who would have been embarrassed for him. His shame was so deep that he kept a close accounting of how much he had received, in the hope that he would one day be able to repay what he considered a debt.

In early November, two weeks before the Dudas fight was scheduled to take place in North Bergen, a few of Braddock's friends, including his sometime sparring partner Pat Sullivan, staged what could be called an intervention. Sullivan in particular had been unimpressed by the quality of Braddock's workouts and disappointed by the length of his training runs. He was working without Gould and Robb, and it showed. His friends told him not to take Dudas lightly. They knew Braddock's habit of winning one, then losing one, and they knew he could not afford to lose this one. Sullivan started sparring with him more frequently and forced him to increase his morning runs to six and seven miles a day. For a week Braddock worked harder than he had ever worked to prepare for a fight; each day he fought the equivalent of twelve rounds with Sullivan and a few other, less hulking sparring partners.

Then Gould resurfaced. He reached Braddock by phone at a local gym. "We finally have another fight, champ," he said.

"But Joe, I lined up a fight myself when I didn't hear from you."

"That's fine. Cancel it. You're fighting John Henry Lewis at the Garden next week."

In 1932, John Henry Lewis had rather easily defeated Braddock in San Francisco. In the two years since, he had established himself as one of the best light heavyweights in the world.

"But Joe, I can't fight as a light heavy. I'm one eighty. Maybe more."

"You don't fight him as a light heavy," Gould said. He was sitting on a desk outside Jimmy Johnston's office, smoking a cigar. "He's willing to fight you as a heavy. Plus it's on the undercard of the Maxie Rosenbloom fight."

Braddock's old friend Rosenbloom was defending his light heavyweight championship against Bob Olin (the only all-Jewish light heavyweight championship fight ever). Braddock and Lewis would fight at the top of the undercard.

"How much?" Braddock asked.

"They're paying seven hundred and fifty dollars."

"That's how much I'm getting to fight Dudas."

"But you need to get back to New York," Gould said between puffs. "You shouldn't be fighting in Jersey."

For a moment Braddock paused to consider what it would mean to cancel the Dudas fight. Then he said, "All right, let's do it."

He broke the news to the New Jersey promoters, canceling

the fight against Dudas, but he continued to train with Sullivan for the Lewis fight. As it would turn out, not a moment of his rigorous training was wasted.

Lewis was a significantly tougher opponent than he had been in 1932. He was smarter, stronger, and more disciplined. He had defeated Rosenbloom twice in nontitle bouts. Jimmy Johnston had signed him to a three-fight contract and expected him to rise quickly to the championship. For Lewis's first fight in New York, Johnston wanted a name opponent who wouldn't give him too much trouble. Despite Braddock's penchant for upsetting the best-laid plans of promoters, he was Johnston's choice. Two years before, after all, he had lost to Lewis by a wide margin, and Lewis had only gotten better.

Of course, Braddock was also a different fighter than he had been in 1932. But there was no good reason to believe, based merely on what he had done against Corn Griffin, that he could handle Lewis, a world-class talent in his prime. Certainly the gamblers didn't think Braddock had a chance — he was a two-to-one underdog. Gould, though, was optimistic. He had always believed in Braddock, especially in the rare instances when Braddock outweighed his opponent (Braddock weighed 187, Lewis only 176).

On November 16, fighting at Madison Square Garden for the first time in years, Braddock gave the greatest performance of his career. For ten rounds he boxed with a great boxer and outpunched him. Lewis dominated with his speed and flash for the first four rounds, but in the fifth round Braddock knocked him down — with his left hand, no less. Shabazian, seated at ringside, was as stunned as Lewis. "The Braddock of 1932 had no left hand," he wrote. "The Braddock of 1934 seemed to be all left hand."

In the seventh round, Lewis lost a point when he hit Braddock below the belt. Still, the fight was close, and when the decision was about to be announced, Braddock was not certain he had won. But he had, once again defying the odds and the wishes of promoters. His conditioning had made the difference. The miles of roadwork, the hours of sparring, the months on the docks, the punching motion of operating the tie hook — all these things had made the Braddock of 1934 superior to all previous editions.

Johnston sought out Braddock in his dressing room after the decision. "You've spoiled two guys for me," he said.

"There's more where that came from," Gould said, answering for his fighter.

After the Lewis bout, Braddock and Gould split $750. Gould was forced to surrender $250 of his share to a creditor. With his share, Braddock took Mae out to dinner for the first time in years. He ordered a steak. Then he ordered another steak. Then he ordered apple pie. The next morning he woke up and walked to the municipal building in North Bergen. Men who had avoided him months earlier now came up to him on the street, newspapers in hand, to talk about the Lewis fight. Braddock was happy to make small talk.

At the municipal building, he found Jimmy Kelly.

"That was a big win, Jimmy," Kelly said. He stood up to congratulate Braddock.

"I want you to take my name off the rolls," Braddock said.

"Are you sure?" Kelly said. "You might still qualify."

"I'm sure," Braddock said, twisting his face into a half-smile. Then he turned around, walked out of the municipal building, and headed home.

13

King Max

....

Cleveland, Chicago, and Miami:
Winter 1934–1935

By mid-December 1934, Max Baer was thoroughly convinced that he was the best boxer in the world. After all, that's what everyone had been telling him for months. His consecutive victories against Schmeling and Carnera, two champions, had made him the biggest sensation in the heavyweight division since the rise of Jack Dempsey. The writers and the general public expected Baer, still only twenty-five, to reign for a decade. Still, a champion needs a challenger, and when Baer surveyed the division, he concluded that none of the challengers was worthy. Who would pay to see him fight Schmeling again? Who would pay to see him fight Carnera again? Who would pay to see him fight Steve Hamas? Or Art Lasky? Or Walter Neusel? No one, Baer thought. Dempsey had had Carpentier, Firpo, and Tunney — opponents crowds could get excited about. How would he ever deliver a million-dollar gate when he was so clearly the best of the heavyweights?

Baer spent a lot of time thinking about this dilemma. Finally he came up with what he considered a brilliant idea, a foolproof plan to draw a million-dollar gate, just as Dempsey so often had. Instead of fighting Hamas and instead of fighting Lasky, the two top contenders, he would fight Hamas and Lasky *on the same night.*

"This is the only way to give the fans their money's worth," he said to a group of writers over lunch in Cleveland, where he was making a charity appearance. "A championship double-header. I'll fight a ten-rounder against Hamas or Lasky, and then the winner will fight the other guy in another ten-rounder."

"How will you decide who gets to fight you first?"

"We'll draw lots," Baer said, scarfing down yet another T-bone. "I don't care."

"How much time between the fights?"

"Five minutes." Baer was, as usual, the best-dressed man in the restaurant. He was careful not to spill any spinach on his blue serge suit.

"Why only five minutes?"

"You don't want to get cold," Baer said. "Once I'm loose, I want to stay loose."

He went on to tell the writers that he thought the double-header would make a million dollars at the gate and that his share would be $400,000. It wasn't Tunney-Dempsey money, but it was as much as he could hope for, considering the quality of his challengers.

"Listen, I don't want to be one of these champions who fights once a year," he said. "I need to fight. Dames are expensive."

Two weeks later, on December 28, Baer stepped into a ring for the first time since the night he took the title from Carnera six months earlier. He was in Chicago, just beginning a five-fight exhibition tour. In the 1930s, heavyweight champions rarely risked their titles more than once a year. To make as much money as possible, they fought meaningless exhibitions in which they were expected to put on a good show for four rounds but not to fight in earnest. In Chicago, though, Baer was fighting a quasi-exhibition. If he were knocked out, he would lose the title. He and his opponent would wear regulation six-ounce gloves, not the eight-ounce gloves usually worn in exhibitions. His opponent was Kingfish Levinsky, the fighter he had twice defeated on points in 1932. It was understood that if Baer and Levinsky boxed fairly evenly for four rounds, they would meet again in the summer of 1935. But Levinsky was a proud, swaggering figure, fighting in his hometown, and he was determined not to play the part of Baer's patsy — and to win the title.

The king of the lackadaisical training camp, Baer was accustomed to horsing around in the ring. Convinced that Levinsky could not hurt him, he was going to put on a show and nothing more. When the bell sounded, he marched out to meet Levinsky and said, "Well, this should be fun." He wound up his right arm in a windmill motion and prepared to deliver a mock punch, and at that moment Levinsky hammered him in the jaw with a straight right. Baer laughed it off. Playing to the crowd, he pretended that the punch had buckled his knees, and he wobbled around the ring. He came at Levinsky again, sticking his chin out to give his opponent an easy target, and again Levinsky punched him hard in the face. "What's wrong with you?" Baer screamed at him. "We're just supposed to be having fun."

When the bell signaled the start of the second round, Baer waited in his corner for Levinsky to come to him. Levinsky instead walked to the center of the ring and waved his fists, inviting Baer to close on him. "That's it," Baer said to Mike Cantwell, his trainer. "The exhibition is over." He then charged at Levinsky, overwhelming him with lefts and rights. Levinsky retreated under the force of the attack, but Baer, grinning ferociously, would not relent. As Levinsky was backpedaling, Baer caught him on the chin with a looping right hand. Levinsky, a veteran who had never been knocked out, who in fact had only once been knocked down, hit the mat with a sickening thud. He was counted out and then carried from the canvas to his corner.

Baer weighed 211 pounds and, the papers noted, "was in magnificent condition."

Baer had again won the battle of the Jewish heavyweights. He had also further demonstrated how much he had improved since 1932, when he had failed to knock out Levinsky over thirty rounds.

Levinsky's manager was furious with him for trying to knock out Baer and thereby ruining their prospects for a fight the following summer. Levinsky's manager was Lena Levy, his sister. She knew that he had just thrown away $20,000.

"The Kingfish got too confident after beating that Baer all over the ring in the first round," Levy, known as Leaping Lena, said after the fight. "He thought he could go on winning just as decisively and did not obey instructions from the corner to be careful in the second round. Why, he was even waving to me that everything was okay when that Baer clipped him on the chin."

During the fight, Baer had noticed an attractive woman seated beside the ring and had had his bodyguard arrange a rendezvous. Hoping not to keep her waiting, he conducted his postfight interviews while he was showering, as he often did. "I guess now folks won't say I am talking out of turn when I say I would like to fight Lasky and Hamas in one night," he said. "Neither of those guys is as tough as Levinsky. That still goes about fighting them both in one night. It won't make any difference to me which one comes in first."

About the fight just concluded, he was almost apologetic. "I didn't want to knock the guy out," he said. "I had hoped that we could go through with a nice fight. But the sucker tried to knock my ears off in the first round and then tried to make me look foolish at the start of the second by standing in the middle of the ring waving his arms at me yelling, 'Come out and fight, you so-and-so.' I said to myself, 'Who does this mug think he is? He's talking to the world's champion.' So I let him have it. Remember what I said about fighting Lasky and Hamas, or Levinsky and Lasky, on the same night? Well, it still goes."

The Levinsky knockout convinced the few remaining doubters that Max Baer was the new Dempsey. "Someone may remove the scalp of Max Baer before 1935 closes out," Grantland Rice wrote in his column on January 4, "but even Dr. Einstein can't think of his name at this moment, using all four dimensions. The unvarnished and unadorned facts are that Max Baer, as heavyweight champion, stands all alone. There is no competition in sight."

Who was Max Baer to disbelieve Grantland Rice?

Reclining in a barber's chair a month later in Miami, as three women were cutting, shaping, and buffing his nails, Baer considered the magnitude of his greatness and decided that only one man from all of history could have whipped him. "A lot of people think I think I'm the hottest heavyweight who threw a right," he said, a bit defensively. "Well, they ain't right. I've been around twenty-five years and I've met one guy who could get in a room with me, lock the door, turn out the lights, and work his way out." For Baer, this was a huge concession.

"The guy? Heck, the ol' man — Jack. The day he licked Willard I'd a been lucky to last a round with him. That's not because I like Jack." At this point Baer was blowing casually on his nails to dry the lacquer. "It's because he could hit harder and move and think faster than I can. But boy, I'd have liked a shot at him, what with all the dough he could pull in that gate. What did he draw with Tunney?"

The reporter told Baer that Dempsey made just about $1 million for the two fights.

"A millon! Listen, I'd fight this room full of wildcats, sailors, and Carneras for that."

Then the reporter asked Baer what he would have done to Tunney.

"The same thing I did to Carnera, Schmeling, and Levinsky,"

Baer said, admiring his dry nails. "All he had was a left hand, and left hands don't hurt. I'd walk in there and plug him with my right."

He leaned back in the barber's chair. Now the scissors were out.

Like Alexander the Great, who at Baer's age realized there were no worlds left to conquer, Baer sighed with boredom at the prospect of defending that which he had already won. He said that the best fighter in the division — other than himself — was Schmeling, a man he had already beaten easily. "He's got a heart, which is more than I can say for Lasky. That Lasky can hit, and he's pretty tough, but he can't take it here," he said, pointing to his heart.

As for Steve Hamas, the former Penn State football star, Baer said, "Steve can hit, that gives him a chance. But listen, I fought a guy in Tampa the other night by the name of Tony Cancela [in an exhibition], and I'll bet a thousand bucks on him against Hamas or Lasky. He's so good I broke a bone in my right hand when I hit him."

Baer considered the significance of what he had said. He was, in his own mind, quite generous. After all, he did say Lasky was tough and Hamas could punch.

Then the reporter asked him one more question. "Is it true, Mr. Baer, that you are engaged to Mary Kirk Brown?" Brown, not to be confused with Mary Ellen Sullivan, had recently been linked to Baer.

The scissors were still working on his curls. Baer tried to be discreet. "I know many girls," he said, "many lovely girls. But I think I shall order à la carte for a while yet. Get me, kid?"

In the winter and spring of 1935, everything on the menu — women, wealth, greatness — was there for the taking for Max Baer.

14

A Shot at Lasky

....

New York: Winter 1935

Now Gould went to work. Braddock's wins over Griffin and
Lewis gave him leverage he hadn't had in years, and he reveled
in it. Writers who hadn't talked to him since before the crash
were now approaching him with notebooks and pens at the
ready. They wanted to know his plans. They wanted to know
where he thought Braddock stood in the heavyweight picture.
They wanted his assessment of the relative strengths of the
contenders.

"Boys," Gould would say, "Jimmy Braddock is one fight away
from wiping that grin off Max Baer's face. He'll make him look
foolish."

Gould didn't mind when the writers laughed at him. As long
as they were writing about Braddock, he was content.

Johnston was putting together an elimination tournament to
determine who would fight Baer in his first title defense, and it
was Gould's mission in life to get Braddock into the mix. Whatever doubts about Braddock's abilities he might have secretly
harbored had been erased by the fighter's win against Lewis —
a win that had deeply impressed Johnston but not the general
public or the writers.

On January 1, 1935, Braddock was not rated among the top
ten heavyweights in the world by the *Ring*. Max Schmeling was

rated higher. So was Steve Hamas, the Jerseyite and former football star. So was Primo Carnera. So was Art Lasky, the Minnesotan who outpointed Baer in Jewishness 100 percent to 25 percent. King Levinsky, Patsy Perroni, Tommy Loughran, Lee Ramage, and a twenty-year-old from Detroit named Joe Louis also rated higher than James J. Braddock. So did Walter Neusel, Charley Massera, Jack Petersen, Johnny Risko, Natie Brown, Abe Feldman, Steve Dudas, Al Ettore, and Buck Everett. In the *Ring*'s year-end roundup of the heavyweight division, Wilbur Wood ranked the top nineteen heavyweights, and Braddock was not among them. To get Braddock a shot at Baer, Gould would somehow have to maneuver him ahead of at least eighteen other fighters. It was a staggering challenge.

Every day Gould parked himself in Johnston's outer office, and every day Johnston assured him that Braddock was in his plans. Gould, of course, wanted more than assurances. He wanted a contract. Meanwhile, Braddock was keeping himself in shape at Stillman's. He seemed to get stronger with each workout. The absence of pain in his right hand was at first slightly distracting. When he hit the heavy bag, he expected to wince. When the pain stopped coming, he almost missed it — it had been with him so long. Slowly, though, he grew accustomed to punching without it. Eventually, as the pain receded in his thoughts, he began to punch harder than he had since before he had broken his hand against Joe Monte's head six years earlier. He had never really noticed how the pain had inhibited his punching power, how it had forced him to pull his punches ever so slightly, diminishing their effectiveness. Now he could punch without thinking about the consequences. He was kicking other habits, too — throwing hundreds of left-handed punches every day, developing his footwork, running great distances to increase his stamina. In the space of just a few months, Braddock had been reborn.

As the days turned into weeks, Gould grew impatient. He

was scared that somehow Braddock's win against Lewis would be forgotten and he would end up the odd man out in the elimination tournament. He intended to prevent any such eventuality by the sheer volume of his verbiage. He talked about Braddock so often, with so many people, in so many different offices, saloons, and steakhouses, that sometimes he lost his train of thought. When this occurred, he would just keep talking, waiting for his thoughts to catch up. He feared nothing as much as silence. The more Gould talked about the state of the heavyweight division, the more convinced he became that of all the top contenders, Art Lasky was the one Braddock was most likely to defeat. He told Johnston that he wanted Lasky.

But Johnston had more pressing concerns. As usual, Schmeling was being difficult. He and Hamas, who had risen to prominence by upsetting and devastating the Black Uhlan a year earlier, were determined to fight a rematch. And Schmeling wanted the fight to take place in Germany. Lured by the promise of a $25,000 purse, Hamas agreed to cross the Atlantic. Another win against Schmeling would virtually guarantee him a shot at the title. At the same time, Carnera signed to fight the equally gargantuan Italian-American heavyweight Ray Impellittiere. Now only Lasky was without an opponent. Finally Johnston suggested Jim Braddock, and the young Minnesotan agreed to fight him on February 1 at Madison Square Garden. Typically for a Braddock opponent, Lasky was immediately installed as a prohibitive favorite.

With a finite goal and an opponent on which to focus his energies, Braddock now immersed himself more deeply than ever in his training. When he wasn't training, he was eating. When he wasn't eating, he was training. Mae saw him even less frequently than when he had worked on the docks. At home the Braddocks were still scrimping, waiting for the Lasky payday, but for the first time in years Jim gave his ambitions free run. He started thinking about what it would mean if he defeated

Lasky. It would mean a shot at the title, which would mean a purse in the neighborhood of $30,000 or more. Just a shot at the title would lift him from poverty to enduring wealth. If he were to win the title — well, that was a thought he was not yet prepared to entertain. It was simply too overwhelming.

At the same time, it was not so wild a dream. Lasky, Hamas, Schmeling, Carnera — Braddock considered them all beatable. Baer scared him least. He had seen Loughran defeat Baer easily at the Garden in 1931. He had watched carefully as the Philadelphia Phantom did to Baer what had been done to him. He said later that Loughran gave him the blueprint for fighting and defeating Max Baer. He would do the same thing: he would box, not slug. But Braddock tried not to think about Baer too often. It was the other Jewish heavyweight whom he first had to defeat. Beat Lasky, get a shot. Beat Lasky, win a million dollars — or at least what seemed like a million dollars.

As the fight approached, Braddock got stronger and stronger. Hoping to get within ten pounds of Lasky's 200, he ate constantly — steaks, ham and eggs, shepherd's pie, ice cream, apple pie, Mae's beef stew. Robb had studied Lasky as closely as possible, talking to trainers and fighters who had seen him as he rose to prominence. Robb and Solly Seeman, another trainer who was working with Braddock, became convinced that Lasky's greatest flaw was his tendency to stick out his chin as if he were trying to get a better look at his opponent. They told Braddock to be ready to nail him in the face when the chin was offered as a target.

On February 1, as Braddock and Gould were preparing to take a ride to the state athletic commission offices for the weigh-in, Johnston called Gould. "The fight's off for now," he said. "Lasky's in the hospital with pneumonia. It's gonna take some time to get back on his feet."

"Why, that kid is yellow," Gould almost screamed.

"Joe, the kid is really sick. Trust me," Johnston said.

"This is going to devastate Jimmy," Gould said, as $4,000 slipped from his grasp.

"He'll get another chance."

Gould told Braddock that the fight was being postponed. Together they went to the hospital where Lasky was laid up and posed with him for the afternoon papers. Then Braddock went back to the gym.

15

The People's Choice

....

New York City: Winter–Spring 1935

In early February, Max Baer went home to San Francisco. Four and a half years after the death of Frankie Campbell, he had not forgotten his pledge to Campbell's widow and son. On February 15, at the Dreamland Arena, he fought an exhibition against Stanley Poreda. The fight raised $10,600 for a fund to benefit Campbell's survivors.

After the benefit, Baer got back on a train for New York. "Listen, fellas, I don't know why Johnston is even bothering with this so-called elimination tournament," he told some reporters when he got there. "I understand that he wants to build up interest in an opponent, but it won't make any difference. None of these guys is fit to lick my boots."

Baer was on a roll. Bleary-eyed, yes, but on a roll. Dressed in a light gray suit, the world's heavyweight champion was taking lunch at Jack Dempsey's restaurant across Eighth Avenue from Madison Square Garden and had invited two dozen of his closest friends in the press to dine with him. Dempsey joined the crowded table and rolled his eyes at Baer's brashness.

"Steve Hamas is a college kid. He's not tough enough to touch me. I've had my way with Schmeling and Carnera. And Lasky hasn't beaten anybody. You guys tell me how Johnston is planning to sell a championship fight against one of them. Fight fans like a little gore, but they don't want to see me kill some-one else."

The writers weren't so sure. "What about Braddock?" The voice — Baer couldn't see the face all the way at the end of the table — belonged to Frank Graham of the *Sun*.

"Braddock?" Baer said dismissively as he fussed with his cufflinks. "You're kidding, right? With all due respect for my elder, he's over the hill. He was over the hill five years ago. Every-one knows he hasn't been the same since Loughran beat him."

"He looked pretty good against Lewis."

"Look, Lewis is a light heavyweight and Braddock barely got the decision. If you put him into the ring against me, what do *you* think is going to happen?"

Graham remained silent.

"He's going to get hurt, that's what's going to happen," Demp-sey interjected. "That is, Max, if you start getting some sleep and stop chasing these women around."

"Chasing women around is the best exercise I know," Baer said. "They're harder to catch than washed-up Irishmen."

Their notebooks filled, the writers put down their pens and cut into their steaks.

Back at home, Jim Braddock felt like a man again. His children had been returned from their grandparents' care, and there was plenty of food on the table. He indulged in a few of his greatest pleasures: playing cards and going to the movies. His favorite card game was hearts; his favorite stars were Charlie Chaplin and Laurel and Hardy. There was no more tossing and turning in bed. There was no more rising at 2 A.M. to pace the streets in frustration. After defeating Lewis, he had not returned to the docks. Still, his future was far from assured. He did not yet dare move out of the basement apartment, and there was no splurg-ing. He woke up at five to run six or seven miles. He took the ferry to the West Side and walked from the river to Stillman's. Lasky's illness was a hard blow, but in the end it might have been the best thing for Braddock, who had more time to condition himself for the fifteen-round fight.

When Lasky was well enough to be discharged, he returned to California, where he was then living, to build up his strength. The fight was rescheduled for the ides of March, the fifteenth. At this time Gould resembled nothing so much as a perpetual motion machine, his head spinning and his legs churning as if he had been drawn by Rube Goldberg. He was constantly running from the Garden to Stillman's, back to the Garden, across the street to Jack Dempsey's, to the offices of the *Sun* and the *Mirror* and the *World*. He needed to know and he needed to plot. Schmeling was going to fight Hamas, who had just boarded a boat for Hamburg. If Hamas won, he might get the shot at Baer. If Schmeling won, he might get the shot. Then Gould worried about Carnera, who had spent most of the year insisting that he had hurt his ankle so badly in the early rounds of the Baer fight that he deserved a rematch. If he defeated Impellittiere, maybe he would get the shot. And then there was Lasky, out in California. He had been eager to fight Braddock, but now it seemed he was considering another opponent — Joe Louis, who was boxing in Los Angeles at the time. Gould got dizzy mulling over all the different possibilities. Powerless in the face of such uncertainty, he started itching for a fight with anyone.

But when Lasky watched Louis annihilate Lee Ramage in Los Angeles on February 21, he changed his mind about challenging Louis, who at the time was referred to as the "Detroit Negro." He wanted Braddock again. He went back to New York. But when he got there, he realized that he had not entirely overcome the lingering effects of pneumonia. His seconds informed Jimmy Johnston that they wanted a one-week postponement, which was granted. When thus informed, on March 5, Gould "hit the roof," as Shabazian put it. He complained bitterly that he and Braddock were being treated shabbily by the Garden, which was true. Johnston, always fond of Gould and Braddock, was nevertheless a businessman. Art Lasky had a future as a drawing card. Jim Braddock did not. Johnston intended to give Lasky a fighting chance to fight well.

After Gould made his displeasure known to Johnston, Lasky's handlers, and virtually every newspaperman in New York, he finally relented. He knew that he had no choice other than to accept March 22 as the new date for the fight. All the ranting did him some good, though. He felt cleansed. Psychologically, it also helped Braddock, who was reassured that Gould would do anything and say anything to press their case, whatever their case might be.

A few days later, though, Johnston told Gould that Lasky's manager, who was also his brother, had changed his mind. Lasky was ready to fight on March 15, and Johnston was prepared to move the fight back to that date to accommodate him. Joe Gould was no man's stooge, and this time he threw a fit worthy of his reputation. He told Johnston that Braddock would fight Lasky on March 22 or not at all. Then he stormed out of Johnston's office and went into hiding. He made it impossible for Johnston to contact him.

As Gould and Johnston sparred, Schmeling and Hamas fought. On March 10, as a sideshow to a Nazi rally, Schmeling took his revenge for the beating he had endured thirteen months earlier, dominating Hamas in front of 30,000 Germans intoxicated by Nazi rhetoric. In the ninth round, Schmeling delivered the knockout blow, and Hamas spent the next several days in a hospital. Gould checked his name off the list of contenders. Hamas eventually recovered, but his career did not.

Five days later, at Madison Square Garden, Carnera and Impellittiere, five hundred pounds of heavyweight between them, fought one of the most lackluster bouts in the history of the arena. Carnera won, but in such disappointing fashion that, Shabazian wrote, "his stock following the fight was lower than it had been prior to the event."

Lou Soresi, Carnera's manager, was convinced that Johnston never intended to give his fighter a shot at regaining the title and had secretly negotiated a battle between the Maxes (Baer and Schmeling) regardless of the outcome of the so-called elimination tournament. In a huff, he stormed out of Johnston's office, walked down the street to the office of the Twentieth Century Sporting Club — Mike Jacobs's rival promoting concern — and signed Carnera to fight Joe Louis, eliminating the former champion from the ranks of those who might fight Baer. Soresi, it turned out, had good instincts. The Garden was indeed planning to match Baer with Schmeling.

But to the considerable surprise and consternation of Johnston, Schmeling was also soon out of the picture. Despite the entreaties of his manager, Joe Jacobs, he made it clear that he was willing to fight Baer, but only in Germany, where he knew there was no chance he would be robbed, as he had been when he fought Sharkey. The German promoter Walter Rothenburg was prepared to offer Baer $300,000 to risk his title, and Schmeling considered the offer too good for Baer to refuse. He was wrong.

Schmeling's stubbornness made one thing very likely: whoever won the Lasky-Braddock fight would then fight Max Baer for the world heavyweight championship.

"You realize what this means?" Gould said to Braddock.

"Yeah, I got to beat Lasky," Braddock said.

"Don't even think about Baer. Let's just get through Lasky."

James J. Braddock had not fought a truly significant fight since 1929. He had had fights that were personally significant, but none that were very closely watched, none that could make an immediate impact on the world of boxing. The Lasky fight, though, was an event of great importance to even casual boxing fans. "Interest in the heavyweight division is at present at white heat," Joseph C. Nichols wrote in the *New York Times* on March 22, 1935, the day of the fight. Then, assessing the qualities of the three-to-one underdog, Nichols wrote, "Braddock is considered to be one of the heaviest hitters in the division, but he is not a scintillating ring general." At the advanced age of twenty-nine, Braddock was considered too old to be able to keep up with Lasky for fifteen rounds. And despite all the steaks he had been eating since defeating Lewis, he still weighed only 182 pounds at the weigh-in. Lasky, despite his recent bout with pneumonia, weighed 197 pounds.

In the first round, Lasky came right at Braddock. When he stuck out his chin, as Doc Robb and Solly Seeman had told Braddock he would, Braddock hit it cleanly. Lasky never recovered from the force of the blow. Using mostly his right hand, Braddock landed punch after punch with spectacular accuracy. Lasky was befuddled. He had never encountered a fighter whose aim matched Braddock's.

Braddock outfought Lasky in eleven of the fifteen rounds. He used his jab to set up his right. He moved gracefully. He looked nothing like the fighter who had struggled for five years against mediocre competition. In the end he won a unanimous decision. "Braddock demonstrated once more, and quite convincingly, that odds mean nothing to him," Nichols wrote after the fight.

But not everyone was convinced. "It was a good fight," Paul Gallico wrote in the *Daily News*, "especially interesting to one who is a keen student of boxing, because the two men fought the entire bout in slow motion."

Braddock and Gould celebrated that night at the Mayflower Hotel on Central Park West. They toasted their comeback. They toasted Tommy Loughran. More than anyone else, they toasted Corn Griffin.

The Monday morning after the fight, eager to collect his share of the purse, $4,100, Braddock walked to Madison Square Garden and sat down in a chair outside Jimmy Johnston's office. He waited for about ten minutes before the door opened and Gould emerged. "What are you doing out here?" Gould said. "Come on in." The leading contender for the heavyweight title was so accustomed to his humble spot *outside* Johnston's office that it never occurred to him that he could walk right in.

Inside Johnston's office, Gould, two other managers, and three writers, including Frank Graham, had been talking about the developing heavyweight situation. A police detective was sitting in one of Johnston's leather armchairs.

Braddock's face showed the marks of the previous night's events.

"Been in a fight?" Graham asked.

"No," Braddock said, "I ran into a door in the dark."

"I never knew you were such a good boxer," the detective said. (He also didn't know that Braddock had a history of assaulting lawmen.)

"You didn't think I knew what to do with my left hand, eh? I was always a pretty good boxer, but when I got in there I usually didn't do much boxing."

"You mean," the detective said, "that fighters don't begin to get smart until they get old."

"You don't get smart in this business," Braddock said. "You just get cute."

"We haven't had a fight around here in a long time that stirred people up like that one," Graham said. "I met some hardboiled guys after the fight that told me they were praying for you. Did you know that?"

Braddock smiled, despite his bruises. Then he said, "The priest over in my parish told me that after mass on Saturday morning he met a lady coming out of the church and she said to him, 'I was listening to Jimmy Braddock's fight on the radio last night, and all the time I was listening to it, I was praying.' And the priest said, 'What do you think I was doing?'"

After Braddock cashed the Garden's check, he took the ferry back to Weehawken — his brother Al was at the helm — and drove with his brother Joe to North Bergen. Joe pulled up in front of the municipal building, and Jim went inside. Again he found Jimmy Kelly, who four months earlier had removed his name from the relief rolls.

"This is for you," Braddock said, handing Kelly an envelope.

"What have you got in there?" Kelly said.

"Just what I owe you."

"What do you mean? You don't owe me anything." Kelly opened the envelope. Inside was three hundred dollars in small bills.

"That's the relief money. I'm paying it back."

"Jim, you know that's not necessary."

"It is to me," Braddock said.

But Kelly wouldn't take Braddock's cash. "Keep the money for now," he said. "You can pay it when you win the title."

Braddock insisted on giving Kelly an IOU, payable July 1.

That afternoon in Manhattan, Joe Gould told Jimmy Johnston that he had no intention of allowing his fighter to get in the ring with Primo Carnera, the recent conqueror of Ray Impellittiere — he was holding out for the title shot. Johnston's elimination tournament, which should have matched Braddock against Carnera and the winner of that bout against Baer, was falling apart. Meanwhile, Carnera had informed Johnston that he had no intention of fighting Braddock and that he would honor his contract to fight Joe Louis. Then Gould told the newspapers that Braddock would fight only Baer or Schmeling. But Schmeling made it clear that he would only fight Baer and only in Germany. Schmeling, Braddock, and Carnera were not under contract to fight for Madison Square Garden, so Johnston was stuck. He didn't relish the thought of matching the world heavyweight champion against Braddock, who was still considered over the hill, despite his three successive victories. But if Schmeling wouldn't budge, Johnston would have no choice.

At its meeting on March 26, with Braddock and Gould in attendance, the state athletic commission took the decision out of Johnston's hands. Phelan, Wear, and Bill Brown — Braddock's biggest fan among the three commissioners — decided that Jim Braddock, rather than the former champion Schmeling or the former champion Carnera, deserved a shot at the title. They unanimously named Braddock the mandatory challenger for Max Baer's heavyweight title.

"The commissioners asked me if I thought I had a good chance with Baer," Braddock told the reporters who were crowding the hallway outside the commission's offices. "I told them I thought I had. I not only have a good right, but I've developed a good left, and I never felt so well before in my life."

Before they dismissed Braddock and Gould, the commissioners insisted that they sign a contract — with each other, in conformity with the commission's rules. They had been working together without a contract since 1927, when their first contract expired.

"How long should I make it for?" Gould asked Braddock.

"Fifty years," Braddock said. "We should both be retired by then."

There was one loophole that could have prevented a Baer-Braddock championship fight. If Schmeling was willing to fight Braddock, the commission would sanction the winner of that fight as Baer's next opponent. But if Schmeling wouldn't fight Braddock, then Braddock would fight Baer.

When Max Baer and Ancil Hoffman were told that Braddock had been designated the official challenger, they scoffed. "Hell," Baer said, "they call me a clown, but I couldn't pull anything funnier than to name such a has-been as a challenger for the title. Why, five years ago that same commission wouldn't let me fight Braddock, told me to find a stronger opponent. And now I'm supposed to fight Braddock! I suppose this Brown is serious about this. But if he is, I suggest Braddock fight my brother Buddy. Buddy will knock him right out of the ring and into Commissioner Brown's lap. There are three better challengers than Braddock. I don't think Braddock can stand up to Carnera, Schmeling, or Joe Louis. I licked Carnera and Schmeling, and Louis's managers say he isn't ready to fight me yet. Let Braddock beat any one of those fellows and Commissioner Brown will have a leg to stand on. I am supposed to be only a dumb fighter, but if I cannot make matches better than the New York commission, I'll go back to herding cows."

"That's a big joke," Hoffman said, reacting to Braddock's designation as the number-one challenger. "Say, I can take Buddy back there and he could knock out Braddock. Braddock wouldn't draw flies. Buddy could beat Braddock and I bet he could knock out Art Lasky in four rounds."

Baer and Hoffman had nothing personal against Braddock. But they were both in the fight game to make money, and they both thought that Braddock would cost them. Baer had lost his passion for the sport five years earlier. Ever since, he had boxed because it was a means to a lucrative end. He had boxed because he was good at it. He had boxed because he liked being famous — and he was good at that too. He had boxed because he thought it made him more attractive to women. He didn't care whether Braddock deserved a shot. "If he needs money so badly," Baer said as he was traveling back east to train for the fight, "I'll let him be one of my sparring partners." In truth, Baer didn't like boxing. And after he had defeated Schmeling and Carnera so easily, his respect for the sport, already minimal, vanished. He reasoned that if he could so thoroughly dominate two champions, boxing couldn't be very difficult.

For Braddock, though, boxing was a way of life. The sport had battered him, and in the end that made him respect it more, the way a cancer survivor learns to respect the disease that almost killed him. Boxing was Braddock's identity. It was his passion. When he stepped into the ring, he did so knowing that he had sacrificed a lot for the sport. He had labored in its dingy clubs. He had sweated and suffered and persevered. Now boxing was finally rewarding him, six years after he lost to Tommy Loughran.

On April 2, despite Braddock's designation as the official challenger, Baer was in Chicago insulting him — and just about everyone else in the heavyweight division. He said Braddock didn't deserve to be mentioned in the same breath with him. Moving on to Joe Louis, he said, "Louis is just a third-rater and no better than my brother Buddy." And referring to the possibility of a rematch with Schmeling, he said, "Max can bring Hitler along to referee a bout if $250,000 is posted."

But three days later, at Jack Dempsey's restaurant, Max Baer and Jim Braddock had lunch together with the media to promote a fight that had yet to be scheduled. Gould was furious with Baer. He and everyone else in the United States had been reading Baer's disparaging comments about Braddock. When he saw the champion, he marched right up to him and wagged a finger at him. "Now tell Jim to his face what you've been shouting to the newspapermen all over the country," he said.

Flummoxed by the short, aggressive man who seemed to be challenging him to a fight, Baer turned to Braddock and said, "Oh, why, hello, Jimmy. I'm glad you licked Lasky, he needed a licking. Congratulations."

"Is that all you've got to say?" said Gould, now shaking with indignation. He wasn't pulling a stunt. He was genuinely angry.

Then, with flashbulbs popping and pens scribbling, Baer took Braddock's hand in his and said, "You can knock anyone down with that right, but if I fight you, I will hurt you."

Braddock did not want to be drawn into a debate, which he knew he would lose. In a strange way, he felt sorry for Baer. Why would Baer bother baiting him if he didn't harbor some self-doubt? So Braddock listened quietly as Gould and Baer sparred and as Baer casually dismissed Braddock's chances of defeating him. "I want three fights this year," Baer said. "And I am willing to fight anyone if I can be shown there will be money in it."

Frank Graham spoke up. "What about Schmeling?" he said.

"I'll meet anyone, anywhere, if they will show me the money, Berlin barred," Baer said.

Meanwhile, Jimmy Johnston was still hoping that he could get Schmeling to agree to fight Baer in the United States. He too was convinced that Braddock "couldn't draw flies," as Hoffman had put it. Finally, though, on April 11 — four days before his contractual deadline to name an opponent for Baer or lose the rights to the title defense — Johnston gave up on Schmeling and accepted the grim reality that James J. Braddock of North Bergen, New Jersey, would fight the great Max Baer for the world heavyweight championship. He told Gould the fight was on, for either June 6 or June 13, at the Madison Square Garden Bowl, the same arena where Corn Griffin had jump-started Braddock's comeback the previous June.

On April 13, with Gould hovering over his shoulder, Braddock signed the contract in Johnston's office, in the presence of several reporters and photographers. He would receive 15 percent of the gate, 2.5 percent more than a challenger would usually receive, with the stipulation that if he won the title, he would make his first defense under the Garden's auspices. If the fight made $200,000 — a conservative estimate — Braddock and Gould would split $30,000. Barring injury, they would be, if not wildly rich, comfortable. Baer would receive 42.5 percent of the gross receipts, $85,000 if the fight made $200,000.

Braddock put down the pen, shook Johnston's hand, stood up, and embraced Gould. He was wearing a gray flannel suit. In stark contrast to Baer, whose suits, shirts, and ties were custom-made and fit perfectly, Braddock in a tie looked like a man with a noose around his neck. Digging his forefinger into the tight space between his neck and his collar, he turned to the reporters and said, "I've studied Baer's style, and I think it's made to order for me. Anyway, I believe that good things come in threes. I've licked two coast battlers [Lewis and Lasky, although Lewis was really an Arizonan and Lasky was a Minnesotan], and Max will be the third."

Braddock didn't quite throw down the gauntlet — that wasn't his style — but he undeniably exuded confidence.

Gould said that he was in the process of locating a training camp, probably somewhere in the Catskill Mountains, about a hundred miles north of the city. They would definitely not set up camp in Saratoga Springs, where Braddock had trained for Loughran. The place was bad luck, Gould said.

Hoffman was still balking. He threatened to accept the offer to fight Schmeling in Germany for $300,000. "Why should we fight Braddock in New York for peanuts?" he said. "We'll go over there and collect the big money, that's what we'll do. Let the New York commission suspend us. So what? When they name an opponent who we figure will draw some money, then we'll return to New York to fight and the suspension will be lifted."

But the German offer wasn't too good to refuse. It was too good to be true. Rothenburg, the German promoter, didn't have the cash. Baer would have to fight Braddock.

"I'll fight Braddock in June," Baer said. "Then I'll fight Louis or Carnera in the fall. That's when I'll make some real money."

As unpopular as Baer had been with the commission prior to the Carnera fight, he had somehow managed to make himself even less popular now. Johnston, who had once seen dollar signs when he looked at Baer, now despised him and Hoffman.

The fight was finally made official. The date was set for June 13. Baer signed his contract. No one seemed to care. It was widely assumed that Braddock was still an unfit opponent for Baer, that Baer would defeat him even more easily than he had defeated Schmeling and Carnera. Hoffman and Baer seemed to be correct: Braddock couldn't draw flies. The newspapermen tried as hard as they could to make his story compelling. They wrote about his months on the docks and the fight against Feldman. They rehashed his numerous upset wins and his mystifying losses. Still, James J. Braddock wasn't connecting with the fighting public, which had been reading about Max the Invincible for almost a year. And of course Baer really did look invincible. He was younger than Braddock, stronger than Braddock, heavier than Braddock; unlike Braddock, he hadn't lost a fight in four years; unlike Braddock, he hadn't lost twenty fights to relative no-names like Al Stillman and Lou Scozza. If Braddock was underestimated, it was only because he deserved to be underestimated.

After a four-year ceasefire, Braddock was back in John Kieran's sights. "Braddock has been around for years," Kieran reminded his readers. "He has lost many fights to run-of-the-mine [sic] heavyweights. He lately staged a belated sprint to make up much lost ground. But he still was James J. Braddock."

On April 25, Baer was in St. Louis to fight an exhibition against Babe Hunt. When asked about his future in the ring, he was completely unenthusiastic. He said matter-of-factly that he would defend his title two or three times and then quit, so that Buddy could succeed him as heavyweight champion. "Three more fights at the most and I'll be able to say goodbye to the fight game," he said. "This racket's too tough. First it will be Braddock. Then Joe Louis — if he beats Carnera — then maybe Schmeling in England. Those fights will give me enough money. And I'll appoint my brother Buddy as my successor and let him defend the title against outstanding fighters."

Back in New York, Dempsey read Baer's comments and groaned. His protégé was a public relations disaster. Fans didn't want a reluctant champion — they wanted a dark destroyer, like Dempsey. They didn't want a conflicted champion — they wanted a proud warrior, like Tunney. It was hard enough getting cash-poor Americans to spend money on boxing without the sport's heavyweight champion sounding like Hamlet. Instead of building up Braddock, Baer dismissed him as if he were an amateur. Instead of generating interest in the fight, he talked about it with no discernible enthusiasm. If Baer didn't care about the fight, why would anyone else? These issues weren't really Dempsey's problems — he had no financial interest in the bout — but it worried him that Baer sounded so flat. Seven weeks before his first title defense, Baer should have been psychologically, if not physically, prepared. But in fact he was distracted and ambivalent.

Hoffman didn't help. As far as he was concerned, the Braddock fight was little more than an exhibition, and he treated it as such. On May 8 he finalized a deal to fight Schmeling on August 17 at Wembley Stadium in London. It is likely that the thought never occurred to him that on August 17, Baer might not still be in possession of the heavyweight championship.

16

Homicide Hall

....

Loch Sheldrake, New York:
Spring 1935

Adhering to a tradition that dates back to the earliest days of prizefighting, Gould searched for a quiet, rural, and remote training camp. Before a big bout, fighters since John L. Sullivan have relocated to the countryside, where it is assumed they can focus more easily on their training, evading the noise and distractions of the city. Gould settled on the Hotel Evans in Loch Sheldrake, New York. In the Catskills, Loch Sheldrake was in fact quiet, rural, and remote. Braddock arrived on April 27, seven weeks before the fight, and moved into a log cabin several hundred yards from the hotel's main building. The cabin featured running water and electricity, but those were the only luxuries.

For the first two weeks Braddock trained in serene solitude, without Doc Robb or Solly Seeman overseeing his workouts, which were limited to long runs and shadowboxing. Every morning at five o'clock he woke up in the darkness. He waited for daylight and then ran eight to ten miles through the chilly countryside, rarely encountering humans or automobiles. By the time he had finished running, the sun was climbing rapidly and it was time to eat an enormous breakfast — a ham steak and six eggs, six pancakes, a loaf of toasted bread, coffee, and juice. Then he would take a nap for an hour. Then he would shadowbox. Then he would eat lunch. Then he would rest or play cards with the brothers who owned the hotel. Then he would eat a steak dinner, with French fries, vegetables, and a chocolate sundae for dessert. In the cool night air, as the sun was setting, he would drink a cup of warm milk. Then, at about eight o'clock, he would go to sleep in the single bed in the cabin.

By the time Robb and Seeman arrived in early May, five weeks before the fight, Braddock was bigger than he had ever before been — in more ways than one. At 220 pounds, he had gained nearly 40 pounds since the Lasky fight just six weeks earlier. More surprising, he had grown a full inch since Robb and Seeman had last seen him and was now six foot three. Lending credence to the widely accepted theory that Irishmen were late bloomers, Braddock said that his father had had a similar growth spurt in his late twenties. Still, the writers who traveled to Loch Sheldrake were astounded by Braddock's physical development. They wrote excitedly about his "amazing transformation." Lud Shabazian, who went to Loch Sheldrake with his wife, Josephine, said that Braddock had undergone a metamorphosis and wondered if he was now *too* heavy.

The weight angle, though, was easily overshadowed by a more compelling development. On May 2, Jim Braddock suddenly and unwillingly became an international celebrity.

Back home in Hudson County, Mayor Julius L. Reich of North Bergen was running for reelection against Commissioner Paul Cullum, at the time a political ally of Commissioner Harry Buesser, Braddock's old friend. The election was two weeks away, and Reich could see that his job was in jeopardy. Cullum and Buesser were aligned with Frank Hague, the mayor of Jersey City and the boss of a powerful political machine. On May 2, in a speech intended to discredit Cullum and Buesser, Reich charged that they had mismanaged the town's relief office. As evidence, he offered the example of James J. Braddock. Reich wanted to know how a man who was about to fight for the world heavyweight championship had managed to qualify for relief. He demanded answers.

When word spread that Braddock was on relief, dozens of reporters pointed their cars for Loch Sheldrake, where they found Braddock in an uncharacteristically snippy mood. He pointed out that he was no longer on relief, explained what the situation had been, and said, "I'm not ashamed. Personally, I didn't mind being hungry, but the kids needed to eat. I had to put food on the table."

Although Reich was wrong, the story was splashed across the front pages of newspapers from San Francisco to London. The Associated Press story that ran in thousands of papers on May 3, 1935, began, "The story of relief case No. 2796 and a battle against odds that dwarf anything James J. Braddock will face in a prize ring June 13 against heavyweight champion Max Baer was revealed yesterday." The story, like dozens, if not hundreds, of others that appeared shortly after Reich's comments, told Braddock's sad tale — how he had lost everything and been reduced to accepting charity from the government. Braddock made sure that everyone knew he had offered to pay back every cent — and then some.

"As soon as I was paid off for the Lasky fight, I gave three hundred dollars to the relief funds of Union City," he told a group of reporters, not getting into details about the IOU. He had interrupted his workout to clear the air and was wearing a gray sweatshirt and sweatpants, and his hair was damp with perspiration. His tone was defensive. "That covered the two hundred and forty dollars I got all told when we were on relief. It was the only fair thing to do."

Even though he repeatedly said he was not ashamed, he *was* ashamed — and angry. He didn't want the world to know how desperate his financial situation had been. He also resented being a political football. The relief story was good for business but bad for his mood. Before the world knew he had been on relief, he had been nearly anonymous. Those who knew him considered him little more than a lamb to be slaughtered by Max Baer. After the relief story broke, he became, overnight, the hero of the masses. In the *Daily News*, Jack Miley described the nature of his newfound appeal: "He has been down and out, on relief, and all but counted out in the game of life. He's an underdog of underdogs, a fellow who has taken his tough breaks without a squawk and has kept on punching — and Joe Public and his pals love this type of guy!"

Interest in the fight, virtually nonexistent on May 2, grew exponentially. Finally the papers had a story to attach to the fight and to sell. Initially indifferent, the London tabloids dispatched correspondents across the Atlantic to chronicle the bout, which was now being billed as Baer the Playboy versus Braddock the Relief Recipient. The *Jersey Journal*'s headline was typical:

COULDN'T LET KIDS STARVE,
SO JIM BRADDOCK WENT ON
RELIEF AND ISN'T ASHAMED

In the annals of political gaffes, Reich's must be accorded special status. Not surprisingly, his attack, aimed at Cullum but implicating and embarrassing Braddock, North Bergen's favorite son, backfired. Responding to Reich's charges, Joe Braddock Junior took the stump for the opposition. "By the power of his brain and brawn, Jim rose to the top of his profession," Joe said during a speech at a fundraising dinner for the local Democratic organization on May 3. "He was always honest and decent, and that is why he is admired all over the country today."

On May 14, Reich was defeated by Cullum, who would remain in office for fifteen years. At Loch Sheldrake, Jim Braddock stayed up unusually late that night, waiting for news of the returns. When Gould told him that Reich had lost, he smiled and went to bed.

"That'll show him," Francis Albertanti, who was in attendance at the challenger's camp, said to Gould.

"Whaddya mean?" Gould said. "We should send Reich a check."

Meanwhile, Baer had pitched camp in Asbury Park on the Jersey shore, the same place he had trained for the Carnera fight. If Braddock's camp was spartan, Baer's was bacchanalian. Once again it was a carnival, replete with strongmen and dwarves. Convinced that Braddock was incapable of defeating him, Baer couldn't bring himself really to fight his sparring partners. Instead he clowned with them and mugged for the writers and fans who stood at ringside. Every day Dynamite Jackson made Baer look awkward, which he was not, and lazy, which he was. Baer was nursing a sore hand and a black eye that he had suffered in one of his exhibition fights. Even wrapped in large, padded gloves, his hands ached whenever he landed a punch.

On May 9, his first full day of training, Baer was, typically, not training too hard. After about an hour of mugging for the fans and waving his fists in mock anger at his sparring partners, he went to the Berkeley Carteret Hotel to rehearse a radio skit. The skit called for him to fire a gun loaded with a blank thirty-two-caliber cartridge, which he prematurely discharged. The wad of paper sealing the powder flew into his chest, producing a six-inch burn. The wad also struck Peggy La Centra, his leading lady, in the face. Together they were rushed to the Hazard Hospital in Long Branch, where they were attended by Dr. Elmer N. Hazard himself. The burn wasn't serious, but there were concerns that an infection would develop. Assuaging the fears of the newspapermen, Johnston, who had been apprised of the accident by Hoffman, said, "They have given Baer an injection of serum as a precaution against lockjaw, and after a few days he will be all right. Unless something unforeseen happens, the fight will be held on June 13."

Two days later Baer was back in his trunks. In the ring, when he was performing for the crowds — fans from New York, curious young women, small boys, and, always, old fighters like Philadelphia Jack O'Brien — he exuded confidence. But as the fight drew closer, he started having doubts. As reports filtered back from Loch Sheldrake, and as details emerged about Braddock's life on the docks and on relief, Baer reconsidered the qualities of the man he had mocked for the previous two months.

"I didn't want the Braddock match in the first place," he told Edward Van Every of the *New York Sun* on May 18, four weeks before the fight. "It's one of those fights in which you get no credit if you win. Of course, I never would have belittled him as an opponent if I had known I was going to get mitts like these." Baer held up his gnarled fists. "Of course I'll belt him out," he continued, "but by being too brash with my tongue, I've put myself on the spot if I don't do the job inside four or five rounds. Now if my hands ain't right, that's not going to be a cinch, but if I say anything of that sort at this stage, they'll say I'm trying to build up Braddock for gate purposes. They'll overlook the fact that Braddock is a guy with a world of heart — he ain't going to go dead on you until he's out. I'm not superstitious, but there's no getting away from it, the breaks are with him. If they weren't, he wouldn't be in there with me, would he? So, here I am with bum mitts, an opponent with a world of guts, fighting in an arena where the title always changes hands, and meeting a man who is desperate to win. Does all that mean I'm in for a helluva time? I may be crazy, but I'm no fool."

A month before the fight, despite his bravado, Baer was setting up his defense in case he lost. It was an odd thing for a champion, especially an enormous favorite, to do. Self-doubt had somehow crept into his mind. For a fighter, self-doubt is a terminal disease.

Baer's camp was similar in every way to his camp a year earlier, except for the absence of Mike Cantwell. After winning the title, Baer and Cantwell — who had trained him for his last four fights — had quarreled and separated. Not surprisingly, Cantwell wanted Baer to spend less time carousing and more time training; Baer finally decided he didn't need a taskmaster. In the weeks leading up to the Braddock fight, Cantwell joined the Braddock camp, where he provided inside information on the champion. More than anything else, he encouraged Braddock to focus his fighting energies on body blows. "Carry the fight to Baer's body," he told Braddock one day while they were playing cards, "and the world's heavyweight championship will change hands." Braddock, looking for any edge, listened closely.

As the camp's resident expert on the enemy, Cantwell was sought out by the writers too. "I was with Baer against Schaaf, Tuffy Griffiths, Max Schmeling, and Carnera, and I know that not one of those boxers paid any attention to Max's midsection," he told them. "Watching Braddock, I perceive that the New Jersey boy can send them downstairs. He uses three punches to the midsection that should have a devastating effect on the champion. His left hook, left uppercut, and right to the kidney are good enough to bring down Baer, who has no defense for these wallops.

"Max and I are good friends," Cantwell concluded, "but that does not blind me to his weaknesses." He could have meant Baer's weakness for women or his weakness for nightlife, but he actually meant his weaknesses in the ring, which had been overlooked as he climbed to the championship.

After the furor over relief case 2796 died down in late May — the reporters finally stopped asking Braddock what it had been like to be so desperate — Loch Sheldrake was curiously, almost eerily, quiet. Barney Ross and Jimmy McLarnin were training nearby for their upcoming welterweight championship fight, and the boxing writers turned their focus to them. What they missed was one of the strangest camps ever.

Even before the fight was scheduled, Gould had decided that the way to defeat Baer was by attrition. His chin was too solid to expect a knockout. Braddock would have to weather a relentless barrage of withering rights, neutralize them with his left hand, and above all else be prepared to fight a full fifteen rounds. Gould thought that Baer would go for the quick knockout; based on what he knew about his training camp, he thought Baer would be in no shape to fight hard for fifteen rounds. If Braddock could withstand his early assaults, Baer would be an easy target in the later rounds.

With that strategy in mind, Gould assembled a murderer's row of sparring partners. There was Paul Pross, a 210-pound German whose father had been killed on the western front the day Pross was born. There was Norman Barnett, who had been a fullback at the University of Maryland. There was Jack McCarthy, a rugged former sparring partner of Jack Sharkey's. And there was Don Petrin, the speediest of the group, who had lost his job sparring with Schmeling in 1930 when he made the Black Uhlan look vulnerable.

The superior quality of the sparring partners wasn't all that made the camp unusual. It was their mandated fierceness. Gould ordered them to give Braddock no quarter. "There are no restrictions on the sparring mates," the *New York Times* reported. "They are under instructions to give Braddock the best they have."

Gould was determined to make Braddock's camp the most grueling ever conceived. The sparring partners switched off after every round, so Robb threw a fresh opponent into the ring every three minutes. When Braddock wasn't sparring, he was running along the country roads, jumping rope, and shadowboxing. When he was sparring, he wasn't really sparring, he was fighting. In the *Daily News*, Jack Miley called the camp "Homicide Hall." Miley's colleague Paul Gallico wrote,

James J. has the roughest crew of spar boys ever assembled at any heavyweight's training camp, and from 4 to 4:45 every afternoon, he amuses himself by prizefighting with them. And when I say prizefighting, that is also what I mean. For this business that goes on by the bonnie banks of Loch Sheldrake can by no stretch of the imagination be called sparring. It is fighting pure and simple. It is really the screwiest training camp you ever saw. Braddock has four big, strong guys, all of whom can fight, and he stays in there for six rounds and fights them while Joe Gould, his manager, sits back on his haunches and rocks with glee.

Gould was as amazed as everyone else by Braddock's physical transformation. By late May, Braddock was a chiseled 198 pounds — the roadwork and the sparring had burned off the excess weight. On May 21, three weeks before the fight, Jack Dempsey drove up to Loch Sheldrake to see the new Braddock, and Homicide Hall, for himself. What he found was an entirely different fighter from the one he had first seen in the 1920s. Braddock was bigger, stronger, and infinitely more nimble in 1935 than he had been in 1928. Dempsey, who joined Braddock and Gould for lunch, was impressed. "Baer better not take Braddock lightly," the Manassa Mauler said within earshot of Braddock. "The kid's training to fight forty rounds."

Still awed by his childhood hero, Braddock, so accustomed to disparagement, was encouraged by Dempsey's compliment. He also knew that Dempsey was well aware of Baer's state of preparedness. If Dempsey said Baer was in trouble, he probably was.

But on the same day that Dempsey visited the Hotel Evans, Baer boxed nine good rounds with five different sparring partners at Asbury Park. "The most impressive feature of his workout was the seriousness with which he attacked his training," Fred Van Ness wrote in the *Times*. "Gone were the clownish antics that have always marked his sparring bouts in camp."

Baer was still favoring his right hand, though, the one that had been injured fighting an exhibition. "The hand is not sore and has come along fine," he said, "but I am not going to take any chances with it. I'm saving it for Braddock."

At Loch Sheldrake, Gould could see that the grueling sparring sessions were achieving the desired effect. Braddock's left hand was evolving into a weapon nearly as potent as his right, and he was in a jovial mood. It helped that Mae was with him. Her presence was a rank violation of boxing protocol, but it was no more exceptional than all the other quirks of the camp. At night, Braddock, Mae, Gould, Robb, the hotel proprietors, and Albertanti played hearts and poker.

As the fight approached, though, Gould got more anxious. He developed a verbal tic: he would repeat, over and over, "Braddock's gonna win, Braddock's gonna win." "If there's a doctor in the house, we think he ought to do something for Mr. Joe Gould," Damon Runyon wrote in the *New York American*, "before paying attention to any other patients."

On Friday, May 24, twenty days before he was scheduled to fight Baer, Braddock and his sparring partners engaged in typically brutal combat. Braddock took a shot to the ribs, a hard, solid punch that made him gasp. He shook it off and kept fighting. But late that night his breathing became labored. Every time he drew a breath, he winced. Finally he had to tell Gould. "Joe, it's my ribs," he said. "They're killing me."

Gould sighed loudly. If Braddock had a broken rib, the fight might have to be postponed, which would be disastrous. Anything could happen before they got back into the ring. Schmeling could change his mind. Baer could decide to fight outside New York State. More than anything else, it would be almost impossible to get Braddock back into peak form.

Gould made a bold decision. "Get in the car," he said. "We're driving back to Jersey. We'll go see Doc McDonnell."

Dr. M. J. McDonnell of North Bergen was Braddock's family physician. His office was more than a hundred miles away. Gould called him and told him to expect them around 2 A.M.

They jumped in the car with Solly Seeman and took off. For two hours, while Braddock sat glumly in the front seat and tried to ignore the pain, Gould plotted. If Braddock was too injured to fight, he would have to ask Johnston for a postponement. It would not be a pleasant conversation. But even if Braddock was not seriously hurt, Gould had to find a way to keep the injury out of the papers. If Baer knew that Braddock's ribs were sore, he would pound at them mercilessly.

When they got to North Bergen, Gould rapped loudly at Doc McDonnell's door. Swearing the doctor to secrecy, he explained what had happened and why his silence was crucial. McDonnell then examined Braddock.

"He has a badly dented rib," McDonnell finally announced. "And some of the muscles underneath the rib are torn."

"How long will it take to heal up?" Gould asked. Braddock remained silent.

"Well, maybe nine or ten days. But he will have to lay off boxing entirely for that period. And he will also have to protect the damaged side with some kind of a brace."

"Please, doc, don't say a word about it to anybody, please."

Gould then made another bold decision. Instead of returning to Loch Sheldrake, he and Braddock would spend the next few days in New York. They could not afford to take the chance that the writers at camp would figure out what had happened. And in any event, Braddock had to be back in New Jersey two nights later for a testimonial dinner being held in his honor. Albertanti would tell the writers at Loch Sheldrake that he had left for New Jersey to see his mother, who had suddenly fallen ill, and that he was staying in the city because it made no sense to make another round trip to attend the dinner on Sunday night.

Fortunately for Braddock and Gould, only one writer showed up at Loch Sheldrake on Saturday, Lud Shabazian. When Albertanti gave him the official story, Shabazian got in his car and drove eight miles down the road to Barney Ross's camp. On Sunday, not a single writer went to Loch Sheldrake. They had all headed back to New York to cover the final preparations for the Ross-McLarnin championship fight, which was to take place Tuesday night at the Polo Grounds.

On Saturday and Sunday, Braddock spent most of his time on the couch in Gould's apartment on Central Park West. He could easily have regretted the brutality of his camp, but he never questioned Gould's strategy. He simply prayed that the rib would heal. If it didn't, he decided, he would fight Baer anyway. There was no way he was risking the loss of $30,000. He had fought for years with excruciating pain in his right hand. The rib had almost three weeks to heal. It would heal, he thought. It had to heal.

On Sunday, Braddock and Gould drove together to the Union City Elks Club to attend the dinner being held in the fighter's honor. A group calling itself the Braddock Boosters had arranged the event. The boosters were eager but, like Braddock, underfunded; the caterer refused to put out the food until he received full payment. The radio announcer Jackie Farrell was the master of ceremonies, and the featured speakers included Jack Dempsey, Jimmy Johnston, former light heavyweight champion Philadelphia Jack O'Brien, three U.S. representatives, and Joseph Braddock, Sr., who said to the crowd of twelve hundred people, "You have paid my boy a fine tribute. May the best man win."

Gene Tunney sent an inspirational telegram that Farrell read aloud. Johnston said in his speech that he had tried to make Braddock go away by matching him against Griffin, Lewis, and Lasky but had been foiled each time. Braddock had made him a believer. "If he is in good condition," he said, unaware that at that moment pain was shooting through Braddock's rib cage, "he will knock Baer's head off."

By all accounts, the crowd showered Braddock with genuine affection. He was moved and more determined than ever to go on with the fight.

"It was the most impressive, spontaneous tribute ever paid

to a fighter," Murray Robinson wrote in the *Newark Star Eagle*. "Baer's dinner stood out in sharp contrast. There was no personal bond between the Californian and the merrymakers. They came chiefly because they wanted to get a closeup of the Livermore Lothario and because the party was thrown at a very nice spot."

Braddock and Gould drove back to Loch Sheldrake immediately after the dinner. Gould was worried that Braddock's injury would be discovered. He really didn't know how he would explain to the writers for five or six consecutive days why Braddock wasn't sparring.

But there were no writers on the grounds of the Hotel Evans on Monday. Or Tuesday. Or Wednesday. Or Thursday. They were all either covering the Ross-McLarnin fight and its controversial aftermath — Ross won a disputed decision — or visiting Asbury Park to see the champion.

As Braddock healed, his anxiety slowly dissipated. It became clear that no one was ever going to know he had been hurt.

"How did we get so lucky?" Gould said to Robb.

"We were due," Robb said.

On Wednesday, Baer looked particularly strong sparring with four different fighters. The *Times* headline said, "Baer Rapidly Nearing Top Form." He injured a knuckle on his left hand when he hit one of his sparring partners on the head, but Hoffman was so confident that he told the writers he was planning for two more fights before the end of the summer, the one against Schmeling in London and one against Joe Louis.

Hoffman's confidence began rubbing off on the media. "Jersey James is just a journeyman pugilist compared to the hard-hitting Harlequin of Hollywood, the playboy of the pugilistic world," John Kieran wrote in the *Times* on May 31, thirteen days before the fight.

In the *New York Evening Journal*, the cartoonist Burris Jenkins sized up Baer versus Braddock. In his sketch, Baer swings with his right, labeled Cold Facts, and Braddock counters with his left, labeled Public Sympathy, Wishes, and Hopes. Next to Baer, Jenkins wrote, "Stronger, Bigger, Tougher, Faster, Younger, Hits Harder, Better Record, Endurance, Thinks Quicker, A Killer When Roused." Next to Braddock, he wrote, "Swell Fellow, Deserves a Break, Dead Game, Wife and Kids, Fighting Heart, Broke Last Year, The Luck of the Irish."

On June 1, after a week's hiatus, Braddock got back in the ring. Despite his supposed lack of drawing power, four hundred writers and fans, none of them aware of his aching rib, showed up to watch him spar six rounds. Gould and Robb had a special leather protector assembled, which Braddock wore under two sweatshirts to conceal it, despite temperatures in the nineties. To Gould's surprise, Braddock looked sharper after a week off than he had looked when he got hurt. Even under the weight of the protector and the sweatshirts, he was moving well and punching crisply. Gould and Braddock both came to realize that he had needed a break — just not a broken rib. "Maybe I should take a few more days off," he joked.

With twelve days to go, Braddock's confidence was restored. The writers were impressed. In the *Sun*, Edward Van Every compared Braddock's sense of himself to Gene Tunney's "on the eve of his first battle with Dempsey." Watching Braddock work out, Trevor Wignall, the dean of the English boxing writers, told Shabazian, "Why, this fellow is a good boxer. I never thought he could move like that. Our impression was that he was a clumsy, slow-footed heavyweight whose right-hand punch was his lone stock in trade." Bill Brown, typically a scold, was also impressed with Braddock, but he issued a warning: "He is a little open for a right-hand punch. He will have to tighten his defense."

On June 6, Frank Graham, Braddock's closest friend among the New York columnists, showed up at Loch Sheldrake. Sitting in the sun outside the log cabin in which the ring had been set up, he and Braddock talked about the remarkable events of the previous twelve months. They talked about the docks.

"I never went down to those piers in the morning without hoping it would be the last time," Braddock said. "I knew that Joe was looking around, trying to find a spot for me, and I figured that someday he'd find one. They keep asking me what's going to happen in this fight. I tell them all I don't know — but it will be a hell of a fight."

Later in the afternoon, Graham talked to Gould, who had just gotten off the phone with Johnston for the fifth time that day. Gould paid tribute to his best friend's toughness. "Here's something I bet you never thought of," he said to Graham. "How is it that Braddock, a big, slow-moving, slow-thinking guy, has outlasted so many fellows of that type who started about the same time he did? Risko, Berlenbach, all those rough, tough fellows like Jim, punchers who would take a punch to land one — they're all washed up, and here, after ten years of it, Jim not only is still fighting, but he's better than ever. Do you know the answer to that one? Well, here it is. He ain't a smart fighter, but he's cute. He gets hit with many a punch, but he don't get hit with the hard ones. Mind, he don't take the others on purpose, but it just seems that when the hard ones come whistling at him, he blocks them or steps back or ducks or something.

"They've been throwing knockout punches at him for ten years, but they haven't nailed him yet. Don't tell me this Baer will nail him either. Max ain't going to be in there this time with a big goop like Carnera that will pull back into the path of those roundhouse rights. He's going to be in there with a guy that's cute."

On Friday, June 8, Braddock turned thirty, though the newspapermen thought he was turning twenty-nine. For some reason, Braddock had been telling people since his pro debut that he was born in 1906, not 1905. He celebrated his birthday by shadowboxing for eight rounds, even though Gould had given him the day off.

The next day, though, his disposition turned sour. He woke up, took one look at the barren log cabin in which he had been living for six weeks, and was suddenly sick of Loch Sheldrake. Instead of greeting everyone from Gould to the writers with a warm "Good morning," he was surly and sullen. It was a sign, Mae told Shabazian, that he was ready to fight. Instinctively, Braddock knew that his training had peaked. At that point, all he wanted to do was get in the ring. *I'm ready,* he kept saying to himself. *Let's go. No more waiting. Nothing good can come from waiting.* The sight of the trees and the flowers, which had soothed him in late April, nauseated him in June.

But on Sunday he was in better spirits. Gould had told him that after he worked out, they would break camp. He went two rounds with Paul Pross and one round with Jack McCarthy; for once they sparred with something less than reckless abandon. Six weeks after his arrival, Braddock left the Catskills weighing 195 pounds — about 10 more than when he got there. His rib had healed completely. He was feeling as fit as he had ever felt.

"The daily boxing bouts have been the marvel of critics," Fred Van Ness, the *Times*'s man at Loch Sheldrake, wrote as camp broke. "They were slugging matches from the start. Almost everything that can happen in a fight has happened in the training ring and Braddock has come through punching harder and better than at any time in his life."

Braddock was anxious but confident. Three consecutive upset victories had made him confident. So had the power he now felt emanating from his left hand. He knew that Tommy Loughran, the last man to defeat Baer, had won by using his left hand and avoiding Baer's right hand. His mind constantly drifted back to that fight, at which he had had a ringside seat. "I seen Tommy Loughran lick him in the Garden," Braddock had said to Shabazian, off the record, "and I boxed Tommy and I knew what kind of a boxer he was, and I said to myself, if I ever fight Baer I'll do the same thing Loughran done with him, the left hand and move."

The ride to New York from Loch Sheldrake was uneventful. With four days to go, Braddock was antsy. He wished the fight were Monday instead of Thursday. He wished he could climb into the ring while he still felt this good. He wished he didn't have to spend another four days waiting for the biggest event of his life. He and Mae checked into the Mayflower Hotel on Central Park West, a block from Gould's apartment. At Loch Sheldrake he had slept ten hours every night, but now sleep wouldn't come. He worried about sleeping awkwardly and injuring his shoulder. Finally, though, exhaustion overtook his anxiety.

The next morning the papers were filled with stories about the upcoming fight. Invariably, Braddock's Irishness was emphasized, though Baer's Jewishness was barely mentioned. Apparently the East Coast writers, many of them Jewish, did not agree with Dr. Goebbels that the champion was actually a Jew. The luck of the Irish was a constant theme in every paper except the *Times*, which usually stayed above the ethnic fray. The writers once again portrayed Baer as a playboy clown and Braddock as the stolid Everyman. Extremely popular earlier in the year, Baer was no match for Braddock as the darling of the casual fan. No one could relate to him — he was too rich, too good-looking, too strong, too talented. Everyone could relate to Jim Braddock, who was not too rich, too good-looking, too strong, or too talented.

In the days leading up to the fight, fan mail started pouring into the Garden's offices, most of it addressed to James J. Braddock. "He receives letters from all parts of the country," Fred Van Ness wrote in the *Times*, "most of them expressing hopes that he will be the next champion." In the *Sun*, Frank Graham quoted Jimmy Johnston, who was one of the few people who said that he had come to believe that Braddock would defeat Baer. "All over the country," Johnston said, "hundreds of thousands, maybe millions of people will be rooting and hoping and praying for Braddock. And if you think you — or Baer — can laugh that off, you're crazy."

"Through these final days before the fight," Van Ness reported, "Braddock appears to be the only calm and collected person in his training entourage." Braddock hid his anxiety, but Gould wore his on his thirty-inch sleeve. He was clearly a wreck. He was still mumbling to himself constantly, repeating the mantra "Braddock's gonna win, Braddock's gonna win" as if he were in a trance.

"A manager easily hypnotizes himself in this manner," Damon Runyon wrote in the *American*,

> but during this phase he usually is quite harmless, and all you have to do is to carry wads of cotton in your pocket and stuff them in your ears at his approach. Presently he will float off in a fog, then you can remove the cotton and continue with your own discourses. But the elbow-jostling stage is quite another matter. At this stage, just attained by Mr. Gould, the cotton is of no avail. The manager suddenly, and at the most inopportune moments, jostles your elbow to attract your attention, and before you can recover he has you by the ear and you are a goner.

At one of the several luncheons held at Jack Dempsey's restaurant in the days before the fight, Gould's jostling caused Bob Ripley — the Believe It or Not Ripley, who, like Runyon, wrote for the Hearst syndicate — to spill clam chowder down the inside of his shirt. He spilled a cup of coffee on Pat Frayne, of the *San Francisco Call-Bulletin*. And he "caused Curley Grieve, of the *San Francisco Examiner*, to severely wound himself on a toothpick," Runyon wrote.

On Monday, June 10, with the fight seventy-two hours away, Braddock returned to Stillman's for one final prefight workout. Just a few months earlier, seeing Braddock laboring at the heavy bag in the same gym, Graham had written, "He would quit the ring and take a job somewhere at twenty-five dollars a week, if he could get it." Now, when Braddock walked into Stillman's, a crowd of more than seven hundred boxing fans and writers greeted him with a raucous yet respectful cheer. Only a few of them had seen him at Loch Sheldrake. The rest were stunned by his physical transformation. They had heard, of course, that he'd put on weight, but most had assumed that a heavier Braddock would be a slower Braddock. When he got into the ring and moved more quickly and gracefully than ever before, they were shocked. Johnny Dundee, one of the sages of Stillman's, said that old fighters never change, except this time. Braddock, he said, was an entirely new fighter.

Baer remained at Asbury Park until June 12, the day before the fight. Walking down the boardwalk with Frank Graham on the afternoon of June 11, he surprised Graham with his lack of confidence. "I will knock Braddock out," he said. "I hope I will."

For years most of the press had swallowed the Baer act whole. It was easy to paint Baer as the fool, the playboy, and the killer. Graham was probably the first to go deeper. In a column titled "The Man Nobody Knows Very Well," based on their conversation of June 11, he wrote,

> Max Baer struts and postures and brags and plays the clown, and you get very tired of him and wish that someone would turn him off. Then you sit down in the quiet of a dressing room with him and you come to the conclusion that he isn't such a bad fellow after all. Indeed, after you have sat there for a while you are convinced that you could walk a long way and not find a more agreeable, more entertaining, more likeable companion. You come away thinking that he is a very unusual fellow and that, because of the several sides to his nature, no one really knows him very well.

On Wednesday, June 12, Braddock slept late. When he awoke in his suite on the sixteenth floor of the Mayflower Hotel, he went for a run in Central Park. Gould, Robb, and Ray Arcel followed in a car. It was a clear day, with the temperature rising into the seventies in the afternoon. Braddock ran strongly, breathing comfortably through his nose, sweating lightly, free of aches and weariness. He peeled off six miles, running around the whole park in less than an hour. The slowest Irishman on the planet wasn't so slow anymore. After the run, Gould put Braddock on a scale. He weighed 190 pounds, which is exactly what Gould wanted him to weigh.

Meanwhile, the morning papers in New York were all telling the same story. Baer was the overwhelming favorite, and Braddock had no shot. The odds against him ranged from six to one to ten to one. Despite all the indications from Braddock's camp that he was in remarkable shape and all the signs that Baer was not fully prepared to defend his title, only a handful of the cognoscenti picked Braddock. "It is even money that Braddock does not come out for the tenth round," Runyon, who had recently dubbed Braddock the Cinderella Man, reported in the *American.*

Seven former heavyweight champions offered their opinions. Jack Dempsey, James J. Jeffries, Primo Carnera, Max Schmeling, and even Gene Tunney, who had once predicted that Braddock would eventually capture the championship, picked Baer. "I feel sure Baer will win," Tunney said. "But Braddock has a chance," Dempscy said generously.

Jess Willard and Jack Sharkey both picked Braddock to win.

Benny Leonard, Joe Gould's childhood friend, said, "Baer has trained faithfully and should win." If training halfheartedly is training faithfully, he was right.

The *New York Times* asked Captain James Horton of the New York Police Department, an aide to Mayor La Guardia, for his pick. "I favor Braddock to win by a knockout," he said. Horton was Irish.

Tommy Loughran, the only living fighter who had defeated them both, hedged. Counterintuitively, he picked Braddock in two rounds or Baer in ten.

For his part, Jimmy Johnston was still concerned that the crowds wouldn't show up to see what the experts said was a mismatch. He tried to even the odds. "Braddock is a sure thing to win," he said — implausibly. "Baer is one of the poorest champions the class has ever known. Luck, a good jaw, and a certain cuteness put him where he is. His cuteness will be discounted by the fact that he is up against a fighter who will take no more notice of his clowning than to crack him on the nose or chin, who will stand up under a punch and punch back and keep punching. Unless Max can rate himself, he is out of luck, and he is out of luck with Braddock."

Johnston, of course, was mostly thinking wishfully. If Braddock won, he would fight his first defense for the Garden. If Baer won, he was a free agent and would probably fight for Mike Jacobs's rival Twentieth Century Sporting Club.

Like Johnston, Braddock's supporters were hopeful but far from confident. "It is unlikely that anything to match this march of Braddock's back from oblivion ever took place in prizefighting before," Frank Graham wrote in the June 13 edition of the *Sun*. "It is almost too much for even his friends to hope that it will be climaxed by a victory over Baer. Yet Braddock, the man who wouldn't give up, will have a chance tonight. It's a long chance, a desperate chance — but it's a chance, and that's all Braddock ever asked in any spot."

When sizing up fights, boxing writers like nothing more than comparing the fighters' records against common opponents, but only five men had fought both Braddock and Baer during the previous seven years. Against Les Kennedy, Baer had lost a ten-round decision and scored a third-round knockout, while Braddock had won a ten-round decision. Against Paul Swiderski, Baer had scored a seventh-round knockout and Braddock had won a ten-round decision. Baer knocked out Tuffy Griffiths in seven rounds, while Braddock knocked him out in two rounds. Baer had both won and lost ten-round decisions against the late Ernie Schaaf, while Braddock had lost a ten-round decision to him. Against Loughran, Braddock had lost a fifteen-round decision and Baer had lost a ten-round decision. With such similar experiences against common opponents, it was hard to use those fights as a basis for intelligent judgments about Baer versus Braddock, except for the fact that Baer's wins had been more recent than Braddock's.

On the day of the fight, the weigh-in was scheduled to take place at noon, at the offices of the state athletic commission on Lafayette Street. Wading through a throng of fans who had gathered outside the building to see the fighters in person, Braddock and Gould walked in at 11:30. Gould was moving quickly, a few paces ahead of Braddock as always, excitedly greeting old friends and acquaintances. Baer arrived at 12:30. When he caught sight of Braddock, he went forward, extended his hand, and said, "How ya doin', kid?" His manner made it impossible to tell that in a few hours he would be defending the most valuable prize in sports. The crowds, the tension, the heat — none of it seemed to affect him.

For his part, Braddock was surprised by Baer's tone, which he sensed was part of his act. Calling Braddock "kid" was a subtle jibe. Nevertheless, Braddock took Baer's hand and shook it. Then he said, "I'll do my talking with you in the ring tonight."

But Gould thrust his full five feet five inches into Baer's personal space and said, at the top of his voice and in his thick New York accent, "You're the guy who kills people in the ring, eh? Well, get out of here, you don't mean a thing to us."

Nonplussed, Baer smiled and walked away.

Stripped to the waist, Braddock mounted the scales first. He weighed 191.75 pounds, almost 10 pounds more than he had weighed against Lasky less than three months earlier. At six foot three he was an imposing presence — not a giant like Carnera, but significantly bigger than most of the men who had been heavyweight champion. Then it was Baer's turn. He dramatically shed his cream-colored double-breasted jacket, white shirt, striped tie, and undershirt, untied his shoes, and stepped on the scale. He weighed 209.5 pounds, close to his ideal weight, and as always his muscles were bulging. His physique — and his tan — made Braddock look anemic.

At a heavyweight fight, of course, the weigh-in is purely ceremonial. Heavyweights can weigh whatever they want. They mount the scales because it's a tradition and because the gamblers like to know how much they weigh. On June 13, 1935, serious issues were addressed after the weigh-in, when Baer, Braddock, Gould, and Hoffman entered the executive chambers of the athletic commission, which had not yet announced who would referee the bout.

Gould had objected to Dempsey as referee — he had made an issue of it on June 2 — and now Hoffman presented the commissioners with a list of referees *he* found unacceptable. Arthur Donovan, who had refereed the Carnera fight 364 days earlier, was at the top of the list, because Baer and Hoffman didn't like the way he had scored that encounter. They then presented a list of referees they *would* find acceptable. None was registered as a referee in the state of New York.

The commission balked. Brown in particular was livid. "We've got plenty of qualified referees in this state," he said to Baer and Hoffman. "We're not going out of state." Then the commission rejected the gloves that Hoffman wanted Baer to use — they were not up to specifications and had been designed specifically to protect his aching hands. Gould also objected to them.

"I've got the champion and they're treating us like we're rubes," Hoffman said as he emerged from the meeting.

At that moment there was a commotion in the crowd. Mike Cantwell had thrown himself in front of Baer. "You're a bum," Cantwell said, mimicking Brown. "Braddock's gonna show you, you big clown." Theatrically, Baer pulled back his right as if he were about to throw a punch. Then he just smiled and laughed.

Braddock watched Baer walk out of the office, turned to Gould, and said, "Come on, let's get back to the hotel." When they left the offices, they found hundreds of people still out on the street waiting to get a look at Braddock. "You see, Jim," Gould said, "they're here for you."

17

A Stout Heart

....

Queens, New York: June 13, 1935

The day before James J. Braddock challenged Max Baer for
the world heavyweight championship, a dozen reporters and
photographers made their way to an apartment on West 64th
Street in Manhattan to attend a séance. Mrs. Felicie Crossley, a
renowned medium who was soon to preside at the International General Assembly of Spiritualists at the Park Central
Hotel, had invited them. To the disappointment of the newspapermen, Mrs. Crossley said she was unable to conduct a séance
because her contacts in the afterlife were otherwise occupied.
She agreed, however, to grant an interview.

In the course of the ensuing interrogation, Mrs. Crossley revealed that President Roosevelt would win a second term in
1936 and that there would be a war in Palestine over rights to
the Suez Canal.

The man from the *Sun* then asked, "What about Judge
Crater?" He was referring to Joseph Force Crater, the New York
state judge who had disappeared without a trace after dining at
a Manhattan restaurant on August 6, 1930.

"Spiritualism," Mrs. Crossley said huffily, "is not a lost-and-
found bureau."

The newspaperman slumped in defeat. But the reporter from
the *Journal* had a question he was hoping she could answer

more easily. "Well, who's going to win the fight tomorrow night," he said, "Baer or Braddock?" He thought he would only confuse the issue by mentioning the wager he was considering placing.

"I am afraid I have no fight guides on the other side," Mrs. Crossley said. "You're on your own."

The interview was over.

Deprived of any insights from the other side, 30,000 fight fans still filed into the Madison Square Garden Bowl the next evening, even though most of them were expecting a lopsided victory for the champion. Throngs of hopeful Irishmen easily outnumbered the Jews supporting Baer. The Italians were there too, and blacks, Poles, and even those of old-fashioned English Protestant stock. There were movie stars and politicians, gangsters and athletes. "It was a crowd that presented a cross-section of American life," James P. Dawson observed, "gathered from near and far, not record-breaking in its numbers but representative in quality."

One thousand policemen were assigned to handle security. They were there generally to keep the peace and specifically to protect the rich and famous seated at ringside — the Whitneys, Chryslers, Baruchs, Warburgs, Singers, and Pulitzers. Tim Mara was there; ten years after buying the New York Giants football team for five hundred dollars, he was still known primarily as a "racetracker." George S. Kaufman, the renowned wit, was among the celebrities occupying the expensive seats.

The expensive seats, in fact, were all filled. There were enough millionaires in New York to buy the several hundred twenty-dollar seats, but the cheap seats were half empty, "mainly for the reason that the lads who used to have two dollars no longer have two dollars, or even one dollar," Runyon wrote from his seat near the swells. "The thing is elementary. If they haven't got it, they can't spend it."

Although millions of people across the country would be listening on the radio and cheering for Braddock, few of his supporters thought he would actually win. Most, in fact, thought he might get hurt. Still, hundreds of fans crowded the roofs of the garage and the apartment building across the street from the arena to watch the fight free of charge.

With so little money at their disposal — and, according to the experts, such a small chance for success — Braddock's fans did not wager much money on the fight. "Probably 90 percent of the fans are pulling for Braddock," Wilbur Wood wrote in the *Sun,* "and some of them will place a small bet for sentimental reasons. Here and there a smart old-timer who knows that any time two game, hard-hitting, durable, well-conditioned fighters meet, the odds should never be eight to one, will take a flyer on Braddock."

The fight was set to begin at ten. So at seven, shortly after getting to his dressing room, Braddock took a nap. Despite all that was at stake, he was, to his own surprise, devoid of anxiety. He had trained intensely for this moment for more than six weeks. In fact, he had worked for this moment his whole life. Now he had to find some serenity before the blows started to fall. He retreated into the cocoon of calmness and sureness under fire that had so often served him well. Once he did, sleep came quickly, and Robb threw a blanket over him. When he woke, after about an hour, he knew that this was the night that would define him, one way or the other, for life.

Meanwhile, out in the open air of the arena, Gould was trying urgently to lay down $25,000 on Braddock to win. Gould admitted that the money wasn't his, but he wouldn't say whose it was.

For the first time, Braddock's father, Joseph Senior, was in attendance at one of his son's fights. At seventy, he was still working as a pier watchman for the Holland America steamship company in Hoboken. All Jim's brothers were there too: Ralph, an assistant yardmaster at the Weehawken depot; Joe Junior, a milkman; Jack, a bookkeeper in a brewery; and Al, still a wheelman on the ferry between Hoboken and West 42nd

Street. Like Jim, the other Braddock men had suffered during the economic downturn. Now they were all together, about to watch one of their own compete for the most coveted prize in sports.

Mae could not bring herself to watch Jim fight in person. She was with the three children at her mother's home in Guttenberg, surrounded by reporters who could not get assigned to the fight.

An unknown number of female fans at the fight were cheering for Baer. Only one, though, was dating him at the time: Mary Ellen Sullivan, the coffee shop manager from the Willard Hotel in Washington. While Braddock was napping, Baer was relaxing in his dressing room in a different way, and with a different woman. When Hoffman discovered what had happened, just a few minutes later, he was incensed. He subscribed to the conventional wisdom of the era, which held that sex sapped a man's energy.

Of the 30,000 people in the Bowl, virtually everyone except the Jews was cheering for Braddock. In 364 days, Baer had squandered all the good will and respect he had built by winning the title. What the public had initially found charming — his swagger, his exuberance, his appetites — eventually came to be regarded as obnoxious. When Baer walked into the Bowl, the odds were on his side; so were talent, youth, strength, and experience in big fights. But he had nowhere to plant his feet, as the trainers liked to say. When a fighter honors the sport by training hard and showing respect for his opponents, he enters the ring with a base; he is fighting with the protection of the fistic fates, as Shabazian might have put it. Baer found very little that was honorable about boxing, and he refused to live by its code. He also believed his opponent was outmatched.

For Jim Braddock, of course, boxing was his code, his calling, his identity. When he stepped into the ring at the Bowl, win or lose, he had somewhere to plant his feet. He could conjure the spirits of the great champions, the Irishmen like Sullivan and Corbett and Tunney who had worn the crown he sought. He derived strength from his losses as well as his wins.

After Braddock woke up from his nap, Robb wrapped his hands and laced up his gloves, with Phelan, Brown, and Hoffman watching. Braddock was not in a talkative mood. He was confident, though. He knew he could beat Max Baer, despite Baer's superior natural ability. He had seen Tommy Loughran do it. He knew that he could best any puncher in the world. Boxers like Loughran and Rosenbloom worried him, but punchers didn't.

The writers at ringside were joking and laying bets — small ones. Simply by showing up, Baer had raised the odds against Braddock. Albertanti was moving in and out of press row, shaking hands and exchanging greetings with Runyon, Rice, Parker, Graham, Dawson, Kieran, Shabazian, Williams, Van Every, Van Ness, Nichols, and the rest. He carried a stack of handouts — a sixteen-page biography of Braddock he had prepared at Loch Sheldrake, which he had also sent to newspapers around the country. He laid one beside each typewriter, and almost to a man, the writers discarded them. They didn't want any clutter, and there was certainly no reason they would have to dig sixteen pages deep into the life story of the longest long shot in heavyweight championship history.

Just after 10 P.M., Baer, Braddock, and all their seconds converged in the center of the ring to listen to referee Johnny McAvoy's instructions. Baer and Braddock were both sweating under their robes and hoods; they had warmed up just before marching into the ring. As McAvoy told them to mind their manners and to remember to retreat to a neutral corner in the event of a knockdown, their eyes met. Baer was grinning, but a sneer lifted the corners of Braddock's mouth. They exchanged a perfunctory glove shake, then wheeled around and walked to their corners.

"Jim, remember, the left, use the left," Gould said. He was so skittish that Braddock thought he might faint.

"Yeah, yeah," Braddock practically growled.

At the bell, Braddock went straight for the champion, cracking him with a left to the jaw and then a right to the body. Baer grinned. He aimed an uppercut at Braddock's chin and missed. They traded off-target left hooks. Baer landed a left on Braddock's ribs, which Braddock answered with a right to Baer's jaw.

Baer did not expect this. He thought Braddock would be nervous, at least at the outset. But Braddock betrayed no anxiety. It was almost as if he were the champion and Baer the challenger. Braddock's punches were crisper and his timing sharper than Baer's — and Baer knew it.

Braddock landed a few more light shots to Baer's head and then the bell sounded, ending the round, which the judges agreed Braddock had won.

In the second round, Braddock again struck first, with a long left to Baer's head. Again Baer smiled. He hit Braddock with another solid body shot, but Braddock responded immediately with three straight rights to Baer's head. Braddock wasn't going anywhere, Baer was realizing, but he was staying out of range of Baer's right hand. Baer missed with a left and then pretended to charge at Braddock, who stood his ground, as if to say, "Go ahead, hit me." Fighting now at full speed, Baer landed a left hook on the point of his chin. "The shock of it," Braddock would later say, "went all the way down to the big toe of my right foot. If there had been a thousand-watt bulb connected with that toe, it would have lit up." But before Baer could follow up, the round ended, and again the judges gave it to Braddock.

Standing behind Braddock in his corner, Gould said, "So that's the heavyweight champion of the world. He's a bum, Jim." Braddock knew better. That left hook had proved to him that Baer was gifted, but he knew he had to resist the temptation to start trading punches. He had to box. He had to use his left. He knew that if the fight came down to who hit hardest, Baer would win.

Gould kept jabbering, his nervous energy manifesting itself in constant chatter. Braddock, of course, was accustomed to Gould's nervous habits. Somehow it had an equalizing effect, Gould's anxiety calming him.

In his corner, Baer's mind was drifting. Typically, he was looking into the crowd for familiar faces. The fight was barely holding his attention. Hoffman was still livid about the sexual encounter in the dressing room. Baer had lost the first two rounds; his legs looked unsteady, and he could not be bothered to pay attention to the entreaties of his corner.

"Max, listen to me," Hoffman said evenly. "This is no joke. You've got to start fighting."

"You see that punch I hit him with? He didn't move. He's a tough guy."

"Hit him with another one and he'll go down."

"Is that Myrna Loy?" Baer was pointing his glove at the crowd.

"Stop it, Max. Come on."

To open the third round, Braddock, sticking with his strategy, fired two lefts into Baer's face. Despite what Braddock had shown against Lewis and Lasky, Baer was still surprised that his left was so strong. Baer responded with a left to Braddock's stomach. The punch was almost low, and Gould started screaming at the champion. On press row, Shabazian allowed himself to imagine for a moment that Baer could not hurt Braddock and that Braddock would actually hold him off to win the title. What had seemed impossible ten minutes earlier was conceivable by the middle of the third round.

Then Baer swung his right arm back behind his head and fired it straight at Braddock's chin. The punch — "I knew it was the best one he had," Braddock said later — landed flush on Braddock's chin. Braddock didn't budge. Reflexively, he shot out his left hand at Baer's head. At that moment he realized he could win — and so did Baer. He had taken Baer's best shot and it had not fazed him. For the first time since before the Loughran fight six years earlier, Braddock could almost taste a championship, even as Baer pounded him in the stomach again. He responded with a right to Baer's jaw. Then Baer landed a left to the head, wincing as it struck Braddock's skull. Braddock landed a right to the head and then a left. The third round was scored even — but psychologically, by withstanding Baer's best punches, Braddock had won.

In the fourth round, Baer started to play to the crowd. Instead of challenging Braddock, whose resiliency was confusing him, the champion mugged and sneered. When Braddock moved in close, crowding him, Baer grabbed him by the shoulders and nearly wrestled him to the canvas. The crowd started booing. McAvoy cautioned him. Baer waved his hand in apology, first at Braddock, then toward the fans, who were now starting to sense that an upset might be in the making. Baer started loading up and firing more rights at Braddock, hoping that one punch would end the fight. But for the most part Braddock managed to stay out of his range. He kept moving to his right, away from Baer's right, waiting for openings created by Baer's lack of discipline.

Hoffman pleaded with Baer to stop fighting merely in spurts, but it was a lecture he should have delivered years earlier. Baer always fought in spurts, and he never listened to Hoffman anyway.

To the men of press row, it appeared that Baer was uninterested in defending his title. None of them had ever seen a champion fight so lackadaisically. But Baer wasn't just uninterested, he was confounded. And he was tiring. The fight was only his third in almost three years. Braddock was fighting for the fourth time in 365 days and had spent most of the previous seven weeks fighting, not just sparring, with tough competition. When Braddock challenged him, Baer had nowhere to go, no strategy to fall back on. He kept looking to land his right, but even when he did, it had no effect. Fighting hard every second, Braddock plugged away, exposing himself to Baer's power only occasionally, never letting down his guard, never looking for the easy way out. His ability to withstand the hardest blows was frustrating Baer, who was interested only in a knockout. Even in a championship fight, Baer could not be motivated to work hard.

In the fifth round, Braddock opened with a short left to Baer's head. Baer countered with a backhand right, an illegal blow, drawing a warning from McAvoy. Now Gould was jumping up and down, screaming at Baer, "Fight clean! Fight clean!" Shabazian thought Gould was going to jump into the ring — which would have disqualified Braddock — but Robb managed to restrain him. Again Baer tried to land several monstrous rights, but each time Braddock avoided them entirely or just took a grazing on the chin. Baer backhanded him again, and Braddock hit Baer with two rights to the chin. Baer hit Braddock with a short right, injuring his hand. The round was nearly even, but Baer lost it because of the fouls.

Between rounds Gould tried to soothe Braddock. Listening closely, Gallico jotted down his words of encouragement. "No mother ever had a tenderer accent in her speech," Gallico wrote in the *Daily News*, "than Gould saying, 'Do you feel all right, Jim? Are you sure you feel all right? Jim, you're doing great. Now get all the rest you can this round. I want you to have a nice rest this round so you'll have plenty of stuff for the finish.'"

At the beginning of the sixth round, Baer charged Braddock, but Braddock stopped him with a jab. At close quarters, Baer landed two uppercuts. Braddock just kept punching. He landed a right on Baer's jaw; the punch exploded with such force that Baer's knees buckled, but he stayed upright. Braddock's corner was growing. Johnston was now standing with Gould, Robb, Arcel, and Whitey Bimstein, another trainer working his corner, shouting as loudly as Gould. Cupping his hands around his mouth, Johnston bellowed at Braddock, "Murder the bum!" Baer was beginning to realize that virtually no one in the arena was cheering for him. The crowd, the commissioners, the police, the newspapermen — they were all rooting for Braddock.

In the seventh round, Baer suddenly started fighting seriously. He rushed Braddock, swinging both hands, landing lefts and rights. Braddock pushed him to the ropes, but Baer responded with a vicious right to the jaw that knocked Braddock's head back. Braddock took several seconds to regain his senses and then fired a right hand that landed solidly on Baer's jaw. Baer smiled and laughed, loudly enough for the writers to hear him. Pressed against the ropes, he lashed out with his right hand, landing several punches to Braddock's head. The round ended with Baer on the offensive.

But in his corner after that round, the champion was breathing hard — too hard. "I don't know if I can make it through fifteen," he said to Hoffman. "I better finish him now."

It had been four years since Baer had been in trouble against anyone. He had no answers for Braddock. Nor did Hoffman.

In the eighth, Baer landed two quick punches to Braddock's head, with no discernible effect. Frustration was setting in. Braddock could see it. And he could sense that Baer was tiring. Still, he knew that Baer was always dangerous, that one punch could end the fight. As his lead piled up, he resolved to fight carefully. He hit Baer with his right, but not solidly. Nevertheless, Baer's knees buckled and he staggered. His eyes rolled back in his head. For a moment it seemed he would topple over. The crowd rose as one to see the champion fall. But suddenly he was back in his fighting stance, rushing at Braddock. He had been playing possum, hoping that Braddock would miscalculate and either approach him with his guard down or turn around. Instead, Braddock's feet never moved. He had been waiting for Baer to try to trick him.

When the crowd realized what Baer had done, they booed him lustily. His trick foiled, he threw a punch at Braddock's head, missing high. Then he moved in and landed several body blows. Braddock got in close and whispered, "Is that as hard as you can punch? Hey, Max, you better get going. You're way behind."

In his corner after the round, Braddock turned to Gould and said, "He's fading."

Gould was now virtually overcome with anxiety. They were six rounds away from winning the championship. In half an hour it would all be over. If Jim just stayed away from the big right hand, he couldn't lose. Meanwhile, Johnston was directing more invective at Baer. "It's over, Max," he said across the ring. No one thought it odd that the promoter was taking sides. Silently, Bill Brown was also cheering Braddock on.

In the ninth round, Baer was again the aggressor. He landed three consecutive left hooks to Braddock's midsection. Then he landed a left below the belt. McAvoy warned him. Gould screamed at him. "Fight clean, you animal," he shouted, his voice rising over the hum of the crowd.

"I am fighting clean," Baer said, turning to Gould, blood and his mouthpiece slurring his speech. At that moment Braddock clipped him with a shot to the head. Now Baer was angry, and for the next two minutes champion and challenger exchanged blow after blow. Because of the foul, the round was officially Braddock's.

As the tenth round began, Baer, despite his fatigue, rushed out to meet Braddock. For three minutes he landed uppercuts, hooks, and short rights. But Braddock was never hurt. He seemed impervious to Baer's punches — the same punches that had toppled Schmeling and Carnera, two champions. Accustomed to fighting in pain, conditioned by a lifetime of receiving blows, he stood his ground in the face of flurry after flurry. Flicking his jab in Baer's face, he kept Baer literally at arm's length, reducing his punching power. And he kept circling away from Baer's right. Finally he threw a left and then a right to Baer's stomach, then landed two rights to Baer's head. Braddock lost the round, but by this time he could lose the fight only by knockout. As long as he could stay out of danger, he was willing to concede points.

In the eleventh, though, Baer found an opening. He landed a huge right hand — "the same punch which had knocked out Schmeling in 1933 and a year later sent Carnera to the boards a dozen times," Shabazian noted — and the crowd once again rose to get a closer look. Braddock staggered, his body shivering as if he had just been dipped in icewater, but he stayed on his feet. There was no way he was going down — not now, not after coming this far. Braddock was numb now, almost unable to feel pain, and he started landing combinations — lefts and rights, one after the other. Then Baer bore in again. Braddock withstood the assault. He landed a backhanded left to the face. Baer smiled. He had won the round again, but it didn't matter. He needed a knockout.

By the beginning of the twelfth round, Baer was exhausted. He chased after Braddock, looking for a knockout, but Braddock kept out of range. As Baer continued to tire, Braddock moved in and landed a series of hard lefts to his chin. Too fatigued to defend himself, Baer got smashed in the face with more than a dozen hard left hands. Braddock was also tired, but he kept punching. Finally Baer started to find his target. For the last thirty seconds of the round, the fighters traded punches to the head and to the body. Even after the bell sounded they kept fighting, Baer landing a left on Braddock's ear.

It was at this moment that Gould jumped through the ropes, screaming wildly at Baer. He charged at Baer's corner but was held back by two policemen guarding the ring. Gould had become unhinged. McAvoy would have been within his rights to disqualify Braddock because of Gould's tantrum, but neither McAvoy nor the policemen, nor anyone else in the arena, wanted to see Braddock lose the fight because his manager had gone crazy. The officers were on the verge of having Gould es-

corted out of the Bowl, but Braddock talked them into allowing
him to stay.

Hoffman was by now overcome with frustration. "What's
wrong with you, Max?" he said. "You've got to knock him out!"

Baer just snarled. He could feel the title slipping away. He
could hear the crowd cheering for his opponent. Here he was,
the ultimate performer, the ultimate crowd-pleaser, and yet the
fans had turned on him. He couldn't understand what he had
done to alienate them. Their betrayal disturbed him more than
the prospect of losing the fight. Throughout his career he had
taken tremendous pride in the entertainment value of his performances, if not their fighting quality. "Did I make a good
fight?" — that was the question he always asked. Now he didn't
really care. It was almost as if he didn't want the title anymore.
Yes, he wanted the trappings — the money, the women, the fame,
the attention. But the title? These ingrates could have it back.

Still, in the final rounds, despite searing pain in both hands,
Baer fought hard. Neither he nor Braddock could move his legs
much anymore. Dehydration had twisted their muscles into
knots. Braddock felt the way he felt after spending an eighteen-
hour day on the docks, but worse. Champion and challenger
stood face to face and swung their arms at each other, Braddock still countering with his left, Baer still barely missing with
his right. In the thirteenth round, Braddock again landed left
jabs and hooks easily. "They poured in on Baer like so much
hail," Shabazian wrote.

"It certainly was a strange sight," Paul Gallico wrote in the
Daily News, "to see the great man-killer Baer cowering behind
his gloves and backing away with his left stuck out to ward off
punishment. He looked exactly like the unpopular school bully
who was receiving a thrashing from the smaller, spunky kid. He
did everything the school bully does but snivel."

In the fourteenth, Baer tried to knock out Braddock with
several uppercuts, but all the power had been sapped from his

arms. In the clinches, Braddock could not be budged. He took punch after punch without flinching. At the bell ending the round, the crowd showered him with cheers. He had not fought brilliantly; he had fought wisely and bravely.

At the beginning of the fifteenth, Braddock and Baer walked out to the middle of the ring and shook gloves. For three minutes they were on top of each other, punching as hard as they could, which by this time wasn't very hard. As the final seconds ticked away, the writers at ringside started scrambling. They needed to know more about the man who was about to become the world heavyweight champion. Some of them had been too lazy to bother to prepare for the possibility that Braddock would win. Everything they needed to know was in Albertanti's handout, the one they had so cavalierly discarded only an hour earlier. Frantically they started searching for it. Some actually climbed under the ring to retrieve wayward copies.

With five seconds left in the fight, Braddock landed two rights to Baer's head. Then the bell sounded. Instantly Gould jumped into the ring, grabbed both of Braddock's legs, and lifted him into the air — a feat of strength made possible only by the euphoria of the moment. Braddock looked down at Gould and said quietly, "We did it. We did it." When Braddock's feet returned to the canvas, Johnston, like a proud father, grabbed him by the shoulder.

Meanwhile, nursing his hands, hanging his head, the smirk wiped from his face, Baer walked back to his corner silently, fully aware of the fact that he was about to surrender the championship.

Al Frazin, the ring announcer, consulted with McAvoy. After thirty seconds, he walked to the microphone dangling from the lights and said, "The winner and new champion —" He was cut off by the crowd, which started cheering again. Mobbed by writers, family, and friends, Braddock lifted his right arm to the sky. He should have raised his left. Baer, ten feet away, on the edge of the crowd surrounding Braddock, was standing by himself, staring at his hands, the once deadly weapons that had betrayed him.

In Guttenberg, Mae Braddock cried and hugged her mother when she heard Frazin announce the winner. But she decided it would be best not to wake the children. After all, it was almost eleven.

Braddock later said that he had a tougher time getting back to his dressing room than he did defeating Baer. Fans reached out for him, struggling to touch the hem of the robe of the new king of the heavyweights. They pulled his hair and grabbed his elbow. The police were powerless to protect him. The writers trailed him closely, with Shabazian, scribbling furiously, practically on his heels. "You showed him, Jim" was the most constant refrain of the fans. "You made us proud" was another. Braddock and Gould clung to each other. Gould, swallowed up in Braddock's robe, grinned wildly. Dazed and ebullient, Braddock was pumping his right fist, his gloves still on. Finally the caravan — Braddock, Gould, the seconds, the police, the writers, Braddock's father and brothers, his friends, celebrities, the commissioners, Johnston — arrived at the small, low-ceilinged building at the edge of the Bowl where Braddock's dressing room was.

The writers didn't initiate the conversation; there were almost too many questions to ask. They waited for Braddock to speak. Surrounded by the "great and the near great," as Gallico recalled, Braddock welled up with emotion. He embraced Gould again and again. Then he spoke. "I'm glad I won," he said, his voice quavering, "because it will please the wife and kids. I've got the prettiest kids in the world, and tonight I can go home to them and say, 'Your daddy is champ.'"

Then Graham asked him what it felt like to be the champion.

"My left arm's sore," Braddock said, taking the question literally. "That's from warding off blows. Baer's a pretty good fighter. He threw plenty of hard punches at me. But from the seventh round on I knew it was mine. I knew I could take him. I had taken a couple of his hard rights to the head, but they didn't hurt me any. He seemed to be getting desperate in the last few rounds. I guess he thought he could nail me."

"Baer claims he broke his hands in the fifth," a reporter said.

This time Gould responded. "Yeah," he said, his face turning red, "that's too bad. Honest, I'm sorry for him."

Braddock's dressing room was so small and so crowded that he could not even shower. He was eventually ushered by police bodyguards through the mob to a taxi. The new heavyweight champion of the world was still speckled with the blood of the immediate former champion. With a police escort clearing a path for his Checker cab, Braddock arrived at the Mayflower Hotel just after 1 A.M. A party was already under way in his suite.

Albertanti was the first familiar face Braddock saw. "Thank God for Corn Griffin," Albertanti said.

"Thank God for Corn Griffin," Braddock agreed.

Every Braddock sibling, cousin, and acquaintance was there. Writers, celebrities, sparring partners — they were all there. One intrepid photographer cut out a paper crown and posed Braddock wearing it. Shabazian was struck by the imagery, which made its way into the title of his soon-to-be-written Braddock biography, *Relief to Royalty*. At about two in the morning, Mae Braddock joined the party. She and Jim embraced, to the snap of a dozen flashbulbs firing simultaneously.

On the big couch in the living room, Gould, chomping a victory cigar, was holding forth for the newspapermen. Already he was making plans for Braddock's first title defense. "Sure, we'll give Schmeling a shot," he said, "and Joe Louis. And Baer and Carnera too. Jimmy will beat each one of them before he's through."

Shabazian dutifully wrote down everything he saw and heard. Braddock's victory was easily the biggest sports story in the history of the *Hudson Dispatch*. New Jersey's first heavyweight champion. Hudson County's most celebrated son. The pride of

North Bergen. The same young man who a decade earlier had fought as Jimmy Ryan. The same young man who had looked so foolish fighting Tommy Loughran. The same young man who had quit the ring after the Feldman fight to work as a longshoreman. The same young man who just a few months earlier had been collecting relief. Jim Braddock, world heavyweight champion. It was preposterous — this was, after all, the same Braddock whose name had not been on the *Ring*'s list of the top *nineteen* heavyweights five months earlier. But Shabazian had seen it happen, each step, the steady progression from Griffin to Lewis to Lasky to Baer. He knew he would never cover a story like this again, and that thought only reinforced the pleasure he was feeling.

All night telegrams poured in. Gene Tunney sent his congratulations. "Thank him," Gould said to Braddock, "but tell him he should have stuck to the ship."

Lou Gehrig sent a telegram. So did Johnny Evers, of Tinker to Evers to Chance fame. So did Jimmy Cagney and Pat O'Brien, who had been telegramming their best wishes all day and night, encouraging their fellow Irishman.

Despite the fractured jaw and eleven feet of fine wire, Pete Latzo sent his congratulations, as did Leo Lomski, Joe Monte, and Art Lasky. They could all now say they had fought the world heavyweight champion.

There was also a telegram from Columbus, Georgia. Gould knew who sent it before he opened it. "Congratulations to the new champion from the cracker who started him on the way up," he said, reading the telegram aloud. "Would like to meet you again."

"Griffin?" Braddock asked.

"Of course," Gould said.

"Thank God for Corn Griffin," Albertanti said.

"Here's to Corn Griffin," Braddock said, and they toasted the terror of Fort Benning.

The reporters surrounded Mae Braddock.

"My husband wasn't seeing Max at all when he was in there in the ring fighting," she said. "What he saw was a fierce ogre, trying to keep him from chasing the big bad wolf from our door. He was thinking of me, and of the kids, every minute of those fifteen terrific fighting rounds."

Braddock, of course, was exhausted. He had fought a hard fight, and his stomach was filled with alcohol. He sat down in a plush armchair, expecting the fatigue to overwhelm him. But his brain wouldn't shut off. His thoughts wandered back to 1929, to the night when Tommy Loughran had made him look so foolish. He remembered the taunts of some of the writers, and the subsequent disappointments, and the outright failures. The days on the docks. The humiliation of relief. All these things were so recent, so vivid. Somehow, though, he had succeeded. He had reversed everything that had come before. He had broken the jinx. How, he wasn't quite sure. But the paper crown he was still wearing proved it wasn't a dream. Finally he shut his eyes and fell asleep.

Three hours later, though, he was awake, too excited to rest any longer. Gould was up too, reading the papers. Together they went through a dozen dailies filled with accounts of the fight and abbreviated versions of Albertanti's handout.

Dan Parker's column was typical:

The crowd was overwhelmingly with Braddock. Here was the ideal hero! An underdog; a modest, likeable fellow; a good family man with a wife and three children; a victim of the depression whose fortune had sunk so low that he had to go on county relief, but whose pride was such that when he got back on his feet, he repaid the county every cent he had received in his lean days; a man whom fortune seemed to have passed by in the ring several years ago, but who realized the dream — all of us cherish — that of getting out of the rut! No wonder almost everyone was pulling for Jimmy to win, though betting the other way.

This was the universal message of the national sporting press in the days after the upset. Braddock as the Everyman. Braddock as the victim of the Depression. Braddock as a source of hope to anyone who had been crushed by the crash.

The feat was so stunning, and the sport so linked to mobsters, that there was some natural skepticism about the outcome. Most of the columnists dismissed the suspicions as balderdash.

"Jimmy deserved to win," Parker wrote. "I'm glad he did win, and there are a hundred million others like me. He'll be a credit to the title he holds and an inspiration to the young folks and the downtrodden, something Baer never was. So, if Baer chucked the fight — and, again, I repeat, I can't imagine why he should — he did boxing a big favor."

Even though Runyon had predicted that Baer would win in nine rounds, he could not pass up the opportunity to say, in effect, "I told you so." "You will recall that we insisted that Braddock was no pop-over for any man," he wrote, "and that besides the stage seemed all set for one of those fistic whimsies in which the pugilistic Fates love to indulge. So we were not at all astonished, and have no brash words to eat, although we admit we did not allow for the mighty Baer stepping in there and putting on a baggy-pants battle."

Eschewing the sarcasm he had reserved for Braddock half a decade earlier, Kieran focused on the uniqueness of the bond between the new champion and his manager. "On the average," he wrote, "a fight manager is a human harpy who squeezes all he can out of the blood and bones of husky and courageous young fellows and then tosses them callously aside when they are battered hulks of no more financial advantage for him. But there are exceptions. Jim drew one of the exceptions in Joe Gould."

Reading Kieran's column, Gould decided he would forgive him. Max Baer, though, was another matter. Baer had posed his hands for the photographers after the fight. The pictures showed two ordinary-looking though swollen hands, but Baer claimed that they had both been broken early in the fight. They probably hadn't been; it was standard practice for defeated champions to scapegoat a sound ligament, tendon, joint, or bone for their losses. Still, Baer was not ungenerous. "I know I deserved to lose the decision," he had said in his dressing room, "and I don't want to take anything away from Braddock. I thought my hands were strong enough when I went into the ring, and it's my own fault that I didn't knock out Jim early. Frankly, I didn't expect the fight to go more than seven rounds."

To no one's surprise, Baer announced that he was through as a fighter — that he was retiring. "I propose to raise white-face cattle on my Western ranch and settle down on the farm," he said. "I've had my hard knocks in the ring and now I am to live my own life."

"Jim," Gould said, passing the paper to Braddock, "Max says he's quitting."

"They always say that when they lose," Braddock said.

In fact, moments after Baer had announced his retirement, Hoffman said, "Don't listen to him, boys. He's obviously upset. He'll get over it."

Amid dozens of withering condemnations of Baer's performance, the harshest was written by his closest friend and mentor. "Max Baer's dilly-dallying and clowning caught up with him in the ring," wrote Jack Dempsey, serving as a special correspondent for the *Times*. "There was not a dissenting voice raised when the long shot was declared the winner. Braddock won cleanly on aggressiveness and clean hitting. I do not wish to take anything from Braddock. He fought his best, and his best was better than Baer's miserable defense of his title."

Nat Fleischer was already describing the upset as the biggest in modern pugilistic history. Even the *Times*'s editorial page offered its opinion. In an item situated higher on the page than one deploring press restrictions in Stalin's Soviet Union, Hitler's Germany, and Mussolini's Italy, the editorialists compared Braddock to David (the one who knocked out Goliath) and to the English navy (the one that knocked out the Spanish Armada).

A few of the writers got a little carried away and let their imaginations get the best of their stories. In the *Daily News*, Jack Miley described Jim's mother, Elizabeth O'Toole Braddock, in her youth as "the fairest colleen of County Galway." If she had ever been in Ireland, that might have been true.

Frank Graham's column — the one he was hoping to write all along, the one celebrating a new champion — was clean and true. "The incredible has happened," he wrote, "and James J. Braddock is the heavyweight champion of the world. Nothing like this has ever happened before in the long history of the prize ring. It just goes to show you how far a stout heart will take a fellow, provided he has a good left hand to go with it."

After digesting dozens of columns and stories, Braddock and Gould took a taxi to Jack Dempsey's restaurant, across the street from the Garden. The media had been invited. As Johnston handed Braddock a check for $31,244.13, the flashbulbs crackled. Of course, even if he had lost the fight, Braddock would have received the check — but no one would have been at Jack Dempsey's taking pictures of him. Braddock and Gould were both puffing on enormous cigars, basking in the moment.

After lunch Braddock took the ferry back to New Jersey. The children were still at their grandmother's home in Guttenberg, where he stopped first, bearing a turtle as a present.

Joseph Nichols of the *Times* asked him, "Why a turtle?"

"Well," Braddock said, "when I left the house to fight Baer, the kids asked me where I was going. I said, 'To get the title.' They thought I said, 'To get a turtle.' So now I've got to pay up."

Braddock slept for a few hours at his mother-in-law's house and then went to see his own mother. Everywhere he went, from Guttenberg to North Bergen, he was mobbed. His face was unmarked, although he had a bandage on the ear that Baer had struck after the end of the twelfth round.

Gould, still in the city, sorted through more than four thousand congratulatory telegrams and dozens of offers for Braddock's services, including many from vaudeville and Broadway producers. The thought of Braddock on stage made him chuckle.

That night, in Jersey City, the Eleventh Ward Democratic Club held a dinner honoring Braddock and Gould. The most reluctant of public speakers, Braddock, who always looked uncomfortable in a tuxedo, made a short speech. "You were all in my corner when nobody else thought I had a chance," he said. "I'll never forget that. And I'll never let you down."

Meanwhile, the papers vied for Braddock's story, which they all agreed made Horatio Alger look like a cynic. Between the allusions to Cinderella and to Alger's heroes, Braddock was reduced quickly from a real, indomitable human being to a fairy-tale cliché. The writers could not resist packaging his story in such a fashion, and the Braddocks played along. The *Daily Mirror* ran a twelve-part series under the byline "Mae Fox Braddock, wife of the new world's heavyweight champion." Her first sentence, which was almost certainly ghostwritten, was "My husband may have been a hobo, but he was never a bum!"

Two days after Braddock won the title, Mae told the *Daily Mirror*, "I don't want Jimmy to stay in the business too long. Another fight or so. Then he should have money enough to retire. We don't need much. Although I like to spend money as well as anybody. So does Jim. But our tastes are simple. And confident as I am in my husband, I endure countless agonies while he is in the ring."

For weeks after the fight, the papers featured photographs of Braddock at various functions. He was almost always in the same pose — at a dining table, staring straight into the lens, slicing into a steak and wearing his crooked smile. There was never any hash in sight.

Epilogue

....

Two days after announcing his retirement, Max Baer came out of retirement. Unlike his loss to Braddock, his change of heart was far from an upset.

Within weeks, Hoffman signed the newly wed Baer — he married Mary Ellen Sullivan sixteen days after losing the title — to fight Joe Louis at Yankee Stadium on September 24. On June 25, Louis had destroyed Carnera, beating him as badly as Baer had. Even while the public was falling in love with Braddock, its new heavyweight champion, it was drawn to the Brown Bomber. Braddock was considered a lucky Irishman who took the title from the lackadaisical Baer, but Louis, at twenty-one, was already being hailed as the most complete heavyweight ever. Still, many people thought that Max Baer was too big and too strong for Louis, who was four inches shorter and twenty pounds lighter.

Baer spent the summer training hard for the Louis fight. Everyone in New York wanted to see the great Joe Louis fight the former champion, who finally had something to prove. But Baer was now suffering from Braddock's syndrome — his hands ached constantly. Like everyone else, he had read all the stories about Louis's power and mercilessness, and for the first time in his career he was scared, because he knew he could barely defend himself. In his dressing room before the fight, a doctor numbed his hands with Novocain so he could use them painlessly. But a thunderstorm delayed the commencement of hostilities, and the Novocain started to wear off. Another injection would have made Baer lose all feeling and could not be risked, so with minutes to go before the opening bell and more than 95,000 fans in attendance, Baer, agonizing in his dressing room, decided he couldn't go through with the fight.

Dempsey, still in Baer's corner despite his criticism after the Braddock fight, shook his head in disgust. "You're going out there and you're going to fight like a champion," he said.

"Jack, my hands are killing me," Baer replied. "He'll slaughter me."

"I don't care if they're both broken," Dempsey said. "You're not quitting now."

In the end, Baer feared Dempsey more than he feared Louis. Utterly defeated before he left his dressing room, he walked out into the night.

Almost immediately Louis reduced him to a bloody heap. In the third round, he caught Baer on the jaw with a volley of rights, and for the first time in his six-year career, Baer was felled by a punch. Bravely, he rose, but he was still dazed. Louis then hit him with a flurry of left hooks, and he went down again. At the count of four, the round ended. Dempsey jumped through the ropes and literally dragged Baer to his corner. But in the fourth round, neither the bell nor Dempsey could save him. Louis hit him with a right high on his temple. Baer went down slowly, "his brain awhirl, his muscles limp," Dawson wrote in the *Times*. Somehow he struggled to one knee. But he couldn't rise. The referee, Arthur Donovan, counted him out.

Back in his dressing room, his face swollen to a high purple sheen and his career shattered, the inevitable question was posed: Did you quit?

All the preening had been beaten out of him. He searched for the right words. "I could have got up, but it wouldn't have done me any good," he finally said. Then he paused. "I wasn't going to get up to be killed just to satisfy the crowd. Believe me, if I'm going to get executed, they'll have to pay more than twenty-five dollars apiece to see it. Quit? Sure I quit. But I was just being smart. I don't want anybody going around telling what a brave guy I was — after I'm dead." In other words, he wasn't going to end up like Frankie Campbell and Ernie Schaaf.

Though Baer continued to fight on and off until 1941 — never getting a shot at reclaiming the title — his comments after the Louis fight were to be his boxing epitaph. They reflected everything Max Baer thought about the sport.

Baer was knocked out twice toward the end of his career by Lou Nova, a legitimate heavyweight contender. In 1941, in their second fight — Baer's last appearance in the ring — he had Nova in trouble. But just when he could have finished off his opponent, Baer turned and walked to the other side of the ring. Nova said he sensed that Baer relented because at some level he was afraid of the damage he might have inflicted. Baer didn't want to end up like Frankie Campbell, and he didn't want any more Campbells on his conscience. An effective fighter can't have a conscience — at least not when he's in the ring.

More than sixty years after his last fight, Baer is still remembered for the crushing force of his right hand — and for squandering its potential.

As Baer's career slid inexorably into irrelevance, Jim Braddock reigned, in Damon Runyon's opinion, as "the most popular champion in the history of the game," which was saying quite a lot just a decade after Jack Dempsey ruled the sport. "He has endeared himself to the American public by his unchanging modesty, his affability, and his sturdy character," Runyon wrote in 1936.

At one of the innumerable testimonial dinners held in Braddock's honor when he was the champion, Mayor Fiorello H. La Guardia addressed him directly. "You can't imagine how interested the general public was in your fight," La Guardia said. "The story of how you were on relief and fought your way to the championship for your wife and three kids did more for boxing than any fight in the last twenty-five years. Why, the first thing my wife asked me at the breakfast table the morning after the fight was, 'Well, did the three kids win?'"

When Braddock won, Gould was elevated too. He was hailed both for his loyalty to Braddock during hard times and his doggedness and cunning in steering him to the championship. It was at this time that Gould, puffed up by the plaudits of the newspapermen, said, "I take my hat off to no manager." Yet his greatest managerial stroke was still to come.

After Louis knocked out Baer, Gould started making plans for a Braddock-Louis showdown for the summer of 1936. The Baer-Louis fight generated nearly $1 million — Baer collected a check for $215,000 — which was the largest live gate since Tunney's and Dempsey's rematch in 1927. It was assumed that a championship fight between Braddock and Louis would easily surpass the million-dollar mark, making Gould and Braddock very rich men. In the meantime, champion and manager would make easy money, fighting exhibitions, appearing on radio shows, and, as was the custom, cashing in on the heavyweight belt in as many ways as possible.

From a distance they watched Louis quickly build his reputation, knocking out Carnera, Levinsky, and Baer in a three-month span. None of those victories particularly impressed Braddock, but they did impress millions of fight fans. Plans for a Braddock-Louis fight, however, were complicated by the rivalry between Jimmy Johnston, at Madison Square Garden, and Mike Jacobs, Louis's promoter. On October 11, 1935, Johnston sent a letter to Louis's managers offering him a shot at the title the following June and requesting a reply within seventy-two hours.

But John Roxborough, one of Louis's managers, had another idea. "We prefer to meet Schmeling in June and Braddock in

September," he told reporters the same day Johnston made his offer.

To say that Roxborough had miscalculated would be a colossal understatement. On June 19, 1936, after a five-month layoff, Louis climbed into the ring at Yankee Stadium to fight Max Schmeling, who was eight years his senior and considered far past his prime. Schmeling hadn't fought in eleven months, since defeating Paulino Uzcudan in a twelve-round decision in Berlin on July 7, 1935. The Black Uhlan was an eight-to-one underdog.

But Schmeling, it turned out, was more than prepared for the challenge. Two minutes into the twelfth round, he stunned Louis with a barrage of right hands to the jaw, and Louis crashed to the canvas. Donovan counted him out.

Gould and Braddock were almost as chagrined as Louis and Roxborough. Schmeling had ruined their million-dollar payday.

When the New York boxing commission insisted that Braddock defend his title against Schmeling, Gould resisted, for any number of reasons, most of them financial. First, the Jewish community in New York was threatening to boycott the fight, which would have greatly diminished the gate. Second, even if the Jews did not boycott, there just wasn't a tremendous amount of fan interest in Schmeling, who by this time was a symbol of Nazi arrogance. Finally, it was widely feared that if Schmeling won, the title would be controlled by the Third Reich and that no Jews or blacks would be accepted as challengers.

Defying the commission, Braddock and Gould negotiated to fight Louis, who had recovered from his loss by knocking out virtually an opponent a month starting in August 1936. Gould proposed a remarkable deal with Mike Jacobs. In exchange for giving Louis a shot at the title, Gould and Braddock wanted 10 percent of Jacobs's earnings from heavyweight championship promotions for a decade — regardless of who was fighting. Jacobs could not be certain that Louis would ever get another shot — Braddock could fight Schmeling, the title could go to Germany, and Schmeling might never risk the title against Louis — so he agreed to Gould's terms.

The deal was made, and the fight was scheduled for June 22, 1937, in Chicago. Braddock would become the first heavyweight champion, white or black, to risk his title against a black man in twenty-nine years, since Tommy Burns had fought Jack Johnson in 1908. When the New York commission sought an injunction to prevent Braddock from fighting Louis, a federal judge ruled in Braddock's favor.

Just before the fight, an article appeared in the *Boxing News* under the headline "I Will K.O. Louis," by James J. Braddock, Heavyweight Champion of the World. Defending himself against the doubters — and they were legion — Braddock wrote, "I can still hit and I can still box. Corn Griffin found out about the punching; Maxie Baer and John Henry Lewis found out about the boxing; and in a short time, Joe Louis will find out about both."

When he stepped into the ring at Comiskey Park to fight Louis, Braddock was the heavyweight champion of the world but he was also the underdog, as he had been against Tuffy Griffiths, Corn Griffin, John Henry Lewis, Art Lasky, and Max Baer. He had won all those fights. He had achieved the biggest upset ever in a heavyweight championship fight, and several other stunning victories. Millions of fans hoped he would do to Louis what he had done to Baer. In the first round, he did — he humbled Louis, with a shot to the jaw that sent the challenger to the canvas. For a moment it was 1935 again, and Braddock let himself dream that Louis would fall before him. Maybe, he thought, Schmeling hadn't been so special that night in 1936 when he had knocked out Louis. Maybe Louis's chin really was easily cracked. But Louis got up quickly, more angry than hurt, and threw several punches that landed with impressive power and astounding speed in Braddock's face. Braddock's brief dream was over. He was wide awake, and he knew he was no match for the younger man. At the end of the round, he headed back to his corner, weary, battered, and determined to lose his championship honorably.

Gould looked at Braddock's face, heard his labored breathing, and said, "Come on, Jim, you've got him. Just look for an opening."

Braddock just grimaced.

In the second, third, and fourth rounds, Louis continued to pummel Braddock, who was nearly defenseless against his swift combinations. He was literally being beaten senseless.

"Joe clipped Jimmy a pretty good shot on the jaw midway in the fifth round and we thought that would be the end," explained Whitey Bimstein, who was working Braddock's corner. "But when Jimmy came back to his corner and we asked him how he felt, he said, 'I'm okay, only the lights are bothering me. I can't see right.' The poor guy didn't realize he was losing. He thought the lights were hurting his eyes. That's why he went in again in the sixth and kept on punching even though he was getting the worst of it."

In the sixth, with each Louis punch, more blood spurted from Braddock's mouth. Louis had opened cuts all over his face, and they were bleeding too. Louis wasn't being cruel. He knew he was fighting a man who had to be beaten soundly to be beaten at all. And he also knew that Braddock still possessed enough power to wreck his career with one punch. Louis could not afford to take any chances.

Between the sixth and seventh rounds, Gould began to fear for Braddock's safety. Braddock was no longer capable of defending himself. There was blood all over his trunks and face. In eleven years in Braddock's corner, Gould had never seen him like this. Arcel, Bimstein, and Gould made a quick decision. It was time, they agreed, to throw in the towel.

"That's it, Jim," Gould said firmly. "I'm going to have the referee stop the fight."

"The hell you are," Braddock said. His face was unrecognizable. His eyes were swollen, and he had a deep gash in his forehead.

"It's time," Gould said.

Spitting blood, Braddock answered with the words that remain his boxing epitaph. "If you do, Joe," Braddock said, "I'll never speak to you again."

The battered champion answered the bell in the seventh and took another horrific beating. After the round, Gould did what he could to ease Braddock's suffering, but he could barely stomach the sight of Braddock's blood flowing in thick rivulets down his face. Shabazian and Graham, at ringside, were struggling to keep their emotions in check as they worked under deadline.

Then, early in the eighth, with Braddock completely spent, Louis landed a brutal left hook to his ribs, immediately followed with another left hook to the jaw, and finally a murderous straight right to the chin. Braddock collapsed to the canvas. The punch had knocked his mouthpiece through his lip, opening a cut that would require twenty-three stitches to close and literally scar him for life. For a full ten minutes he lay semiconscious in the middle of the ring. His two-year reign had ended with him on his back. He had lost like a champion — it was a cliché, but one that mattered to him.

"Even when he was knocked out and we brought him back to his senses, the first thing he asked was, 'Did I make a good fight?'" Bimstein said. "There may be better fighters than Braddock, but there'll never be a gamer one."

In the *Daily Mirror*, Dan Parker wrote, "The exhibition of courage the gallant Anglo-Irishman gave before that final bolt of lightning struck him on the side of the jaw awakened admiration and compassion for him in the heart of everyone in that vast crowd."

"The old champion was as game as a butcher's chopping block," Bugs Baer — no relation to Max — wrote for the Hearst syndicate.

Braddock's purse was more than $320,000. He and Gould ended up splitting another $150,000 over the next ten years, per their agreement with Jacobs.

For the rest of his life, Louis said that Braddock was the bravest man he ever fought. Over the years, Braddock and Louis saw each other fairly frequently at fights and black-tie dinners. Louis always greeted Braddock the same way: "Hello, champ." He fought eight world heavyweight champions, more than any other fighter ever, but he never called anyone but Jim Braddock "champ."

In retirement, Baer and Braddock were as different as they had been in the ring.

Always hungry for the spotlight, Baer gravitated to show business. He and Maxie Rosenbloom had a popular nightclub act. He made commercials and starred in radio shows. He was a celebrity referee.

On the morning of November 21, 1959, three days after refereeing a nationally televised heavyweight fight, Baer was in Los Angeles to film a series of television commercials. As he was shaving in his room at the Roosevelt Hotel, he felt a burning sensation in his chest. He called the front desk and said, "I'm having chest pains. I need a doctor."

"The house doctor will be up in a minute," the desk clerk said.

"House doctor?" Baer replied. "No, dummy, I need a people doctor."

Baer, who, like Braddock, had become the loving father of two sons and a daughter, was dead within the hour, of a heart attack, at the age of fifty. More than twenty-four years after surrendering his title to Braddock, his death was reported on the front page of the *New York Times*. That would have pleased him.

After Baer died, Braddock called him the hardest puncher he ever fought, another tribute that would have pleased Baer.

By the late 1960s, Braddock, never a good businessman, had spent all the money he had made as champion and from Mike Jacobs's promotions. Still strong and full of vitality, he was working for the Franklin Contracting Company, operating heavy machinery. "If you feel good," he said on his sixty-fourth birthday, in 1969, "you might as well keep at it, and I'm outdoors in that great Jersey air." Still married to Mae, he lived comfortably in the house he had bought in North Bergen shortly after winning the title.

In his lifetime, his celebrity never completely faded. Up until the end, he received three or four letters a week from people all over the world who had been inspired by his story, which remains a testament to the indomitability of the human spirit. In the record books, where his name will always appear alongside those of John L. Sullivan, Jack Dempsey, Joe Louis, and Muhammad Ali, he is still called the Cinderella Man and remembered as the quintessential fighter's fighter. When pride still mattered, no one displayed more than Jim Braddock.

James J. Braddock died in his sleep in North Bergen on November 30, 1974, at the age of sixty-nine. In the *New York Times*, Red Smith wrote, "If death came easily, it was the only thing in his life that did."

Appendixes

Notes

Acknowledgments

Index

Appendix A

THE HEAVYWEIGHT CHAMPIONSHIP

The champions listed here are the lineal champions—the men who beat the men, back to Sullivan. This list does not include the various alphabet-soup champions who have proliferated since the 1970s.

Champion	Nickname	Reign
John L. Sullivan	The Boston Strong Boy	1885–1892
James J. Corbett	Gentleman Jim	1892–1897
Bob Fitzsimmons	Ruby Robert	1897–1899
James J. Jeffries	The Boilermaker	1899–1905, ret.
Marvin Hart	The Fightin' Kentuckian	1905–1906
Tommy Burns	The Little Giant of Hanover	1906–1908
Jack Johnson	Li'l Arthur	1908–1915
Jess Willard	The Pottawatomie Giant	1915–1919
Jack Dempsey	The Manassa Mauler	1919–1926
Gene Tunney	The Fighting Marine	1926–1928, ret.
Max Schmeling	The Black Uhlan of the Rhine	1930–1932
Jack Sharkey	The Boston Gob	1932–1933
Primo Carnera	The Ambling Alp	1933–1934
Max Baer	The Livermore Larruper	1934–1935
James J. Braddock	The Cinderella Man	1935–1937
Joe Louis	The Brown Bomber	1937–1949, ret.
Ezzard Charles	The Cincinnati Cobra	1949–1951
"Jersey" Joe Walcott	Jersey Joe	1951–1952
Rocky Marciano	The Brockton Blockbuster	1952–1956, ret.
Floyd Patterson	—	1956–1959
Ingemar Johansson	Ingo	1959–1960
Floyd Patterson	—	1960–1962
Charles "Sonny" Liston	Sonny	1962–1964
Cassius Clay	The Louisville Lip	1964–1970, ret.
Joe Frazier	Smokin' Joe	1970–1973
George Foreman	—	1973–1974
Muhammad Ali	The Greatest	1974–1978
Leon Spinks	Neon Leon	1978
Muhammad Ali	The Greatest	1978–1979, ret.
Larry Holmes	The Easton Assassin	1980–1985

Champion	Nickname	Reign
Michael Spinks	—	1985–1988
Mike Tyson	Iron Mike	1988–1990
James "Buster" Douglas	Buster	1990
Evander Holyfield	The Real Deal	1990–1992
Riddick Bowe	Big Daddy	1992–1993
Evander Holyfield	The Real Deal	1993–1994
Michael Moorer	—	1994
George Foreman	Big George	1994–1997
Shannon Briggs	The Cannon	1997–1998
Lennox Lewis	—	1998–2001
Hasim Rahman	The Rock	2001
Lennox Lewis	—	2001–2004, ret.

Source: The Cyber Boxing Zone (www.cyberboxingzone.com).

Appendix B

JAMES J. BRADDOCK'S RING RECORD

46–23–4 (27 wins by knockout)

Date	Opponent	Place	Result
1926			
Apr. 13	Al Settle	Union City, N.J.	ND 4
Apr. 22	George Deschner	Ridgefield Park, N.J.	KO 2
May	Phil Weisberger	Jersey City, N.J.	KO 1
May	Jack O'Day	Jersey City, N.J.	KO 1
May	Willie Daily	Jersey City, N.J.	KO 1
June 18	Leo Dobson	Jersey City, N.J.	KO 1
June 28	Jim Pearson	Jersey City, N.J.	KO 2
July 9	Walter Westman	Jersey City, N.J.	TK 3
Sept. 7	Gene Travers	Jersey City, N.J.	KO 1
Sept. 13	Mike Rock	Jersey City, N.J.	KO 1
Sept. 16	Ray Kennedy	West New York, N.J.	KO 1
Sept. 30	Carmine Caggiano	West New York, N.J.	KO 1
Nov. 12	Lou Barba	New York, N.Y.	W 6
Dec. 4	Al Settles	New York, N.Y.	W 6
Dec. 8	Joe Hudson	New York, N.Y.	W 6
Dec. 20	"Doc" Conrad	Jersey City, N.J.	ND 4
1927			
Jan. 28	George LaRocco	New York, N.Y.	KO 1
Feb. 1	Johnny Alberts	Wilkes-Barre, Pa.	KO 4
Feb. 15	Jack Nelson	Wilkes-Barre, Pa.	W 6
Mar. 3	Lou Barba	New York, N.Y.	W 4
Mar. 8	Nick Fadil	New York, N.Y.	W 6
Mar.	Tom McKiernan	—	KO 2
Apr. 19	Frankie Lennon	Wilkes-Barre, Pa.	KO 3
May 2	Stanley Simmons	Jersey City, N.J.	TK 1
May 11	Jack Stone	West New York, N.J.	ND 10
May 20	George LaRocco	New York, N.Y.	D 6
May 27	Paul Cavalier	Rochelle Park, N.J.	ND 10
June 8	Jimmy Francis	West New York, N.J.	ND 10
July 13	Jimmy Francis	Union City, N.J.	ND 10
July 21	George LaRocco	New York, N.Y.	W 6
Aug. 10	Vic McLaughlin	West New York, N.J.	ND 10
Sept. 21	Herman Heller	West New York, N.J.	ND 10

Date	Opponent	Place	Result
Oct. 5	Joe Monte	New York, N.Y.	D 10
1928			
Jan. 6	Paul Swiderski	New York, N.Y.	W 8
May 7	Jack Darnell	Jersey City, N.J.	KO 4
May 16	Jimmy Francis	West New York, N.J.	ND 10
June 7	Joe Monte	New York, N.Y.	L 10
June 27	Billy Vidabeck	West New York, N.J.	ND 10
July 25	Nando Tassi	New York, N.Y.	D 10
Aug. 8	Joe Sekyra	New York, N.Y.	L 10
Oct. 17	Pete Latzo	Newark, N.J.	W 10
Nov. 30	"Tuffy" Griffiths	New York, N.Y.	KO 2
1929			
Jan. 18	Leo Lomski	New York, N.Y.	L 10
Feb. 4	George Gemas	Newark, N.J.	KO 1
Mar. 11	Jimmy Slattery	New York, N.Y.	TK 9
Apr. 22	Eddie Benson	Buffalo, N.Y.	KO 1
July 18	Tommy Loughran**	New York, N.Y.	L 15
Aug. 27	Yale Okun	Los Angeles, Calif.	L 10
Nov. 15	Maxie Rosenbloom	New York, N.Y.	L 10
Dec. 7	Jack "Jake" Warren	Brooklyn, N.Y.	KO 2
1930			
Jan. 17	Leo Lomski	Chicago, Ill.	L 10
Apr. 7	Billy Jones	Philadelphia, Pa.	L 10
June 5	Harold Mays	West New York, N.J.	ND 10
July 2	Joe Monte	Boston, Mass.	W 10
Aug. 11	Alvin "Babe" Hunt	Boston, Mass.	L 10
Sept. 19	Phil Mercurio	Boston, Mass.	KO 2
1931			
Jan. 23	Ernie Schaaf	New York, N.Y.	L 10
Mar. 5	Jack Roper	Miami, Fla.	KO 1
Mar. 30	Jack Kelly	New Haven, Conn.	W 10
Sept. 3	Andy Mitchell	Detroit, Mich.	D 10
Oct. 9	Joe Sekyra	New York, N.Y.	L 10
Nov. 10	Maxie Rosenbloom	Minneapolis, Minn.	NC 2
Dec. 4	Al Gainer	New Haven, Conn.	L 10
1932			
Mar. 18	Baxter Calmes	Chicago, Ill.	L 10
May 13	Charley Retzlaff	Boston, Mass.	L 10
June 21	Vincent Parille	Long Island City, N.Y.	W 5
July 25	Tony Shucco	Long Island City, N.Y.	L 8
Sept. 21	John Henry Lewis	San Francisco, Calif.	L 10
Sept. 30	Dynamite Jackson	San Diego, Calif.	W 10

Date	Opponent	Place	Result
Oct. 21	Tom Patrick	Hollywood, Calif.	L 10
Nov. 9	Lou Scozza	San Francisco, Calif.	LT 6
1933			
Jan. 13	Martin Levandowski	Chicago, Ill.	W 10
Jan. 20	Hans Birkie	New York, N.Y.	L 10
Mar. 1	Al Ettore	Philadelphia, Pa.	LF 4
Mar. 21	Al Stillman	St. Louis, Mo.	TK 10
Apr. 5	Martin Levandowski	St. Louis, Mo.	L 10
May 19	Al Stillman	St. Louis, Mo.	L 10
June 21	Les Kennedy	Jersey City, N.J.	W 10
July 21	Chester Matan	West New York, N.J.	W 10
Sept. 25	Abe Feldman	Mount Vernon, N.Y.	NC 6
1934			
June 14	"Corn" Griffin	Long Island City, N.Y.	TK 3
Nov. 16	John Henry Lewis	New York, N.Y.	W 10
1935			
Mar. 22	Art Lasky	New York, N.Y.	W 15
June 13	Max Baer*	Long Island City, N.Y.	W 15
1937			
June 22	Joe Louis*	Chicago, Ill.	KO'd by 8
1938			
Jan. 21	Tommy Farr	New York, N.Y.	W 10

Note: There are a few conflicts in Braddock's ring record that should be addressed here. Most are explained by the fact that in the 1920s many fights were officially scored as no-decisions but scored by newspaper reporters as wins, losses, or draws. For instance, the record is not quite clear concerning the three fights between Braddock and Jimmy Francis in 1927 and 1928. The record books score all three as no-decisions, but in one reference, Lud Shabazian says Braddock won all three fights. In another, though, Shabazian writes that Braddock and Francis fought no-decisions in their first two fights while Braddock won their third fight, on May 16, 1928. Shabazian also writes that Braddock knocked out Leo Dobson in two rounds. The record books say it was a first-round knockout.

Sources: The Cyber Boxing Zone (www.cyberboxingzone.com); Lud Shabazian, *Relief to Royalty* (Union City, N.J.: Hudson Dispatch, 1936); James Roberts and Alexander G. Skutt, *The Boxing Register*, 3d ed. (Ithaca, N.Y.: McBooks, 2002).

Key

W: Won decision	NC: No contest
KO: Won by knockout	D: Draw
LT: Lost by technical knockout	ND: No decision
KO'd by: Lost by knockout	TK: Won by technical knockout
LD: Lost decision	*: For the heavyweight championship
LF: Lost on foul	**: For the light heavyweight championship

Appendix C

MAX BAER'S RING RECORD

72–12 (53 wins by knockout)

Date	Opponent	Place	Result
1929			
May 16	Chief Caribou	Stockton, Calif.	KO 2
June 6	Sailor Leeds	Stockton, Calif.	KO 1
July 4	Tillie Taverna	Stockton, Calif.	KO 1
July 18	Al Ledford	Stockton, Calif.	KO 1
July 24	Benny Hill	Oakland, Calif.	W 4
July 31	Benny Hill	Oakland, Calif.	W 4
Aug. 28	Al Ledford	Oakland, Calif.	KO 2
Sept. 4	Jack McCarthy	Oakland, Calif.	LF 3
Sept. 25	Frank Rujenski	Oakland, Calif.	KO 3
Oct. 2	George Carroll	Oakland, Calif.	KO 1
Oct. 16	Chief Caribou	Oakland, Calif.	KO 1
Oct. 30	Alex Rowe	Oakland, Calif.	KO 1
Nov. 6	Natie Brown	Oakland, Calif.	W 6
Nov. 20	Tillie Taverna	Oakland, Calif.	KO 2
Dec. 4	Chet Shandel	Oakland, Calif.	KO 2
Dec. 30	Tony Fuente	Oakland, Calif.	KO 1
1930			
Jan. 15	Tiny Abbott	Oakland, Calif.	LF 3
Jan. 29	Tiny Abbott	Oakland, Calif.	KO 6
Apr. 9	Jack Stewart	Oakland, Calif.	KO 2
Apr. 22	Ernie Owens	Los Angeles, Calif.	W 10
May 7	Tom Toner	Oakland, Calif.	KO 6
May 28	Jack Linkhorn	Oakland, Calif.	KO 1
June 11	Ora "Buck" Weaver	Oakland, Calif.	KO 1
June 25	Ernie Owens	Oakland, Calif.	TK 5
July 15	Les Kennedy	Los Angeles, Calif.	LD 10
Aug. 11	Meyer "K.O." Christner	Oakland, Calif.	KO 2
Aug. 25	Frankie Campbell	San Francisco, Calif.	KO 5
Dec. 19	Ernie Schaaf	New York, N.Y.	LD 10
1931			
Jan. 16	Tom Heeney	New York, N.Y.	KO 3
Feb. 6	Tommy Loughran	New York, N.Y.	LD 10
Apr. 7	Ernie Owens	Portland, Ore.	KO 2

Date	Opponent	Place	Result
May 5	Johnny Risko	Cleveland, Ohio	LD 10
July 4	Paolino Uzcudun	Reno, Nev.	LD 20
Sept. 23	Jack Van Noy	Oakland, Calif.	TK 8
Oct. 21	Jose Santa	Oakland, Calif.	KO 10
Nov. 9	Johnny Risko	San Francisco, Calif.	W 10
Nov. 23	Les Kennedy	Oakland, Calif.	KO 3
Dec. 30	Arthur DeKuh	Oakland, Calif.	W 10
1932			
Jan. 29	King Levinsky	New York, N.Y.	W 10
Feb. 22	Tom Heeney	San Francisco, Calif.	W 10
Apr. 26	Paul Swiderski	Los Angeles, Calif.	KO 7
May 11	Walter Cobb	Oakland, Calif.	TK 4
July 4	King Levinsky	Reno, Nev.	W 20
Aug. 31	Ernie Schaaf	Chicago, Ill.	W 10
Sept. 26	"Tuffy" Griffith	Chicago, Ill.	TK 7
1933			
June 8	Max Schmeling	New York, N.Y.	TK 10
1934			
June 14	Primo Carnera*	Long Island City, N.Y.	TK 11
1935			
June 13	Jim Braddock*	Long Island City, N.Y.	LD 15
Sept. 24	Joe Louis	New York, N.Y.	KO'd by 4
1936			
June 15	Tony Souza	Salt Lake City, Utah	W 6
June 17	Bob Frazier	Boise, Idaho	TK 2
June 19	Harold "Millionaire" Murphy	Pocatello, Idaho	W 6
June 23	George Brown	Tyler, Tex.	KO 3
June 24	Wilson Dunn	San Antonio, Tex.	KO 3
July 2	Alfred "Butch" Rogers	Dallas, Tex.	KO 3
July 13	Jim Merriott	Oklahoma City, Okla.	KO 2
July 16	Junior Munsell	Tulsa, Okla.	KO 5
July 18	Cecil Smith	Ada, Okla.	W 4
July 24	Bob Williams	Ogden, Utah	KO 1
Aug. 19	James J. Walsh	Vancouver, BC, Can.	KO 1
Aug. 20	Nails Gorman	Marshfield, Ore.	TK 2
Aug. 25	Cecil Myart	Portland, Ore.	W 6
Aug. 29	Al Frankco	Lewiston, Idaho	KO 2
Aug. 31	Don Baxter	Coeur d'Alene, Idaho	KO 1
Sept. 2	Al Gaynor	Twin Falls, Idaho	KO 1
Sept. 3	Eddie Franks	Provo, Utah	KO 3
Sept. 8	Sammy Evans	Casper, Wyo.	KO 4
Sept. 14	Ed "Bearcat" Wright	Des Moines, Iowa	W 6

Date	Opponent	Place	Result
Sept. 21	Andy "Kid" Miller	Sheldon, Iowa	W 6
Sept.	Cyclone Bench	Rock Springs, Wyo.	KO
Sept. 30	Babe Davis	Keokuk, Iowa	W 6
Oct. 6	Tim Charles	Evansville, Ill.	KO 4
Oct. 8	Art Oliver	Platteville, Wis.	LD 6
Oct. 19	Dutch Weimer	Toronto, Ont., Can.	KO 2
1937			
Apr. 15	Tommy Farr	London, Eng.	LD 12
May 27	Ben Foord	London, Eng.	TK 9
1938			
Mar. 11	Tommy Farr	New York, N.Y.	W 15
Oct. 27	Ellsworth "Hank" Hankinson	Honolulu, Hawaii	KO 1
1939			
June 1	Lou Nova	New York, N.Y.	LT 11
Sept. 4	Ed Murphy	Silver Peak, Nev.	KO 1
Sept. 18	Babe Ritchie	Lubbock, Tex.	KO 2
1940			
July 2	Tony Galento	Jersey City, N.J.	TK 8
Sept. 26	Pat Comiskey	Jersey City, N.J.	TK 1
1941			
Apr. 4	Lou Nova	New York, N.Y.	LT 8

Sources: The Cyber Boxing Zone (www.cyberboxingzone.com); Nat Fleischer, *Max Baer, the Glamour Boy of the Ring* (New York: O'Brien, 1941); James Roberts and Alexander G. Skutt, *The Boxing Register*, 3d ed. (Ithaca, N.Y.: McBooks, 2002).

Key

W: Won decision
KO: Won by knockout
LT: Lost by technical knockout
KO'd by: Lost by knockout
LD: Lost decision
LF: Lost on foul
NC: No contest
D: Draw
ND: No decision
TK: Won by technical knockout
*: For the heavyweight championship

Notes

Preface

viii "typified the plight": "Women Will Seek $3,000,000 for Idle," *New York Times*, Nov. 24, 1932, p. 30.

ix "His time was the Great Depression": Red Smith, "A Champion for His Time," *New York Times*, Dec. 1, 1974, p. 255.

x "the Cinderella Man": Peter Heller, *In This Corner . . . !* (New York: Da Capo, 1994), p. 173.

xi "Jack Johnson's impact": John Lardner, *White Hopes and Other Tigers* (Philadelphia: Lippincott, 1951), p. 13.

    "Who was that man?": Ibid.

xii "Outlined against": Grantland Rice, *The Tumult and the Shouting* (New York: A. S. Barnes, 1963), p. 177.

    "It was Granny": Arthur Daley, "The Little General from Notre Dame," *New York Times*, Jan. 27, 1965, p. 38.

    "I don't want": Lud Shabazian, *Relief to Royalty* (Union City, N.J.: Hudson Dispatch, 1936), p. 1.

1. Corn and Hash

1 In eighty pro fights: *The Boxing Register: International Boxing Hall of Fame Official Record Book*, 3d ed. (Ithaca, N.Y.: McBooks, 2002), p. 65.

2 His parents: Lud Shabazian, *Relief to Royalty* (Union City, N.J.: Hudson Dispatch, 1936), p. 12.

3 Braddock announced his retirement: When he eventually won the championship, it was frequently written that he had retired twice from boxing. The *Ring* calls him "twice retired" in 1935 in a story titled "Dame Fortune Smiles on Braddock," by George T. Tickell. The sources, though, are inconsistent. The retirement question is clouded by the fact that a boxer like Braddock in the early 1930s, unranked and with no

prospects, could have informally retired a dozen times without anyone's noticing.

5   Unlike Jim Braddock: Much of the information about Corn Griffin in this chapter came from Shabazian, *Relief to Royalty,* and Frank Graham, Jr., "Relief to Royalty on Hope, Hash and Corn," *Sports Illustrated,* Apr. 15, 1963.

"Griffin," someone once wrote: Graham, "Relief to Royalty."

6   It was widely assumed: John Lardner, "The Big Man with the Biggest Punch," *New York Times,* Aug. 26, 1956, p. SM9.

Carnera was also the sad inspiration: Thomas Hauser and Stephen Brunt, *The Italian Stallions, Heroes of Boxing's Glory Days* (Toronto: Sportclassic Books, 2004), p. 27.

"Carnera was the only": Paul Gallico, "Pity the Poor Giant," in *The Fireside Book of Boxing,* W. C. Heinz, ed. (New York: Simon & Schuster, 1961), pp. 151–52.

"For breakfast": Lawrence Ritter, *East Side, West Side: Tales of New York Sporting Life 1910–1960* (Toronto: Sportclassic Books, 1998), p. 110.

7   "Carnera encountered": Joseph C. Nichols, "Carnera Engages in Speedy Session," *New York Times,* June 4, 1934, p. 21.

"As a sparring partner": Frank Graham, Jr., *A Farewell to Heroes* (New York: Viking, 1981), p. 62.

"Two years from now": Graham, "Relief to Royalty."

8   "started in New York": John D. McCallum, *The World Heavyweight Boxing Championship: A History* (Radnor, Pa.: Chilton, 1974), p. 194.

9   "It's a deal": Frank Graham, Jr., tells the story this way in *It Takes Heart,* written with Mel Allen (New York: Harper, 1959), p. 83. But other accounts of the meeting between Johnston and Gould paint a different picture of the proceedings. According to some, it was Johnston, not Gould, who suggested Braddock as an opponent for Griffin, and it was Gould, not Johnston, who feared for Braddock's safety. In Shabazian's account, Johnston supposedly told Gould, "You're always on my neck for a bout for that washed-up heavyweight of yours, but when I give you one, you turn around and offer to fight somebody else. Well, you'll fight Griffin or you won't fight at all" (*Relief to Royalty,* p. 96).

10   "I had about two days' notice": Frank Graham, "Setting the Pace," *New York Sun,* June 7, 1935, p. 30.

It was opened in 1921: Ritter, *East Side, West Side,* p. 181.

11   "Fresh air?": Ronald K. Fried, *Corner Men: Great Boxing Trainers* (New York: Four Walls Eight Windows, 1991), p. 37.

"Big or small": Ibid., p. 38.

12   "We wuz robbed!": Ibid., p. 110.

16   "Corn's in worse shape": William R. Conklin, "Braddock Strikes Blow," *New York Times,* Feb. 3, 1956, p. 30.

16 "He had me on the deck": Peter Heller, *In This Corner . . . !* (New York: Da Capo, 1994), p. 172. Gould predicted in 1934 in a Frank Graham column in the *Sun* that Braddock would defeat Lasky because he always had success against left hookers.

2. The Battle of Nurge's Field

18 On July 8, 1889: Nat Fleischer, *The Heavyweight Championship: An Informal History of Heavyweight Boxing from 1719 to the Present Day* (New York: Putnam's, 1949), p. 94.

19 "Dad was a fighting Irishman": James Lambert Harte, *The Amazing Story of James J. Braddock* (Emmaus, Pa.: Rodale, 1938), p. 21.

21 "There were thirty-five boys": Ibid.

When Braddock was ten: Mrs. Mae Fox Braddock, as told to Frank Doyle, "Irish Eyes Smile on Braddock," *Sunday Mirror*, June 16, 1935, p. 3.

"It was so cold": Lud Shabazian, *Relief to Royalty* (Union City, N.J.: Hudson Dispatch, 1936), p. 16.

22 "If I happened": Harte, *Amazing Story*, p. 10.

"Serene was Braddock": Jimmy Cannon, "Pity the Poor Fighters," *New York Post*, Jan. 11, 1998, p. 79.

23 "I hardly think": Willard expressed these sentiments consistently for more than fifty years. "If Johnson was going to take a dive," he said, "I wish he'd have done it sooner. It was hotter than hell out there" ("Our Man in Havana and His View of the Great White Hoax," *Canberra Times*, Aug. 23, 1998, p. 14).

24 "managed himself": John Lardner, *White Hopes and Other Tigers* (Philadelphia: Lippincott, 1951), p. 72.

25 His curiosity satisfied: Dick Snider, "Is Jack Dempsey the Greatest Sports Figure of All Time?" *Topeka Capital-Journal*, Oct. 2, 2000.

32 "I feinted him": Lud Shabazian, *Relief to Royalty* (Union City, N.J.: Hudson Dispatch, 1936), p. 33.

34 "You want to make five bucks?": This story is recounted in several sources, including Shabazian, *Relief to Royalty*, and Frank Graham, "He Never Had Many Street Fights," *New York Sun*, Nov. 21, 1934. Graham also offers an account of Braddock's first meeting with Gould in the *Sun* on Sept. 24, 1942, in a column titled "It Began in a Gymnasium in Hoboken." I often quote the dialogue in Graham's columns verbatim. It was widely thought that he possessed the best memory and the best ear of any of his contemporaries; when he quoted people, they said it, which wasn't always the case with other columnists. Gould told the Galfund story hundreds, if not thousands, of times, and it appeared in varying forms in dozens of newspapers.

36 "Tell him I'll be here": Harte also retells the Galfund story, and much of the dialogue in my account is similar to his.

3. The Meat Inspector

39   Suddenly most certified meat inspectors: Meat inspection had finally become a serious business in the U.S. armed forces. Tragically, when Fiorello La Guardia, the future mayor of New York, was in his youth, his father contracted hepatitis serving in the U.S. Army during the Spanish-American War — after ingesting rancid meat. Six years after the war, never having recovered from the infection, Achille La Guardia died. The circumstances of his father's death shaped La Guardia's reformist outlook.

"Just imagine": Lud Shabazian, *Relief to Royalty* (Union City, N.J.: Hudson Dispatch, 1936), p. 42.

40   Gould liked to tell a story: Frank Graham, "All the Way to the Grave," in *The Fireside Book of Boxing*, W. C. Heinz, ed. (New York: Simon & Schuster, 1961), p. 165.

41   "In spite of a compulsion": John Lardner, *White Hopes and Other Tigers* (Philadelphia: Lippincott, 1951), p. 17.

"I take my hat off": Ibid.

"The manager may be": Ibid.

42   "They looked like Mutt and Jeff": John D. McCallum, *The World Heavyweight Boxing Championship: A History* (Radnor, Pa.: Chilton, 1974), p. 192.

43   When Dobson, who was black: The Dobson weigh-in story was gleaned in bits and pieces from several sources, including Francis Albertanti, "Relief to Royalty," *Ring Magazine*, and Frank Graham, *New York Sun*, Nov. 21, 1934.

46   "Sure, bye": Francis Albertanti, "Braddock's Mother Behind His Startling Rise," *Ring Magazine*, Feb. 1929, p. 23.

4. The Livermore Butcher Boy

47   "That's right": John D. McCallum, *The Encyclopedia of World Boxing Champions Since 1882* (Radnor, Pa.: Chilton, 1975), p. 41.

48   "the New Deal": John D. McCallum, *The World Heavyweight Boxing Championship: A History* (Radnor, Pa.: Chilton, 1974), p. 175.

"Above all else": Ron Fimrite, "Send in the Clown," *Sports Illustrated*, Mar. 20, 1978, p. 67.

49   "Max was the most misunderstood": Peter Heller, *In This Corner . . . !* (New York: Da Capo, 1994), p. 125.

"Our father's a champion": McCallum, *World Heavyweight Championship*, p. 178.

50   He claimed that when he was attacked: *Oakland Post-Enquirer*, "Life of Max Baer," ch. 1, in *New York Daily Mirror*, June 18, 1934, p. 2.

"A lucky punch": Baer told this story frequently. His son Max Junior recounted it for me, and it also appears in Nat Fleischer, *Max Baer, the Glamour Boy of the Ring* (New York: C. J. O'Brien, 1941), p. 5, and Nat

Loubet, "Max Adelbert Baer: The Magnificent One," *Ring Magazine*, Feb. 1960, p. 39.

51 The receipts: John Lardner, *White Hopes and Other Tigers* (Philadelphia: Lippincott, 1951), p. 150.

"Even the subway": "Fight Nightlights and Some Shadows," *New York Times*, Sept. 15, 1923, p. 2.

"It was not a boxing match": Frank Menke, "Dempsey-Firpo," in *The Fireside Book of Boxing*, W. C. Heinz, ed. (New York: Simon & Schuster, 1961), p. 291.

52 "I fell right on top": Heller, *In This Corner*, p. 60.

"The crowd saw four minutes": Lardner, *White Hopes*, p. 150.

"It was the most dramatic": "Morning Briefing: You're Only as Old as They Say You Are," *Los Angeles Times*, Sept. 14, 1988, p. S2.

"The fighting instinct": Fleischer, *Max Baer*, p. 6.

53 Before Baer turned eighteen: Al Santoro and John Walbridge, "Life of Max Baer," ch. 2, in *New York Daily Mirror*, June 19, 1934, p. 33.

54 "Max worked for me": Fleischer, *Max Baer*, p. 9.

55 "a hard-bitten hombre": Ibid., p. 11.

56 "Hello, I'll bet": Santoro and Walbridge, "Life of Max Baer," ch. 24, in *New York Daily Mirror*, July 11, 1934, p. 29.

He arrived in a sixteen-cylinder limousine: Fimrite, "Send in the Clown," p. 72.

57 Campbell's real name: My account of the Baer-Campbell fight and its aftermath relies heavily on the reporting of the *San Francisco Chronicle*, the *Oakland Post-Enquirer*, the *Sacramento Bee*, and the *Sacramento Union*, as well as subsequent accounts by Nat Fleischer and Ron Fimrite. See also Le Pacini, "The Most Infamous Fight," *San Franciscan*, n.d.

58 "Frankie had better not": In Fimrite, "Send in the Clown," p. 70.

59 "keep fighting": Ibid.

"Something feels like": Ibid., p. 72.

"seemed to carry": Rudy Hickey, "Stricken Lad Allowed to Stay on Ring Floor for Thirty Minutes," *Sacramento Bee*, Aug. 27, 1930, p. 14.

60 "As the fans milled around": Rudy Hickey, "Campbell Never Regained Consciousness," *Sacramento Bee*, Aug. 27, 1930, p. 14.

"he just stood there": Fimrite, "Send in the Clown," p. 72.

"It's all right": "Young Widow Absolves Baer of All Blame," *San Francisco Chronicle*, Aug. 27, 1930.

"Campbell's brain": "Baer Fight Death Under Double Sift," *San Francisco Chronicle*, Aug. 27, 1930, p. 1.

The complainant: Associated Press, "Baer Arraignment Postponed," *Sacramento Union*, Aug. 28, 1930.

61 "I went into the ring": Pacini, "Most Infamous Fight."

"He should have stopped": "Campbell's Manager Criticizes Referee," *Sacramento Union*, Aug. 27, 1930.

61   "According to the ethics": Hickey, "Campbell Never Regained," p. 14.
62   "Max is heartsick": Pacini, "Most Infamous Fight."

5. Spooked by the Phantom

67   "The punch was a Firpo-like club": "Monte Stops Muskie in Second Round," *New York Times*, July 22, 1927, p. 10.
68   "What did he want": See John D. McCallum, *The World Heavyweight Boxing Championship: A History* (Radnor, Pa.: Chilton, 1974), p. 152.
71   "Almost exclusively a counter-fighter": James P. Dawson, "Sekyra Is Victor Against Braddock," *New York Times*, Aug. 9, 1928, p. 13.
72   "Only a superman": "Dempsey Says Only a Superman Will Beat Heeney," *New York Times*, July 23, 1928, p. 19.
     "The youngster gave indications": Ibid.
73   "After all, we beat": See Lud Shabazian, *Relief to Royalty* (Union City, N.J.: Hudson Dispatch, 1936), p. 59.
74   Lou Stillman made him feel welcome: In the Nov. 28, 1928, edition of the *Sun*, Wilbur Wood wrote, "There was more tongue-wagging around Lou Stillman's gymnasium during and after Tuffy Griffiths's workout there yesterday than in many a moon. It was the mob's first chance to get a peek at the Sioux City light heavyweight with gloves on his hands and the place was packed" ("Griffiths Has Class in Drill," p. 28). In the Nov. 30, 1928, edition of the *New York American*, on p. 9, under the headline "Griffiths in New York Ring Debut Tonight," Ed Fayne wrote, "For months word has been coming from the wide open spaces of the sensational doings of young 'Tuffy' Griffiths." Two days earlier in the *American*, the caption accompanying a photograph of Griffiths and his manager, Jack O'Keefe, said, "Gymnasium critics went wild over 'Tuffy' Griffiths when he made his first appearance here yesterday."
78   "No one who saw that fight": Shabazian, *Relief to Royalty*, p. 59.
79   "Young man": The Muldoon anecdote is another oft-told chapter of the Braddock story. See Shabazian, *Relief to Royalty*, p. 60, and "Muldoon Prophecy True," *New York Times*, June 14, 1935, p. 29. George T. Tickell also quotes Muldoon: "If you handle this boy right, he'll climb high. Right now he could make lots of trouble for any of the leaders in his class, and you're a lucky fellow to have him in your stable" ("Dame Fortune Smiles on Braddock," *Ring Magazine*, July 1935, p. 15).
80   "I am happy": Francis Albertanti, "Braddock's Mother Behind His Startling Rise," *Ring Magazine*, Feb. 1929, p. 23.
81   "Looks like they are picking": Ibid., p. 22.
     "Nobody chops wood": "Sports World Specials," *New York Times*, Dec. 27, 1982, p. C2.
     "In more ways than one": Albertanti, "Braddock's Mother," p. 23.
82   "He'll knock out Lomski": "Favors Braddock to Beat Lomski," *New York Times*, Jan. 14, 1929, p. 28.

83 "The trouble with Braddock's work": James P. Dawson, "18,000 see Lomski Defeat Braddock," *New York Times*, Jan. 19, 1929, p. 16.

84 "He was a brilliant boxer": Shabazian, *Relief to Royalty*, p. 62.
"Reports from there": "Braddock Engages in Strenuous Drill", *New York Times*, Mar. 8, 1929, p. 27.

85 "James J. Braddock advanced": James P. Dawson, "Slattery Stopped by Braddock in 9th," *New York Times*, Mar. 12, 1929, p. 36.

87 "He was a guy": Peter Heller, *In This Corner . . . !* (New York: Da Capo, 1994), p. 173.
"Tommy won't be 27": John Kieran, "Sports of the Times," *New York Times*, July 18, 1929, p. 19.

88 "A gent who doesn't care": In Shabazian, *Relief to Royalty*, p. 68.
"That guy will be duck soup": Mrs. James J. Braddock, as told to Frank Doyle, "Floored by Love, Jinx Pursued Braddock, His Wife Says," *New York Daily Mirror*, June 21, 1935.
"Braddock is the picture": "Braddock to Insist on New Bout Terms," *New York Times*, July 17, 1929, p. 30.
"The fight had hardly started": Shabazian, *Relief to Royalty*, p. 69.

90 "He couldn't hit me": Heller, *In This Corner*, p. 124.
"Hit him with your right hand": Frank Graham, "Setting the Pace," *New York Sun*, Sept. 24, 1942, p. 22.
"In the fourteenth": James P. Dawson, "Braddock Is Beaten by Tommy Loughran," *New York Times*, July 19, 1929, p. 22.
"The way Loughran boxed": In Shabazian, *Relief to Royalty*, p. 72.
"Jimmy looked like he had been run through": Mrs. James J. Braddock, "Floored by Love."

91 "He didn't land his right": Shabazian, *Relief to Royalty*, p. 73.
"It was a very bad night": Graham, "Setting the Pace."
"No fighter ever had": Ibid.
"It always seemed to me": McCallum, *World Heavyweight Championship*, p. 192.

92 "That was a comedy interlude": John Kieran, "Sports of the Times," *New York Times*, June 30, 1931, p. 20.

6. The Great White Way

93 "That dough lasted": Nat Fleischer, *Max Baer, the Glamour Boy of the Ring* (New York: C. J. O'Brien, 1941), p. 15.
"She was a type": Ibid., p. 17.

96 "an erroneous impression": "Sees Relief Abused in Bread Lines Here," *New York Times*, Dec. 16, 1930, p. 3.

97 "There was a young scrapper": Fleischer, *Max Baer*, p. 18.

98 "Not yet": Wilbur Wood, "Baer Talks a Great Fight," *New York Sun*, Dec. 4, 1930.
"I figure the fight game": Ibid.

98 "They were a handsome": Fleischer, *Max Baer*, p. 18.
100 "Ernie Schaaf": James P. Dawson, "Schaaf Triumphs in Bout with Baer," *New York Times*, Dec. 20, 1930, p. 24.
101 "Round after round": Wilbur Wood, "Baer, a Throwback to Dempsey," *Ring Magazine*, June 1934, p. 3.

"We boxed ten rounds": Peter Heller, *In This Corner . . . !* (New York: Da Capo, 1994), p. 125.

He was meeting: The breakfast scene at the Warwick, including the dialogue here, is recounted in Grantland Rice's autobiography, *The Tumult and the Shouting* (New York: Barnes, 1954), p. 128.
103 "One reason he failed": Fleischer, *Max Baer*, p. 22.

7. The Crash and the Jinx

105 "We in America today": "America in 1929: The Prosperity Illusion," *Business Week*, Sept. 3, 1979.

By 1929: "Roots of Disaster," *Business Week*, Sept. 3, 1979, p. 6.
106 "Sooner or later a crash": "Babson Predicts Crash in Stocks," *New York Times*, Sept. 6, 1929, p. 12.

"What can be said": "Comment of Press on Crash in Stocks," *New York Times*, Oct. 30, 1929, p. 7.
108 "It was a nice club": Mrs. James J. Braddock, as told to Frank Doyle, "Floored by Love, Jinx Pursued Braddock, His Wife Says," *New York Daily Mirror*, June 21, 1935.
110 "That's another point": John Kieran, "Sports of the Times," *New York Times*, Nov. 15, 1929, p. 32.
111 "fled from the building": Lud Shabazian, *Relief to Royalty* (Union City, N.J.: Hudson Dispatch, 1936), p. 75.

"As soon as they started trading": Mrs. James J. Braddock, "Champ's $20,000 Lost in Stocks," *New York Daily Mirror*, June 22, 1935.

"I'm disgusted": Shabazian, *Relief to Royalty*, p. 75.
112 "While the action": "Verdict of Draw Changed 11 Days After Bout," *New York Times*, Jan. 29, 1930, p. 27.

"Announcer Smith grabbed": Ibid.
113 "Any time now": John Kieran, "Sports of the Times," *New York Times*, Jan. 30, 1930, p. 28.

"I have received": Shabazian, *Relief to Royalty*, p. 77.

"Everything looked rosy": Mrs. James J. Braddock, "Floored by Love."
114 All the money: Shabazian, *Relief to Royalty*, pp. 78–79.
115 "sensational ten-round battle": "Hunt Outpoints Braddock," *New York Times*, Aug. 12, 1930, p. 24.

"There is no profession": Francis Albertanti, "Braddock's Mother Behind His Startling Rise," *Ring Magazine*, Feb. 1929, p. 23.

"He got married": Frank Graham, "Setting the Pace: He Never Had Many Street Fights," *New York Sun*, Nov. 21, 1934.

118 "A majority of the slim crowd": James P. Dawson, "Schaaf Wins Bout Against Braddock," *New York Times*, Jan. 24, 1931, p. 21.

"After watching James J. Braddock": John Kieran, "Sports of the Times," *New York Times*, Jan. 25, 1931, p. S2.

"James J. Braddock is an exponent": John Kieran, "Sports of the Times," *New York Times*, Jan. 30, 1931, p. 26.

119 "It was pathetic": John Kieran, "Sports of the Times," *New York Times*, Dec. 18, 1931, p. 34.

"I wept and wept": Mrs. James J. Braddock, "Champ's $20,000 Lost."

"Never mind, baby": Ibid.

120 "In return for pledges": "Purses of Fighters Ordered to Charity," *New York Times*, Nov. 12, 1931, p. 32.

The only explanation: Mrs. James J. Braddock, "Champion Is Overjoyed by Arrival of Son," *New York Sunday Mirror*, June 23, 1935, p. 12.

121 At lunch they would share: Gould often described his relationship with Braddock during the hardest times. Shabazian mentions the meals Gould and Braddock split, as does Lemuel F. Parton, "Win or Lose Gould and Braddock Will Eat at the Crillon," *New York Sun*, June 14, 1937.

At the time boxers wore: Personal interview with George Horowitz, Everlast Sporting Goods Company, June 2004, New York, New York.

122 Parrille, who outweighed: "Retzlaff Triumphs in Fight at Bowl," *New York Times*, June 22, 1932, p. 28.

Just as they were being booked: "Jim Braddock Breaks Police Captain's Nose in Free-for-All at Headquarters," *Jersey Journal*, July 7, 1932, p. 1.

123 Two policemen: Ibid.

"Braddock was ranked": Ibid.

127 "Them knockout sensations": Shabazian, *Relief to Royalty*, p. 81.

128 "a slow-motion picture": James P. Dawson, "Birkie Is Victor," *New York Times*, Jan. 21, 1933, p. 18.

132 Braddock went back: Red Smith, "A Champion for His Time," *New York Times*, Dec. 1, 1974, p. 255.

8. The Lord of the Jungle

135 Later, the *Oakland Post-Enquirer*: Al Santoro and John Walbridge, "Life of Max Baer," ch. 21, in *New York Daily Mirror*, July 8, 1934, p. 33.

136 "You can never tell": Wilbur Wood, "Baer, a Throwback to Dempsey," *Ring Magazine*, June 1934, p. 3.

137 "You can sweat out beer": Quoted in A. J. Liebling, *Back Where I Came From* (New York: Sheridan, 1938), p. 94.

"Stanley Ketchel was twenty-four": Tom Callahan, "Boxing's Allure," *Time*, June 27, 1988, p. 66.

138 "while a fashionable audience": Associated Press, "Max Baer Weds in Reno," *New York Times*, July 9, 1931, p. 6.

139 "Hence, loathed Melancholy": John Kieran, "Allegro di Bravura," *New York Times*, Jan. 29, 1932, p. 22.

140 "I'll make Baer jump": Wood, "Baer, a Throwback," p. 48.

142 He was unconscious: Schaaf was the first boxer mortally wounded in a fight at Madison Square Garden. Benny Paret was the second, on March 24, 1962, in a fight against Emile Griffith.

9. Star of David

145 "He was supposed to be": Bill Gallo, "A Bare Baer Couldn't Make the Cut," *New York Daily News*, Aug. 25, 1996, p. 92.

"You can tell those people": Ron Fimrite, "Send in the Clown," *Sports Illustrated*, Mar. 20, 1978, p. 75.

147 "Max Schmeling's most popular": "Schmeling Began Ring Career at 19," *New York Times*, June 13, 1930, p. 28.

"Listen, kid": John D. McCallum, *The World Heavyweight Boxing Championship: A History* (Radnor, Pa.: Chilton, 1974), p. 140.

149 "I'll beat that Hun": Wilbur Wood, "Baer Revives an Old Stunt," *New York Sun*, Apr. 19, 1933.

150 "He is as playful": Ibid.

151 "I see three of him": Fimrite, "Send in the Clown," p. 75.

"Baer started out like a human tornado": James P. Dawson, "Baer Knocks Out Schmeling in 10th," *New York Times*, June 9, 1933, p. 21.

"That's one for Hitler": "Nazis Still Irked by Baer's Remark," *New York Times*, Mar. 14, 1935, p. 26.

152 "I'm gonna win": "Baer Now Looks to Title," *New York Times*, June 9, 1933, p. 21.

"A new star": Dawson, "Baer Knocks Out Schmeling," p. 21.

155 "Separated and reconciled": "Will Divorce Max Baer," *New York Times*, Nov. 28, 1933, p. 25.

"Mrs. Dorothy Baer": "Mrs. Max Baer Wins Divorce in Mexico," *New York Sun*, Oct. 4, 1933.

156 "Max Baer may have astonished": Mordaunt Hall, "The Screen: Max Baer, Myrna Loy and Walter Huston in 'The Prizefighter and the Lady,'" *New York Times*, Nov. 11, 1933, p. 10.

"It is reliably reported": George T. Pardy, "Gold Versus Glory," *Ring Magazine*, 1933–34, p. 14.

157 "scruples against the film": John Elliot, "Nazis Ban Film Starring Baer," *New York Herald-Tribune*, Mar. 30, 1934.

"They didn't ban": Associated Press, "Baer Pities Poor Frauleins," *New York Herald-Tribune*, Mar. 30, 1934.

10. On the Waterfront

158 "After the fight": Mrs. James J. Braddock, "Champion Is Overjoyed by Arrival of Son," *New York Sunday Mirror*, June 23, 1935, p. 12.

162 "Mae, what's going on?": Mel Allen and Frank Graham, Jr., *It Takes Heart* (New York: Harper, 1959), p. 81.

163 Gould had borrowed: Lud Shabazian, *Relief to Royalty* (Union City, N.J.: Hudson Dispatch, 1936), p. 87.

164 "Mae, please believe me": Mrs. James J. Braddock, "Mrs. Braddock Tells Mental Agony Jim Suffered," *New York Daily Mirror*, June 24, 1935.
"Darling, I can't stand": Mrs. James J. Braddock, as told to Frank Doyle, "Champ's Wife Says Love Inspired Him to Title," *New York Daily Mirror*, June 25, 1935, p. 6.

11. Last One Up's a Sissy

166 "It was all I could do": Harry Cross, "Baer Will Fight Only If Dempsey Shares Profits," *New York Herald-Tribune*, Dec. 11, 1934.

169 "Baer is a bum": See, for example, John D. McCallum, *The World Heavyweight Boxing Championship: A History* (Radnor, Pa.: Chilton, 1974), p. 168.
"There must be something": Edward Van Every, "Baer Declared Physically Fit to Box Carnera," *New York Sun*, June 8, 1934, p. 1.
"The trouble with Max": Ibid.
"The newspapermen are friends": Ibid.

170 "I'm not like Carnera": Joseph C. Nichols, "Baer Uses His Feet in Testing Defense," *New York Times*, June 1, 1934, p. 34.
"He is at just the right peak": "Baer Speeds Work; Boxes Nine Rounds," *New York Times*, June 5, 1934, p. 31.
"Carnera looks good?": John Kieran, "Sights and Sounds at Asbury Park," *New York Times*, June 4, 1934, p. 24.
"But just as sure": Ibid.

171 "With his bronzed features": Ibid.
"You know that movie": Ibid.
Cantwell's doubts: Wilbur Wood, "Baer's Manager Sees Delay," *New York Sun*, June 7, 1934.
"Baer's timing": "Baer Pilot Seeks to Put Off Fight," *New York Times*, June 7, 1934, p. 30.

172 "On what Baer showed me": Van Every, "Baer Declared Physically Fit," p. 1.
"Baer has had plenty": "Garden Wants No Delay," *New York Times*, June 7, 1934, p. 30.
"I will not stand": "Carnera Is Adamant," *New York Times*, June 8, 1934, p. 25.

173 "Here comes the stunt business": Nat Fleischer, *Max Baer, the Glamour Boy of the Ring* (New York: C. J. O'Brien, 1941), p. 30.
"You maka me": Ibid.
"Our opinion": Joseph C. Nichols, "Baer Is Found Fit for Carnera Fight," *New York Times*, June 9, 1934, p. 10.

174 "The contestants": Van Every, "Baer Declared Physically Fit," p. 1.
"Look at all the excitement": Ibid.
"You can't convince me": Nichols, "Baer Is Found Fit," p. 10.

175 "Max wore down": John Kieran, "Sports of the Times," *New York Times*, June 13, 1934, p. 28.

176 "See, I'm a wrestler": Joseph C. Nichols, "Baer Clowns Way Through Workout," *New York Times*, June 10, 1934, p. S8.
"It was plain to see": Ibid.
"I licked Carnera": "Carnera Predicts Victory in Title Bout," *New York Times*, June 10, 1934, p. S8.
"I am in good shape": Ibid.

177 "Baer can hit harder": "Ross Picks Baer to Win," *New York Times*, June 13, 1934, p. 30.

178 "Get out": Telephone interview with Max Baer, Jr., Sept. 15, 2004.

180 "Take care of Harry": Fleischer, *Max Baer*, p. 2.

181 "How's Harry?": Ron Fimrite, "Send in the Clown," *Sports Illustrated*, Mar. 20, 1978, p. 76.
"I lose, don't you see?": "Beaten Champion Weeps Like a Child," *New York Times*, June 15, 1934, p. 27.
"I guess Primo": "Baer Loquacious After the Fight," *New York Times*, June 15, 1934, p. 27.

183 "We've been separated": Jeannette Smits, "'No More Women,' Max Vows, as He Pens *My Life and Loves*," *New York Journal*, June 16, 1934, p. 1.
At the Park Central: The Park Central had already achieved widespread notoriety as the site of the murder of Arnold Rothstein. The gambler who fixed the 1919 World Series was gunned down in 1928 in room 349, after a three-day poker game in which he lost $320,000. The killer thought, perhaps rightly, that Rothstein wasn't good for the money. Twenty-nine years later, on October 25, 1957, Albert Anastasia, the gangster known as the Lord High Executioner, was gunned down in the Park Central's barbershop.
"If Max Baer tried to keep": Edward Van Every, "Girl Secretary Shields Baer," *New York Sun*, July 2, 1934.
"For I'm fed up": Ibid.

184 "Max Baer, My Heart": Jane Franklin, "Baer Love Letters on Asbestos," *New York Daily Mirror*, June 21, 1934.
"My dear Max": Ibid.

185 "Baer Never Learned": *New York Evening Journal*, June 18, 1934, p. 25.
"if there was a yellower fellow": Max Baer, "Unkissed and 'Yellow' at 19, 'Bashful' Champ Admits," *New York Mirror*, June 18, 1934.
"Flood of Mash Notes": *New York Daily Mirror*, June 19, 1934, p. 3.
"Loving Letters": *New York Daily Mirror*, June 18, 1934, p. 3.
"Too Bad, Girls!": *New York Daily Mirror*, June 16, 1934.

185 "Ma Baer Not Reading": *New York Daily Mirror*, June 20, 1934, p. 4.
"That's absurd": "Baer Challenges Mdivani Royalty," *New York Mirror*, Sept. 9, 1934.

12. Another Upset

191 "Over there, for instance": Frank Graham, "Setting the Pace," *New York Sun*, Sept. 17, 1934.
193 "The Braddock of 1932": Lud Shabazian, *Relief to Royalty* (Union City, N.J.: Hudson Dispatch, 1936), p. 101.
194 "You've spoiled two guys": Ibid., p. 103.

13. King Max

196 "Listen, I don't want": Associated Press, "Baer Would Fight Twice in a Night," *New York Times*, Dec. 13, 1934, p. 31.
197 "That's it": Wilbur Wood, "Champion Loses His Temper," *New York Sun*, Dec. 29, 1934.
198 "The Kingfish got too confident": Associated Press, "Knockout Victory Cost Baer $50,000," *New York Times*, Dec. 30, 1934, p. S9.
"I guess now folks": "Baer Repeats Challenge," *New York Sun*, Dec. 29, 1934.
"I didn't want": Associated Press, "Knockout Victory."
199 "Someone may remove": Grantland Rice, "The Sportlight: Champions and Their Chances for 1935," *New York Sun*, Jan. 5, 1935.
"A lot of people": On January 24, 1934, Baer gave a lengthy interview to the United Press, whose story, "Admits He Is Not Invincible," appeared in the *New York Sun* on Jan. 25, 1935.

14. A Shot at Lasky

202 Wilbur Wood ranked: Wood's rankings appeared in both the *Ring* and the *Sun*, Jan. 3, 1935, in a story titled "Champion Has Perfect Score."

15. The People's Choice

206 The fight raised $10,600: "Mrs. Frankie Campbell's Fight Benefit Fund Placed in Trust," *San Francisco Chronicle*, Feb. 27, 1935.
209 "his stock following the fight": Lud Shabazian, *Relief to Royalty* (Union City, N.J.: Hudson Dispatch, 1936).
210 "Braddock is considered": Joseph C. Nichols, "Lasky Is Favored to Beat Braddock," *New York Times*, Mar. 22, 1935, p. 30.
211 "Braddock demonstrated once more": Joseph C. Nichols, "Braddock Defeats Lasky on Points," *New York Times*, Mar. 23, 1935, p. 19.
"It was a good fight": Ed Fitzgerald, "Cinderella Jim," *Sport*, Feb. 1950, p. 68.
212 "The priest": Frank Graham, Jr., *A Farewell to Heroes* (New York: Viking, 1981), pp. 65–66.

213 Braddock insisted: "Braddock Pays ERA Debt 2 Weeks Before It Is Due," *New York Times*, June 23, 1935, p. 25.

214 "The commissioners asked me": Fred Van Ness, "Match Between Schmeling and Lasky's Conqueror Urged by Commission to Determine Next Foe for Baer," *New York Times*, Mar. 27, 1935, p. 26.

"Fifty years": This story was told often. See Shabazian, *Relief to Royalty*, p. 32, and Frank Graham, "Give Joe Gould a Big Hand, Too," *New York Sun*, June 15, 1935, p. 32.

"Hell," Baer said: Shabazian, *Relief to Royalty*, p. 116.

215 "That's a big joke": Associated Press, "Hoffman Scoffs at Match," *New York Times*, Mar. 27, 1935, p. 26.

216 "Louis is just": United Press, "Baer Would Even Stand for Hitler's Referee," *New York Sun*, Apr. 3, 1935.

"I'll meet anyone": Fred Van Ness, "Baer, in City, Indicates Braddock Will Be Opponent Here in June," *New York Times*, Apr. 6, 1935, p. 20. Sixty years later, in the film *Jerry Maguire*, Cuba Gooding would popularize the phrase "Show me the money." Baer said it first.

217 "I've studied Baer's style": Louis Effrat, "Braddock Formally Signs to Box Baer for Title at Garden Bowl," *New York Times*, Apr. 14, 1935, p. S8.

219 "Braddock has been around": John Kieran, "Sparring with the Fight Program," *New York Times*, May 20, 1935, p. 22.

"Three More Fights": Associated Press, "Baer, an Eye Black, Talks of Retiring," *New York Times*, Apr. 26, 1935, p. 27.

16. Homicide Hall

223 "I'm not ashamed": "Dole Repaid by Braddock," *New York Sun*, May 3, 1935.

"The story of relief case No. 2796": Associated Press, "Braddock, Relief Case Last Year, Is Now on the Road to Wealth," *New York Times*, May 3, 1935, p. 26.

"As soon as I was paid off": Ibid.

224 "He has been down": Jack Miley, "Braddock's Life — Saga of a Setup," *New York Daily News*, June 16, 1935, p. 72.

"Couldn't Let Kids Starve": Associated Press, "Couldn't Let Kids Starve, So Braddock Went on Relief and Isn't Ashamed," *Jersey Journal*, May 3, 1935, p. 1.

"By the power": "Joe Braddock on the Stump," *Jersey Journal*, May 4, 1935, p. 8.

225 "They have given Baer": "Baer Burned on Chest by Blank Cartridge Wad," *New York Times*, May 10, 1935, p. 27. According to John V. Gromback, the "accident" was a stunt to get publicity for his radio show; see *The Saga of Sock* (New York: A. S. Barnes, 1949), p. 159.

226 "I didn't want the Braddock match": Edward Van Every, "Baer Sees Title Threat in Braddock," *New York Sun*, May 18, 1935.

227 "Max and I are good friends": Joseph C. Nichols, "Challenger's Punishing Body Blows in Evidence at His Upstate Camp," *New York Times*, June 5, 1935, p. 27.

228 "There are no restrictions": "400 at Braddock's Camp," *New York Times*, June 2, 1935, p. 54.

"James J. has the roughest": Lud Shabazian, *Relief to Royalty* (Union City, N.J.: Hudson Dispatch, 1936), p. 135.

229 "The most impressive feature": Fred Van Ness, "Baer Bars Clowning as He Boxes 9 Fast Rounds With 5 Partners," *New York Times*, May 23, 1935, p. 33.

"The hand is not sore": Ibid.

230 "If there's a doctor": Damon Runyon, "Both Barrels," *New York American*, June 13, 1935, p. 17.

231 "Please, doc": Shabazian, *Relief to Royalty*, p. 138.

232 "If he is in good condition": Ibid., p. 141.

"It was the most impressive": Ibid., p. 143.

233 "Jersey James": John Kieran, "Sports of the Times," *New York Times*, May 31, 1935, p. 23.

234 "on the eve": Shabazian, *Relief to Royalty*, p. 146.

"Why, this fellow": Ibid.

"He is a little open": Ibid., p. 147.

235 "I never went down": Frank Graham, "Setting the Pace: A Year Ago in Braddock's Life," *New York Sun*, June 7, 1935, p. 30.

"They've been throwing": Ibid.

236 "The daily boxing bouts": Fred Van Ness, "Braddock in Shape as He Breaks Camp," *New York Times*, June 10, 1935, p. 21.

"I seen Tommy": Peter Heller, *In This Corner . . . !* (New York: Da Capo, 1994), p. 175.

237 "He receives letters": Fred Van Ness, "Impressive Exhibition Given by Braddock as He Finishes Boxing Drills Here," *New York Times*, June 11, 1935, p. 28.

"All over the country": Frank Graham, "The Man Who Wouldn't Give Up," *New York Sun*, June 13, 1935, p. 30.

238 "Through these final days": Van Ness, "Impressive Exhibition," p. 28.

"A manager easily hypnotizes: Runyon, "Both Barrels," p. 17.

"caused Curley Grieve": Ibid.

"He would quit the ring": Frank Graham, Jr., *A Farewell to Heroes* (New York: Viking, 1981), p. 60.

239 Johnny Dundee: Van Ness, "Impressive Exhibition."

"I will knock": Frank Graham, "Setting the Pace: The Man Nobody Knows Very Well," *New York Sun*, June 12, 1935, p. 34.

"Max Baer struts": Ibid.

240 "It is even money": Heller, *In This Corner*, p. 173. Braddock told Peter Heller that Runyon coined the nickname, and most sources agree. How-

ever, in his book *The Heavyweight Championship*, Nat Fleischer writes that Albertanti dubbed Braddock the Cinderella Man (p. 235).

Counterintuitively, he picked: "Five Ex-Champions Select Baer to Win," *New York Times*, June 13, 1935, p. 27.

241 "Braddock is a sure thing": Edward Van Every, "His Conqueror Says Braddock Is Sure to Win," *New York Sun*, June 13, 1935, p. 30.

"It is unlikely": Graham, "The Man Who Wouldn't Give Up," p. 30.

242 "I'll do my talking": Some reporters thought the comment came from Gould, not Braddock.

"You're the guy": "Air of Belligerency Marks Weighing In," *New York Times*, June 14, 1935, p. 30.

243 Theatrically: Ibid.

17. A Stout Heart

246 "I am afraid": "Spiritualist Fails to Bare Mysteries," *New York Times*, June 13, 1935, p. 25.

"It was a crowd": James P. Dawson, "Braddock Outpoints Baer to Win World Ring Title," *New York Times*, June 14, 1935, p. 1.

"mainly for the reason": Damon Runyon, "Braddock Defeats Baer for Heavy Title," *New York American*, June 14, 1935, p. 1.

247 "Probably 90 percent": Wilbur Wood, "Expert Opinion May Jinx Max," *New York Sun*, June 12, 1935, p. 34.

248 While Braddock was napping: Telephone interview with Max Baer, Jr., Sept. 15, 2004.

250 "The shock of it": Arthur Daley, "The Stroke of Midnight," *New York Times*, Sept. 26, 1962, p. 44.

"So that's the heavyweight champion": Paul Gallico, "How It Feels," *Daily News*, June 15, 1935.

251 "I knew it was the best": "Won Title in 3rd, Braddock Says," *New York Times*, June 14, 1935, p. 29.

253 "No mother": Gallico, "How It Feels."

255 "I am fighting clean": Lud Shabazian, *Relief to Royalty* (Union City, N.J.: Hudson Dispatch, 1936), p. 169.

257 "They poured in": Ibid.

"It certainly was a strange": Gallico, "How It Feels."

259 "I'm glad I won": Ed Fitzgerald, "Cinderella Jim," *Sport*, Feb. 1950, p. 69.

"My left arm's sore": "Ex-Champ Retires; New King's Family to Celebrate," *New York Journal*, June 14, 1935, p. 1.

260 "Yeah," he said: Shabazian, *Relief to Royalty*, p. 173.

261 "Thank him": Ibid., p. 174.

"Congratulations to the new": Ibid., p. 175.

262 "My husband wasn't seeing": Mae Fox Braddock, "Wife Reveals Jimmy Braddock as Most Bashful Fighter," *New York Daily Mirror*, June 17, 1935, p. 5.

262 "The crowd was overwhelmingly": Dan Parker, "Punchinello of Pugilism Passes," *New York Daily Mirror*, June 15, 1935, p. 23.

263 "Jimmy deserved": Ibid.

"You will recall": Damon Runyon, "Both Barrels," *New York American*, June 15, 1935, p. 19.

"On the average": John Kieran, "Lucky Jim," *New York Times*, June 16, 1935, p. 52.

264 "I know I deserved": Joseph C. Nichols, "Braddock Likely to Risk Newly-Acquired Heavyweight Title in September," *New York Times*, June 15, 1935, p. 9.

"I propose to raise": Murray Lewin, "Through with Ring Says Baer," *New York Daily Mirror*, June 14, 1935, p. 38.

"Don't listen": Ibid.

"Max Baer's dilly-dallying": Jack Dempsey, "Baer's Clowning Is Hit by Dempsey," *New York Times*, June 14, 1935, p. 30.

265 "the fairest colleen": Jack Miley, "Champ, Descendant of Irish Kings, an Alger Hero," *New York Daily News*, June 15, 1935, p. 32.

"The incredible has happened": Frank Graham, "Setting the Pace: Up from the Floor to Glory," *New York Sun*, June 14, 1935, p. 28.

"Well," Braddock said: See Frank Graham, Jr., *A Farewell to Heroes* (New York: Viking, 1981), p. 69.

266 "My husband may": Mrs. Mae Fox Braddock, "Champ's Wife Lauds Her Jim," *New York Daily Mirror*, June 17, 1935, p. 3.

"I don't want Jimmy": Mae Braddock, "Wife Reveals," p. 5.

Epilogue

268 "I don't care": Arthur Daley, "The Big, Bad Baer," *New York Times*, Nov. 25, 1959, p. 32.

"his brain awhirl": James P. Dawson, "Louis Stops Baer in 4th at Stadium as 95,000 Look On," *New York Times*, Sept. 25, 1935, p. 1.

"I could have got up": Frank Graham, "Extra! Baer Knocks Out Louis," *New York Sun*, June 24, 1938.

269 "the most popular champion": Lud Shabazian, *Relief to Royalty* (Union City, N.J.: Hudson Dispatch, 1936), p. 3.

"You can't imagine": Ibid., p. 132.

270 "We prefer to meet": "Roxborough Tells Plans," *New York Times*, Oct. 12, 1935, p. 22.

272 "I can still hit": James J. Braddock, "I Will K.O. Louis," *Boxing News*, n.d., p. 5.

273 "Joe clipped Jimmy": Ronald K. Fried, *Corner Men: Great Boxing Trainers* (New York: Four Walls Eight Windows, 1991), p. 210.

274 "Even when he was knocked out": Ibid.

"The exhibition of courage": In James Lambert Harte, *The Amazing Story of James J. Braddock* (Emmaus, Pa.: Rodale, 1938), p. 137.

274 "The old champion": Bugs Baer, "Epigrams," in *The Fireside Book of Boxing*, W. C. Heinz, ed. (New York: Simon & Schuster, 1961), p. 26.

Baer, who, like Braddock: Associated Press, "Max Baer, 50, Dies," *New York Times*, Nov. 22, 1959, p. 1.

276 "If you feel good": "Braddock at 64: Baer Hit Hard but Louis Was Faster," *New York Times*, June 8, 1969, p. S5.

"If death came easily": Red Smith, "A Champion for His Time," *New York Times*, Dec. 1, 1974, p. 255.

Acknowledgments

I am deeply indebted to the men — many of them enduring giants of the press box and press row — who covered James J. Braddock, Max Baer, and boxing in the 1920s and 1930s: Grantland Rice, Frank Graham, Sr., James P. Dawson, Nat Fleischer, Fred Van Ness, Joseph C. Nichols, John Kieran, Joe Williams, Jimmy Cannon, Damon Runyon, Wilbur Wood, Paul Gallico, Westbrook Pegler, W. O. McGeehan, Edward Van Every, Dan Parker, Murray Lewin, Jack Miley, Red Smith, and, of course, Lud Shabazian, among others. I never had the opportunity to meet any of them — most have been dead for decades — but I wish I had. I relied heavily on their colorful accounts of the lives of Braddock and Baer and of the events at which they had ringside seats, literally and metaphorically.

In particular, I culled an enormous amount of information from Lud Shabazian's 1936 biography of Jim Braddock, *Relief to Royalty*. Nat Fleischer's brief biography, *Max Baer, the Glamour Boy of the Ring*, was also invaluable, particularly concerning Baer's youth and early professional career. These two books, as well as the archives of the *New York Times*, *New York Sun*, *New York Daily Mirror*, *New York Journal*, *New York Herald-Tribune*, *San Francisco Chronicle*, *Ring Magazine*, and *New York World-Telegram*, formed the backbone of my research, but I repeatedly turned to several other sources: James Lambert Harte's 1938 biography, *The Amazing Story of James J. Braddock*; Frank Graham, Jr.'s account of the Braddock-Griffin fight in *Sports Illustrated*, his memoir, *A Farewell to Heroes*, and, by Graham and Mel Allen, *It Takes Heart*; Ron Fimrite's definitive *Sports Illustrated* profile of Max Baer,

"Send in the Clown"; Ed Fitzgerald's 1950 *Sport* profile of Braddock, "Cinderella Jim"; *The Fireside Book of Boxing*, edited by W. C. Heinz, and *The Book of Boxing*, edited by Heinz and Nathan Ward; Michael Silver's *Ring Magazine* profile of Braddock, "The Cinderella Man Whose Clock Never Struck 12"; Tom Hauser and Stephen Brunt's *The Italian Stallions*; Larry Ritter's *East Side, West Side*; John Lardner's *White Hopes and Other Tigers*; Peter Heller's *In This Corner . . . !*; *To Absent Friends from Red Smith*, edited by Dave Anderson; Ronald K. Fried's *Corner Men: Great Boxing Trainers*; John D. McCallum's *The World Heavyweight Boxing Championship* and *The Encyclopedia of World Boxing Champions*; Marcus Griffin's *Wise Guy: James J. Johnston: A Rhapsody in Fistics*; Nat Fleischer's *The Heavyweight Championship: An Informal History of Heavyweight Boxing from 1719 to the Present Day*; Richard Bak's *Joe Louis: The Great Black Hope*; and *The Encyclopedia of New York City*, edited by Kenneth T. Jackson.

Many of the stories in the book were culled from not one but several of the aforementioned sources. For instance, there are at least a dozen nearly contemporaneous accounts of the day in 1926 on which Jimmy Braddock embarrassed Harry Galfund as they sparred at Joe Jeannette's gym in West Hoboken, piquing the interest of Joe Gould. Lud Shabazian's account is slightly different from Frank Graham's, which is slightly different from Red Smith's. In the interest of historical accuracy and narrative flow, I have included the details and dialogue that I thought were most credible.

Speaking of dialogue, the vast majority of the dialogue in the book was extracted from contemporary accounts. For the most part, I have tried to use wherever possible the exact words recorded by the reporters who were scribbling the words down as they were spoken. But on occasion I have, necessarily, taken some license in embellishing and editing the dialogue. I have endeavored to remain true to the essential facts and convictions of the men and women who grace these pages, and always I have done so only in service to the story.

This book could not have been written without benefit of the talent and patience of Susan Canavan, my editor at Houghton Mifflin. For better or worse, *Cinderella Man* is as much her book as mine.

Scott Waxman, my literary agent, first attracted me to the idea of writing a book about Jim Braddock. From the beginning, his support and encouragement helped keep me going.

I am also grateful for the contributions of Martha Kennedy, who designed the evocative cover; Liz Duvall, who cleaned up my prose; Carla

Gray, Houghton Mifflin's marketing guru; and Gracie Doyle, the house publicist extraordinaire.

I must also thank the small army of men and women whose research assistance helped make the story of Braddock and Baer come alive for me. The incomparable Joe Goldstein burrowed deep into the recesses of the New York Public Library to find essential primary sources. Willie Weinbaum, my colleague at ESPN, the best reporter I know, tracked down dozens of people who knew Baer and Braddock. Dave Smith of the New York Public Library pointed me to the books, magazine profiles, and clippings on which I most relied. Aron Heller, Larry Friedman, Max Greengrass, Jordan Koss, and Rick Manista all spurned more lucrative summer jobs that might have situated them at pools or beaches to research the lives of two boxers whose names were previously unknown to them. Jeff Brophy of the International Boxing Hall of Fame, in Canastota, New York, generously provided ancient stories from the *Ring* and located long-forgotten minutes of meetings of the New York State Athletic Commission. Johnny Miller at the *San Francisco Chronicle* and Susan Lintelmann at the United States Military Academy library were invaluable sources for material on the deaths of Frankie Campbell and his son, cadet Francis Camilli, Jr. Bert Sugar shared details of the lives of Braddock and Baer that only he knew. Greg Payan found the photographs that illustrate this book. Dan Weinberg located video copies of the critical fights that defined the careers of Braddock and Baer. Peter Heller was kind enough to provide a copy of the complete interview he conducted with Jim Braddock that was excerpted in his book *In This Corner . . . !* W. C. Heinz and Jimmy Breslin allowed me to tap into their estimable brains for Baer and Braddock tidbits. Bob Shabazian and Max Baer, Jr., shared with me vivid memories of their fathers. Joseph Mallon, Joseph Kraljic, and Mike Viola all submitted to interviews about Jim Braddock, while Sam Bercovich, Sam Gold, Jack and Elaine La Lanne, and Harvey Taub all submitted to interviews about Max Baer. Diane Camilli Abraham, Bill Camilli, Doug Camilli, Jack Camilli, and Richard Camilli were all interviewed about Frankie Campbell.

I was also helped by Bob Foster at the Hoboken Museum, Cynthia Harris at the Jersey City Library, and Estela Longo at the West New York Library.

Mike Lupica, Vince Doria, Gare Joyce, Bud Morgan, Evan Kanew, and Tim Hays formed a sage focus group that helped shape *Cinderella Man* as it was written.

Thanks also to Farley Chase, Sarah Gabert, Kate McKean, Melissa

Jacobs, Don Barone, Nicole Noren, Dave Herscher, Ellen Harrilal, and Sue Friedmann for all their help.

Finally, I want to acknowledge the contributions of Ralph Wiley, a friend, colleague, and mentor whose premature death stole from us a gifted and unique voice. His book, *Serenity: A Boxing Memoir,* made me a fan of the sweet science. The week before he died, we talked about James J. Braddock, Max Baer, and the process of writing a book. He called it a forced march. Like most everything Ralph told me in the fifteen years we knew each other, his description was on the mark — but at least I had plenty of good company.

Index